Phyllis Nagy
Plays: 1

Weldon Rising, Butterfly Kiss, Disappeared, The Strip

'Young playwrights don't come much hotter than Phyllis Nagy.'
Daily Telegraph

Weldon Rising: 'Here is the best new play I have seen in many
months . . . This play is exciting because it is well written,
unusually constructed and morally serious. It is also frequently
funny.' *Financial Times*

Butterfly Kiss: 'Nagy captures the texture of a life and writes short,
vivid, often disturbingly erotic scenes . . . it's a play that leaves me
proclaiming Nagy a writer of real talent.' *Guardian*

Disappeared: 'A piece that gets right under your skin . . . There's no
neat solution to Nagy's conundrum, just a fog of fear, despair, and
most remarkably of all, a final mirage of escape. Spine-tingling
stuff.' *Daily Telegraph*

The Strip: 'kaleidoscopic and hugely accomplished dissection of fate,
love and chance.' *Independent*

Phyllis Nagy was born in New York City and has lived in
London since 1992. Her plays, including *Weldon Rising*, *Butterfly
Kiss*, *Disappeared* and *The Strip*, have been produced throughout the
world and have received awards including the Writers' Guild of
Great Britain Award, a Mobil Prize, a Susan Smith Blackburn
Prize, the Eileen Anderson/Central Television Award, two
National Endowment for the Arts Fellowships and a McKnight
Foundation Fellowship. Phyllis is currently under commission to
the Royal Shakespeare Company, Nottingham Playhouse and the
Royal Court Theatre, where she was recently writer-in-residence.
She has adapted Patricia Highsmith's *The Talented Mr Ripley* for the
Watford Palace Theatre and her new play, *Never Land*, opened at
the Royal Court Theatre in January 1998.

PHYLLIS NAGY

Plays: 1

Weldon Rising
Butterfly Kiss
Disappeared
The Strip

Introduced by Michael Coveney
With a preface by the author

Methuen Drama

METHUEN CONTEMPORARY DRAMATISTS

This collection first published in Great Britain in 1998
by Methuen Drama
Methuen Publishing Ltd
215 Vauxhall Bridge Road
London SW1V 1EJ

www.methuen.co.uk

Methuen Publishing Ltd reg. number 3543167

Caution

Contents

Chronology

October 1992	*Weldon Rising*, Royal Court Theatre and Liverpool Playhouse
January 1993	*Entering Queens*, Gay Sweatshop
March 1994	*Trip's Cinch*, Actors Theatre of Louisville (USA)
March 1994	*Girl Bar*, Celebration Theatre Los Angeles (USA)
April 1994	*Butterfly Kiss*, Almeida Theatre
April 1994	*The Scarlet Letter*, Denver Centre Theatre (USA)
February 1995	*Disappeared*, Leicester Haymarket and Royal Court Theatre – Midnight Theatre Company and Chapman Duncan Associates
March 1995	*The Strip*, Royal Court Theatre

Preface

Since much of my work thus far has concerned itself with the ways in which individual destiny (sometimes seemingly random and sometimes seemingly spooky and pre-ordained) controls individual morality (and vice versa), it seems entirely appropriate that my plays have been produced in an almost random order bearing no particular relationship to when they were written.

Weldon Rising was completed in early winter 1992 – written over the euphoric two months between my first visit from New York to the Royal Court Theatre and my return to London in order to settle for good. It was produced well before both *Disappeared* and *Butterfly Kiss*, but was written later than either of them. *Butterfly Kiss* was completed in 1989 but existed in an earlier, nearly unrecognisable student incarnation in 1983 and *Disappeared* was written over a week in the summer of 1991. *Girl Bar*, the earliest of my professional efforts, dates from early 1988 but was produced after nearly all the others.

I, of course, put this all down to blind fate. While I lived and worked in America, I did not receive a single professional production of any play. But the moment I *did* arrive here, *all* of the plays were produced in fairly swift succession. Most of the time I spent being the best-known-unproduced-playwright-in-America was fairly miserable, but in retrospect, those pressure-free years afforded me the opportunity to develop a precise and rigorous working method – for which I am now terribly grateful.

I have plenty of folk to thank for rescuing me from early obscurity and would like to take the opportunity to do so here. Elyse Dodgson, Stephen Jeffreys, James MacDonald, Bo Barton, Jo Town, Anne Mayer, Lisa Makin, Marieke Spencer, Paul Arditti, Carl Miller and Graham Cowley – past and present staff at the Royal Court – have offered

their advocacy and talents throughout these six years.
Ramin Gray, Kate Rowland and Lois Weaver trusted the
work and gave me crucial early productions. Derek Wax,
Guy Chapman, Paul Kerryson and John Blackmore were
key to the success of *Disappeared*. Jonathan Kent and Ian
McDiaramid will always hold a place in my heart for
Butterfly Kiss – it remains my favourite production
experience. I owe a huge debt of gratitude to all the actors,
directors and designers with whom I've worked, but
especially to Melee Hutton, Nancy Crane and Andrew
Woodall, the actors who've been with me through most of
the plays and to Steven Pimlott, whose wise, witty and
courageous direction of my work is responsible for a
significant portion of its success. Two good and loyal
friends, Giles Croft and Peggy Butcher, deserve all the
gratitude I can give them for their unstinting generosity
and good humour through dark times. Finally, my undying
love and eternal thanks to the two people without whom
none of this would have taken place: Stephen Daldry, who
produced my work first and has continued to do so ever
since and Mel Kenyon, whose love, support and fierce
intelligence keeps me writing plays.

Phyllis Nagy
September 1997

Introduction

The four plays collected in this volume emerged in London (one of them, *Disappeared*, at first on tour) in a concentrated period of just over three years in the early 1990s and established Phyllis Nagy as a playwright of distinction and individuality.

She has not (obviously) been lumped in with the new laddish and loutish drama that has made such an impact in the wake of *Trainspotting* (novel, stage play and film). Nor does she quite tally with the feminist writers of the Royal Court in the 1980s, many of whom bit the bullet on sexual politics, parturition and mother-daughter relationships without really challenging ideas of form and style.

The first thing you notice about these plays, apart from their continuous, restless theatrical dynamic, is the line by line quality of the writing. Expletives and slang are deployed rhythmically, never gratuitously. Whereas much contemporary playwrighting is egregious, anorexic, short-winded and uncultured, Nagy writes sinuously and elegantly, working consistently towards a theatrical coalescence of plot, dialogue and swiftly changing scenic representation that is as exciting as it is unusual.

And she sounds up to date. Well, she is up to date. The Luxor Hotel in Las Vegas, whose Sphinx-like exterior dominates the action of *The Strip*, was only built in 1993. The climactic mood of meltdown and Armageddon in *Weldon Rising* reflects the author's visceral response to recent waves of violence and paranoia, some of it homophobic, some of it general, on the streets of the West Village in her home city of New York.

The characters are in search of destinations, new adventures, changes of pace, alternative varieties of excitement. Their stories are tales of exodus and disenchantment, of fear and loathing, of mystery and imagination.

In *Weldon Rising*, the bereaved Natty Weldon, consumed with cowardice and dismay, steps finally through a giant

onstage map of the meat-packing district and out of the
play. In *Disappeared*, a tense mystery thriller revolves around
the unexplained exit of Sarah Casey from a bar in Hell's
Kitchen.

In *Butterfly Kiss*, Lily's decisive act of matricide – an
ultimate statement in social and domestic defiance – is
unravelled within an antiseptic white New York prison cell.
And in *The Strip*, Ava Coo's cross-country mission to hit the
cabaret circuit in Las Vegas is complemented by other
pursuits – spiritual, criminal and investigative – in a rich
transatlantic tapestry of coming and going.

This may be fanciful, but I suspect that the writer
herself, an American now living in London – she visited
the Royal Court on assignment for two weeks in 1991, fell
in love, and stayed – is fired by her own experience to
express and explore other dreams of leaving. And it is
because these stories are bedded in ideals of emotional and
sexual possibility and of fulfilment that they resonate so
effectively in performance.

Their tone is deceptively flippant, because, outside of
Tom Stoppard, Caryl Churchill and David Hare, we have
become accustomed to the unmusical and the unpolished in
modern British playwriting. Nagy has a sardonic, mordant
and often playfully cruel tone in her writing that fits the
fantastical scenarios and defines her world of strange
contemporaneity.

The opening line of *The Strip* – 'Female impersonation is
a rather curious career choice for a woman, Miss Coo' –
has already achieved classic status not only for its
deliciously subversive sentiment, but also for its alliterative
beauty and its unexpected emergence from an opening
sequence of Madonna's 'Rescue Me' and introductory
tableaux involving all the characters.

Other favourite lines of mine include, 'There really
aren't any junkets to Siberia', the bad news for a client in
the wonderful travel agency scene in *Disappeared*; the pay-off
to the parenthetical story, in the same play, of Sarah's
fiancé's uncle trying to breach the closed-down Sea World
at San Diego on an away-day trip and impaling himself

fatally on the railings – 'At least he didn't stay in
California long enough to catch the cancer'; and the
exasperated response of the redneck mass murderer Lester
in *The Strip* on hearing Yvonne Elliman's beautiful
recording of 'I Don't Know How to Love Him' – 'I know
it comes from some fucked-up Limey musical thee-a-ter
thingamajig with a band of hippies humping Jesus . . .'

Weldon Rising has a good first line, too: 'I might have
been beautiful.' This sounds both romantic, like Tennessee
Williams, and wistful, like Sir Andrew Aguecheek in *Twelfth
Night*. The physically nerdish Natty, trapped in the
epicentre of a city on heat, is a discreet homosexual ('I
can't dance and leather makes me squeamish') who sells
lamps while the lights are going out all over town. His
lover has been murdered, stabbed rashly by a rude boy
shouting 'fuckface faggot'.

The incident was witnessed, and is re-enacted, under the
gaze of two quarrelsome neighbourhood lesbians, Tilly and
Jaye, whose own relationship floods the stage in tandem
with the main event. Further commentary is provided by
an outrageous transvestite, Marcel, who speaks only in the
third person (because he *is* the third person, he explains).

The quartier is vividly imagined, as in a Williams play of
the steamy South, and the rising heat feeds back reports on
the radio of a plane exploding on take-off, of a bus melting
on entering the Holland Tunnel, and of all the bridges
collapsing ('So much for the bridge and tunnel crowd' is a
typical Nagy reaction quip). The play is drawn into this
terrifying situation, its theatricality defined in the fate of
characters cast adrift but bravely trying to reclaim the
world and each other. Natty embodies feelings of both guilt
and helplessness. The lesbians, who met by chance at the
airport, cool down with crates of stolen beer and finally
resolve a physical impasse by making gloriously explicit love
in the white heat of apotheosis.

A similar, though cooler, poetic and musical synthesis
informs *Butterfly Kiss*, which is not to be confused with a
rather vulgar British lesbian road movie of the same title
that subsequently appeared. Lily is indeed a musician who

promises her mother a concert of songs before shooting her
in the head.

The theatrical cross-fading and flash-backing demanded
by the play was beautifully realised in Steven Pimlott's
Almeida Theatre production, which seemed nonetheless to
be played in a constant theatrical present.

The play in performance achieves, or should achieve, a
Mozartian classicism in its deployment of information.
Aspects of Lily's experience are revealed cumulatively,
though not chronologically. Her father, a lepidopterist, sets
her up as a girlfriend for his ex-Marine buddy. The actress
has to segue from being a fourteen-year-old beach tease
into casually flirting with her future female lover in a
woman's bar. The Lolita parallels – and Nabokov was a
lepidopterist – are obvious but the variations anything but.

At the same time, Lily's relations with her mother and
equally obnoxious grandmother are spikily chronicled in
scenes that are as hard-edged as they are dazzlingly well
written. Her mother, a former switchboard operator, thinks
that, because she drinks, she looks like Tallulah Bankhead,
which puts one unavoidably in mind of the attraction the
role of Regina Giddens in Lillian Hellman's *Little Foxes* held
for the real-life Tallulah: 'a rapacious, soulless, sadistic bitch
who would've cut her own mother's throat.'

If Tennessee Williams comes to mind during *Weldon
Rising*, the technique of poetic deliquescence in *Butterfly Kiss*
surely owes something to Arthur Miller in *Death of a
Salesman*. There is even a tawdry variation on Willy
Loman's motel mistress, a spurious Countess of the cabaret
and lover of Lily's father who declares her seedy aspirations
with the triumphant remark 'J'habite Queens'.

A more conventional sort of unsolved mystery is the
subject of *Disappeared* in which, like Lily, the heroine Sarah
Casey disavows all domestic expectations and strikes out
into uncharted territory. The discussion of what may or
may not have happened is bookended by the present tense
scenes in the mid-town bar where Sarah was last spotted
alive.

Nagy always intermingles her lead stories with other,

complementary narratives, and although she may not get
the interaction quite right here, she does create a superb,
secondary lost soul figure in the character of Elston Rupp,
who accosts Sarah in the bar in the guise of an enter-
tainments attorney. Rupp, in another guise of a bankruptcy
trustee, seeks that junket in Siberia. So, who is he? We
learn of his employment in a thrift shop, where he assumes
the identity, and the clothes, of donating customers before
penetrating the world and pursuing his dastardly business.
The play has a nagging thriller richness and a valedictory
tone that may well reflect Nagy's own farewell to New
York.

Like Tony Kushner, whose landmark *Angels in America*
was first acclaimed in London before becoming a hit in
New York, Nagy has made a reputation here partly,
perhaps, because her local obsessions come up sharper
when seen out of their immediate cultural context. We can
relish her characteristic exotica, her details of language and
topography, in a fiercer focus, as we do those of Sam
Shepard, another great poetic American monitor of specific
landscapes and weird and winding adventures.

The playwright's ambition (to date) peaks in *The Strip*,
where all the various strands of action seem to be
manipulated by Otto Mink, a sleazy, shadowy figure not
unlike, as my colleague Paul Taylor pointed out, the Duke
of dark corners in *Measure For Measure*. Ava Coo, a big-
busted butch amalgam of Madonna and Judy Garland,
may be no virginal Isabella, but there are Pompey Bums
and Elbows around in the shape of a gay fitness freak,
Martin, and his dissatisfied pawnbroker friend, Tom.

While redneck Lester unwittingly wanders into a gay bar
in Earl's Court (just like a place back home, 'where a fella
can hook up with his buddies, take a break from the missus
and the kids') and meets Martin, his wife, plus baby
redneck, diverts to Liverpool with Tom.

Meanwhile, a lesbian journalist turned private detective
pursues Lester. And Ava, equally adored by the repo man
who has come to impound her car, and the journalist,
takes off to Las Vegas where, coincidentally, her mother is

cleaning toilets at the club and recording letters to her
daughter which she never sends.

This is a dizzyingly complicated narrative, but one in
which all the strands are meticulously controlled and
brought climatically together in Las Vegas where the entire
cast witnesses an eclipse of the sun in the shadow of the
Luxor Hotel.

The play's structure is both a variation, and a
sophisticated advance, on that of *Weldon Rising*, and I
remember leaving the theatre amazed by the achievement
and struck with the sort of terrifying panic over writing
about it that a critic only feels after seeing the best work of
either Tom Stoppard or Sam Shepard.

I think a reading of these plays will convince you that
Nagy belongs to the top class. She has managed to strike a
rich and personal seam of experience without sounding as
though she is fulfilling an agenda. All the time, she is
trying to write great theatre, not setting out to shock, or to
catch the latest wave in the fashion stakes.

I count it pertinent that she admits to having once been
a devilish and pernickety researcher on the *New York Times
Magazine*; she's a theatrical intellectual who cares deeply
about words and their meanings and inflections. That's the
Stoppard strain. (Maybe this has something to do with her
Hungarian antecedence; Stoppard's is Czech.)

And the Shepard? She loves sports, music, gambling. She
knows a lot about all three. And, like Shepard, she has a
fantastic knack of translating those enthusiasms, and her
lust for life and travel, into the quintessence of art and the
registration of human endeavour, and of love, both
transient and lasting, in a bristling network of damn good
stories and startling theatrics.

Michael Coveney
July 1997

Weldon Rising

To Mel

*So if you ever felt something behind you, when you weren't even one,
like a welcome heat, like a bulb, like a sun, trying to shine right
across the universe — it was me. Always me. It was me. It was me.*
(Martin Amis)

Weldon Rising was first produced by the Royal Court Theatre in association with the Liverpool Playhouse. The play opened at the Liverpool Playhouse Studio on 27 October 1992 and the first London performance was at the Royal Court Theatre Upstairs on 3 December 1992. The cast was as follows:

Natty Weldon	Simon Gregor
Marcel	Andrew Woodall
Tilly	Melee Hutton
Jaye	Rosie Rowell
Jimmy	Paul Viragh
Boy	Matthew Wait

Directed by Penny Ciniewicz
Designed by Ruari Murchison
Lighting by Jon Linstrum

Characters

Natty Weldon, *35. Distressed by his ordinary good looks. Adrift, guilty, obsessive. However, his self-effacing sense of humour enables him to fight rather than crumble.*

Tilly, *not quite 30, but older than she'd like to be. Pretty enough, which is problematic for her. Naturally curious and incongruously romantic.*

Jaye, *not quite 30. Very fit, clean and thoroughly gorgeous. Mean, caustic and not afraid of being unsympathetic. Not at all coy or girlish, but not butch either.*

Marcel, *stunning young transvestite without a permanent address. Very much a man. Not at all effeminate or mincing.*

Jimmy, *Natty's lover. He's everything Natty isn't: tall, beautiful, outspoken.*

Boy, *so beautiful and dangerous that no two people can remember him in quite the same way. Very young and unfailingly polite, even when violent. The sum of all fears.*

The Setting
Little West 12th Street, a cobbled back street in New York City's meat-packing district. Factory buildings that may or may not be deserted. Shadowy, all of it. One surface must be covered entirely by a detailed map of the meat-packing district. The map is enormous, overwhelming. One area of the stage, preferably above street level, represents Tilly and Jane's apartment during the first several scenes of the play. The apartment should not be represented naturalistically. What's important is the sense that the women watch Natty and Marcel from a separate space. It is the hottest evening of the year.

Note
The music should be treated as an integral part of the text rather than as background noise. Therefore, it is especially important that the versions of the songs indicated are used in production.

Much of the punctuation used in the play is not standard and is intended to create a non-naturalistic pattern to the language. The play works best in performance when strict attention is paid to the specifics of the punctuation. Similarly, the use of capitals in some lines does not necessarily indicate an increase in volume; rather, it is meant to indicate shifts in thought.

Lights up on **Natty Weldon**. *He's in the street. He wears boxer shorts and a wool beret. He sits before an art deco vanity, the surface of which is covered by bottles of cologne. The vanity's mirror is pasted over with postcards. Open boxes scattered about. Clothes overflowing from them. A portable steel clothing rack, full of men's stuff. There is a Walkman and two tiny speakers set up on one edge of the vanity.* **Natty** *douses himself with cologne from every bottle.*

Lights up on **Marcel**. *He wears something ridiculous, like a plastic dress and platform shoes, but looks dazzling nonetheless. He is meticulously washing out a pair of pantyhose in a ceramic basin.*

Natty I might have been beautiful. I think. In Morocco. Ann Arbor. Montreal. San Francisco. Brisbane. Detroit. In transit. I used to be a little beautiful in transit.

Marcel Marcel says: you were never beautiful. Marcel says: you're a liar. Marcel says: YOU STINK.

Natty *switches on the Walkman. It's Led Zeppelin's 'Trampled Underfoot'.* **Natty** *begins to unpack the boxes, hanging the clothing on the rack.*

Marcel Marcel says: shut that shit off. Marcel says: SHUT THAT SHIT OFF.

Lights up on **Tilly** *and* **Jaye**. *They observe the scene from their apartment.* **Tilly** *drinks beer and eats popcorn, totally fascinated by the proceedings. Empty beer bottles are scattered around them.*

Tilly He's very skinny. Arms like twigs. That's unhealthy.

Jaye I despise men with skinny arms.

Tilly We should feed him. Maybe.

Jaye He's way past the stage for feeding. Forget it.

Marcel Marcel is displeased. Marcel wants some quietude in which to wash her tights.

Natty *ignores* **Marcel** *and continues unpacking clothes.* **Marcel** *hurls the Walkman and speakers into the street. Music out.*

Marcel Marcel detests rock and roll. And queer boys who smell of marzipan.

Natty That was Jimmy's favourite. I used to be beautiful.
A little. With Jimmy.

Lights down on **Natty** *and* **Marcel**.

Tilly Men are violent. Even when they wear dresses.
Let's stay home for ever.

Jaye *kisses the back of* **Tilly**'*s neck while* **Tilly** *continues to
observe the unseen scene.*

Jaye Hold still and let me bite your neck.

Tilly It's too fucking hot for that. Do we have any more
beer? I drink too much beer.

Jaye You don't drink enough. You're coherent when
you're drunk.

Tilly It's a hundred and twenty degrees and if I don't
have another beer I'm gonna . . . ouch. Stop that. You're
hurting me.

Jaye When you're drunk, you let me bite your neck.

Tilly You know, he's really very skinny. But he has a
nice ass. WOULD YOU PLEASE STOP MAULING ME.

Jaye Sorry. No more beer. We're dry.

Tilly Liar. You're hoarding it. Under the floorboards.

Jaye Tough. No sex, no booze.

Tilly I can't believe you're doing this to me. It's
blackmail.

Jaye Hey. These are the rules. I bite your neck, you get
a beer. I rip off your clothes, you get another beer.

Tilly Don't be such a boy.

Jaye Listen to yourself. Since when did you decide to be
celibate?

Tilly Since it's gotten so hot I can't think straight. Jesus.
I need a drink. Please.

Jaye   Bulldyke.

Tilly   Flattery just won't work any more, honey. Look. That silly drag queen is washing his pantyhose.

Jaye   You've been at that window for weeks. Talk to me, Tilly.

Tilly   I wonder what size he wears. I hate my name. It's withered. We got any more popcorn?

Jaye   Pay some attention to me or I'll get another girlfriend.

Tilly   I bet he wears queen-sized. Long legs. Yeah. Well. Who are you kidding? Nobody else would have you. You're a mess.

Jaye   Fuck off.

Tilly   No, really. You're worse than me. And you got no booze in the house, no food and you got no air-conditioning. Why don't we have air-conditioning?

Jaye   I like the heat. It's unpleasant.

Tilly   And why does this skinny little fuck keep packing and unpacking clothes? I mean, why doesn't he just trash them?

Jaye   I'm out of here.

Tilly   Oh yeah? Where you going?

Jaye   I told you. I'm on the prowl.

Tilly   I hate it when you're pathetic.

Jaye   Okay. So I might be persuaded to stay home and hook you up to a beer i.v.

Tilly   Don't go out.

Jaye   Why not? I look good under lampposts. Cheap and sexy. That's me.

Tilly   You might lose your keys. Then what. Then you'd be lost to the streets.

*Jaye turns **Tilly** towards her.*

Jaye You ought to get out, too. Come with me.

Tilly I can't. My hair's dirty. I smell.

Jaye Tilly. It's all right to go outside now. It's all over.

Tilly We should have helped him. We should have run out into the street then.

Jaye I'm not listening to this any more.

Tilly Why didn't we help him? Now look at him. Nearly naked and still trying to hide his bald spot.

*Jaye holds out a beer to **Tilly**, as if from nowhere.*

Jaye Whoops. Look what I found. It's a . . . Corona.

Tilly I knew you were holding out on me. Bitch. Give it here.

Jaye Fuck me first.

Tilly Were you always this mean?

Jaye Yup. Now. What's it gonna be?

Tilly We used to be civilized, you know.

Jaye Too late for that. I'll count to ten. One. Two.

Tilly I can't help this, Jaye. I can't. We watched a man die and I can't move now. I want to sit at the window and rot. And drink till I drop.

Jaye Three. Four. I swear, when I get to ten, this all goes down the drain. Five. Six.

Tilly For chrissakes. Just let me have the fucking beer, all right?

Jaye Seven. Eight.

Tilly Okay. OKAY. STOP. What do you want? I'll do it.

Jaye On your knees.

Tilly *drops to her knees.* **Jaye** *goes to her, opens the beer.*

Jaye Mouth open, head tilted back.

Tilly *complies.* **Jaye** *feeds beer to* **Tilly**.

Jaye We did what we could. We called the cops. We're not responsible.

Tilly Just . . . shut up and feed me.

Jaye *bends to kiss* **Tilly**.

Jaye What do you love more: me or booze?

Tilly Shut up. Feed me.

Jaye *kisses* **Tilly**. *Lights down on them. Lights up on* **Natty**. *He cuts his toe-nails.*

Natty One night's like the next. I'm indecisive. I don't know which tie to wear. I can't choose between Chinese takeout or pizza. I think if I cut long and hard enough my feet will bleed and I won't be able to go out. We'll have to stay home, but no. Jimmy's ready to go and I can't stop him. We argue. I choose my most unfashionable tie, hoping he'll be embarrassed to be seen with me. But no. We go. We leave the apartment. We're on the street. We're moving.

Jimmy *enters.*

Jimmy It'll be good for you. Get out and meet your peers.

Natty They're not my peers. I own a small business. I have customers. I'm not political. They're your peers.

Jimmy Dances are fun, Natty. Not political.

Natty You can dance. I can't. You know I look like Peter Lorre in *M* when I dance.

Jimmy You have no gay friends.

Natty I'm not good-looking enough to have gay friends. You go. I'll go home and bake muffins. But please, Jimmy, don't make me go to a dance where I'll meet lots of boys who can't have sex, looking to have it anyway.

Jimmy   You've become so unfair in your old age. A shame. Come on. Have fun with me. Like in the old days.

Natty   Every day of my life is an old day.

Jimmy   Natty, everybody knows you're queer. Even your . . . customers.

Natty   Who told you that?

Jimmy   You don't fool anybody. Besides, it's not like we skip down the avenue holding hands and singing Judy Garland songs.

Natty   I don't see any reason to broadcast my sexuality.

Jimmy   Yeah, yeah. I know this story already.

Natty   Really. In fifteen years have you learned nothing about me? I'm discreet.

Jimmy   You're invisible.

Natty   I think you need drugs. Valium.

Jimmy   Maybe I'd like to hold your hand. Walk along Eighth Avenue and spit at passers-by.

Natty   You spit. I'll crawl under a manhole. Jimmy: I DON'T WANT TO GO. I don't do witty repartee. I sell lamps. I sometimes wear polyester. I can't dance and leather makes me squeamish. I don't vote. I don't go to bars. My only friends are miserably unhappy straight girls who hover in cabarets. We sing along to every show tune ever written and weep at last call. I've never done a popper in my life. I just . . . do you. Come home and watch *Now Voyager* with me.

Jimmy   I need people. Music. Smoke-filled rooms.

Natty   Fine. I'll smoke a carton of Camels for you. Just come home. With me.

Jimmy   Be more dangerous for me.

Natty   Love me for my cowardice.

Jimmy   I've done that for fifteen years. It's time for a change.

Natty   I'm allergic to change.

Jimmy   We haven't been out as a couple in ages. The boys don't believe me when I say I have a lover. You ought to prove I'm not a liar.

Natty   But I *am* a liar. I'm pathological. I lie about everything. I crave it.

Jimmy   I've got to be with people. Men. Happy sweaty men. Pressed together. Dancing for joy.

Natty   On the train this morning, I was reading something German. Told the sexy kid next to me that I was taking a PhD in German literature. Told him it was the wave of the future. He was impressed. Gave me his phone number. Would you like his number? I bet *he* dances.

Jimmy   I don't want a catalogue of your lies.

Natty   When I met you, I told you my mother was Sonja Henje. That she dropped me out on the ice in the middle of a double toe-loop.

Jimmy   I thought it was a lovely image. I still do.

Natty   If I lie enough, it keeps me healthy. But in order to lie successfully, one can't participate too much. In life.

Jimmy   There's nothing wrong with selling lamps, Nathaniel.

Natty   You call me Nathaniel when you're angry with me. You've called me that a lot lately. The thing about lamps is, as you get older, it's less and less flattering to bathe yourself in light. I replaced all the bulbs in the shop with 40-watters.

Jimmy   I won't indulge you.

Natty And another thing. I'm really fat. Yesterday I gained twenty pounds when you weren't looking.

Boy *enters. He lights a cigarette, watches them. They watch him.*

Jimmy My God. Remember when you looked like that?

Natty I never looked like that.

Jimmy What a face.

Natty Sure. It's not dropped yet. Wait ten years and oh . . . a few hundred thousand cigarettes later.

Jimmy He smokes like he's waiting to be fucked.

Natty No doubt he is. Waiting. For sure.

Jimmy Are you jealous?

Natty I'm not in a position to be jealous. People like me are grateful for any attention paid to us. We're happy for crumbs. Morsels.

Jimmy You're jealous. It's fantastic. Come on. Let's go.

He holds out his hand to **Natty**. **Natty** *doesn't take it.* **Jimmy** *smiles at* **Boy**.

Jimmy (*to* **Boy**) Excuse us. We do this all the time.

Boy What? What do you do all the time?

Jimmy Argue in public.

Boy I wasn't listening.

Natty All right. You win. Let's go. I'll cringe in a corner and watch you dance.

Boy Have you got the correct time?

Natty I . . . you talking to me?

Boy Yes. The time. What is it?

Natty It's . . . late. I don't know.

Boy Don't you have a watch?

Natty Oh God. Don't hurt me.

Jimmy Natty...

Boy Hey. Fuck off asshole. I asked you for the time.
That's all.

Jimmy It's 10.45.

Boy Oh yeah? Where you going?

Natty That's really none of your business.

Boy Are you a faggot?

Jimmy Come on, Natty. Let's go.

Natty (*to* **Boy**) What does that mean? What kind of a
question is that to ask a total stranger?

Boy You're a faggot. Right? I know you are.

Natty Listen. You've got it ... all wrong.

Jimmy No he doesn't.

Natty Be quiet, Jimmy. Let me handle this.

Boy I asked you for the time. You were rude. I don't like
that. I don't like you.

Jimmy (*to* **Boy**) Leave him alone.

Boy *advances on* **Natty**.

Boy Awww. Isn't that sweet? Your man's protecting you.
I'm touched. I'm fucking nauseous.

Jimmy Leave my lover alone.

Boy Well. Hmmmm. And where does that leave us? I
come out for some air. Want to see myself a little scenery.
And all around me there are faggots.

Jimmy Nobody asked you to come here.

Boy What. Do I need an invitation to walk down the
street?

Jimmy No. Do we?

Boy   Smartass invert.

Natty   Wait. Wait. Let's be reasonable.

Boy   You. You piece of shit. What's reason? You can't reason with sickness. You can't talk man to man or nothing like that. Can you?

Boy *advances on* **Natty**.

Natty   Please don't hurt me.

Boy *advances on* **Natty**. **Boy** *breaks up into hysterical laughter.*

Boy   Oh man. Oh SHIT. I really had you going there, didn't I?

Natty   I ... I ...

Boy   HA-HA. You should have seen your face. What a scream.

Jimmy   What the fuck are you doing?

Boy   Go on. Get outta here. Have a nice night.

Natty   You scared me. How dare you scare me.

Jimmy   We're out of here. Natty. Leave this moron alone. You know, you're real pretty. An asshole. But pretty.

Boy   You think I'm pretty? Do you?

Natty   How dare you frighten me. You ought to be ashamed of yourself.

Boy   But I'm not. Fuckface. Fuckface faggot.

Boy *pulls out a knife. It's a casual gesture, as if he's lighting a cigarette.*

Natty   Oh God. Pease. I'm ... I'm not a faggot. I'm not. Don't hurt me.

Jimmy (*comes very close to* **Boy**)   You're such an asshole, Natty. (*To* **Boy**.) Get out of here. GET THE FUCK OUT OF HERE BEFORE I TAKE MY FAGGOT FISTS AND RAM THEM DOWN YOUR THROAT, PUNK.

Boy *stabs* **Jimmy** *repeatedly.* **Natty** *runs away.*

Boy   WHO'S PRETTY NOW. WHO? WHO?

Boy *continues to stab* **Jimmy**. *Lights down on them. Lights up on* **Tilly** *and* **Jaye**. **Tilly** *applies polish to* **Jaye**'s *toe-nails. A radio report is heard.*

Radio   Current Central Park temperature is a staggering one hundred and twenty with no drop-off in sight. Temperature expected to climb to one hundred and forty by daybreak.

Tilly   It's gotten hotter every night since that night.

Jaye   What night?

Tilly   Don't play dumb with me. You get laid and you lose your memory? You know. That night.

Jaye   I told you. I'm not talking about that any more.

Tilly   One day it's sixty degrees. The next day it's a hundred. Weather doesn't happen that way. Look. It's so hot the polish won't dry. It cracks. Like tiny faultlines.

Jaye   It's cheap polish, Tilly. What do you expect from something I lifted off the discount rack at Leroy Pharmacy?

Tilly   You stole this.

Jaye   Uh-huh. On an impulse.

Tilly   Slut.

Jaye   You're a fine one to talk. I saw you stealing fruit at the grocers. Apples. Oranges.

Tilly   I tried to steal bananas but I couldn't fit them in my bra.

Jaye   I don't know if I approve of this.

Tilly   Listen. I stole useful items. I stole food. You indulged yourself. The theft of cheap red nail polish is not exactly defensible.

Jaye   So. Turn me in. I don't care. I hear there's lots of sex in prison.

Tilly   You never let up, do you?

Jaye   Nope. Get used to it.

Tilly   I used to have standards.

Jaye   And then you met me.

Tilly   Jaye. We're middle class. We don't steal.

Jaye   We're impulse thieves. It's probably an illness. Like compulsive shopping. Except we don't pay. And we can't afford to pay, anyway. We spend all our pennies to make rent on an unglamorous shitbox in a menacing neighbourhood. It's an illness. Trust me. God. I love it when you're on your knees.

Tilly   I'm kind of dizzy. Is it possible to get heat-stroke at night?

Jaye   Silly bitch. Do my nails. Go on.

Tilly   I'm thirsty. And cranky. Jaye. Are we unhappy? Are we so unhappy that we steal to fill a void? My God. There are so many things I'd like to take. I'd like to run through the city with enormous shopping carts and fill them with everything.

Jaye   I'd like to fill my shopping cart with multiples of your tongue. And maybe your hands. That way, I wouldn't have to hear you go on and on about this stuff.

Tilly   Take me someplace.

Jaye   You're already someplace.

Tilly   I was thinking ... a beer run would be nice right about now.

Jaye   Okay. We'll drag out the carts and go shopping. Wake everybody up. Get wild.

Tilly   But then I think, well, I really can't bear to walk past him. He's diminishing. Daily. I don't know whether to laugh or cry.

Jaye   Why not both. If you hit the extremes, you'll eventually get to the middle.

Tilly   You know what. We witnessed a horrible crime.

Jaye   I really can't wait to get back to work. The office is air-conditioned.

Tilly   We witnessed a horrible crime and we've responded by becoming criminals ourselves. We never talk to him. Why not?

Radio static is heard.

Radio   The latest reading from Central Park is a hundred and thirty degrees. An astonishingly rapid increase in temperature has been noted over the last half hour. The Mayor has ordered that all businesses operating within the five boroughs close until further notice. It's . . .
VACATION TIME.

Jaye   It's time to make that beer run.

Lights down on **Tilly** *and* **Jaye**. *Lights up on* **Marcel**, *on the job. Every few seconds, we see headlight beams come and go. Lights up on* **Natty**. *He sits at the vanity. As he speaks, he touches the postcards taped to the mirror, one by one.*

Marcel (*to the passing cars*)   Marcel says: Stop. Come directly to jail. Do not pass go. Marcel collects two hundred dollars.

Natty   Morocco has much to recommend it. Sand, for one thing. And intrigue, for another. And of course, there are the boys.

Marcel   Slow down. What's your hurry? Marcel can provide motion in the comfort of your imitation leather interior. All you need's a decent car stereo and a wad of cash to make Marcel a happy camper.

Natty   And Paris, well. It's natural that I would be attracted to the city of light. I love places where I can't understand one damned word spoken. Life's a breeze then.

Marcel   So much traffic and so little time. Boys. BOYS.
Take a breather. It's hot and Marcel is sooooo cold.
Marcel has a brilliant theory which Marcel will reveal in
due course.

Natty   Amsterdam. Now *that's* a city. The prince of cities.
I could get lost there. I could. Lost among the blonds.
Blonds love me. They don't take me for a coward.

Marcel   Marcel's radiant theory is this: it's so hot that
people are keeping to their cars. They mindlessly travel the
same stretch of the West Side highway for hours so they
can be in the only air-conditioning that still works. But oh,
all my children, let me tell *you* what will happen when
those cars fizzle out.

Natty   I'm sure I was braver in another life. I just don't
know which one. London. I stayed indoors and avoided the
food. Jimmy had a splendid holiday while I watched the
World Scrabble Championships. I've got to take Jimmy's
ashes to Westminster Abbey and hide them under the
coronation chair. I mean, who will care?

Marcel   Oh my honey-pants, all of you. Your cars will
self-destruct on this particular stretch of the gloomy
highway. In the sweltering heat you will stagger from the
intensity of moiself. And Marcel will wait for you. With a
pitcher of ice water and clean pantyhose. Marcel prepares
for your coming catastrophe.

Headlights beam directly at **Marcel**. *He's ablaze in light.*

THAT'S RIGHT, HON. COME CLOSER. CONSUME
ME.

Headlights disappear.

Shitshitshit. Marcel's gonna collapse from boredom.
Marcel's gonna starve and faint from lack of nourishment.
(*Turning his attention to* **Natty**.) Excuse me, Charles Atlas.

Natty   Brave. Braver. Bravest. Seattle. Salt Lake City.
Cincinnati.

Marcel   Marcel said: PARDON MOI MR FUCKING
UNIVERSE. Marcel would like some food. Marcel would
like *you* to provide hors d'oeuvres.

Natty   You broke my music. You scream at me. And you
want me to *feed* you?

Marcel   You've invaded Marcel's space. And now you
must pay up. Food. Glorious food. That is Marcel's desire.

Natty   I have clothes. I can give you a hat. Or a necktie.

Marcel   Marcel says: you are a silly queen. Marcel says:
my splendiferous wardrobe is quite complete. AND WHO
NEEDS CLOTHES IN THIS AWFUL HEAT.

Natty   Courage is a state of mind. A state. Connecticut.
California. Calgary.

Marcel   You are depriving Marcel of a livelihood.
Potential clients take one look at the skinny buttless wonder
of you and they FLEE. Marcel holds you personally
responsible. Marcel finds it a DISGUSTING
PERVERSION when moneyed queer boys take to the
streets. GET OUT. YOU ARE ECLIPSING THE SUN
THAT SPELLS M-A-R-C-E-L.

Natty   I haven't eaten for weeks. I think.

Marcel   Marcel commands you to return to your hovel
and whip up some ... RATATOUILLE.

Natty   Why doesn't Marcel go *home* and cook up some
... RATATOUILLE?

Marcel   *Nature* is Marcel's home. *Nature* nourishes Marcel.
When it rains, Marcel's slender neck drifts elegantly back,
Marcel's perfect lips part, and the *rain* feeds Marcel. And
sometimes Marcel is nourished by unsuspecting gay boys
who stay too long on Marcel's nature preserve.

Natty   I must unpack Jimmy's clothing. I must make
contributions to charity.

Marcel   Charity begins at home. Charity begins at night.

Charity begins with Marcel. Nourish Marcel. NOW.

Natty   Jimmy always said you were sad.

Marcel   Marcel has serviced the needs of . . . of . . .
Neanderthal, Cro-Magnon and Renaissance man. Marcel
does not recall a Jimmy man.

Natty   Marcel watched him die.

*Headlight beams swing by. A constant stream of light that suggests a
mass exodus.*

Marcel   Take a break oh all my weary travellers. The
night sky burns your eyes, but Marcel has a magic balm.
Marcel is but a reflection of the company he keeps. Stop.
STOP. TWO ROADS DIVERGED ON A HIGHWAY
AND I COMMAND YOU TO TAKE THE ONE THAT
LEADS TO ME.

Headlights disappear. **Marcel** *returns to his ceramic basin. Takes
many panthose from his purse and washes them carefully. He lays
them out in the street to dry.*

Natty   A thousand years ago, when I was a boy and still
had hair, I lived above a club on the highway called Ten
West. At the time, I was a pharmacist's assistant. I wore
white smocks to convince myself I was a professional. At
night, I locked myself into my studio apartment and
fantasised to the thumping and throbbing music that
vibrated beneath my feet. One night, I stood before a
mirror and combed my hair for three hours. Beneath me,
Donna Summer and Sylvester wailed on. That night, I
unlocked my door and entered paradise. I drank a vodka
tonic and cried at the bar. Nobody talked to me. I figured
it was because in my haste to leave locked doors behind
me, I forgot to remove my pharmacist assistant's white
smock. On my ninth vodka tonic, I met Jimmy. He tapped
me on my shoulder and asked if I was a doctor. I said, no.
I'm Natty. He said, so you are. So you are.

Music in: 'Johnny Come Home' (Fine Young Cannibals).

Headlights beam directly as **Marcel**.

Marcel A PENNY FOR YOUR THOUGHTS, SWEET THING.

Headlights disappear.

Natty Natty says: Marcel can use Natty's clothing rack. For the pantyhose. So they dry.

Marcel You wearing that ugly beret because you're bald?

Natty No. No. I have some hair. Some.

Marcel Marcel's tits are melting from the heat and you've got this . . . woollen monstrosity . . . perched on your head. You're sick.

Natty I'm modest.

Marcel Then do us a favour and cover that mass of undernourishment you call a body. Marcel is not comfortable around starvation.

Natty I shaved off all my body hair.

Marcel How nice for you. Marcel knows all about that kind of thing so please spare Marcel the details.

Natty I'm swimming to England. I've got to bring Jimmy's ashes to Westminster Abbey.

Marcel Marcel believes we are living in the age of supersonic transport. So you ought to grow back your leg hair and FLY.

Natty I'm not afraid of flying. But I fear water. So I must . . . swim. Brave. Braver. Bravest.

Marcel Marcel thought you were harmless. Marcel thought your major problem was that you smelled like an almond. But Marcel is no longer so sure. And . . . WHERE IS THAT DIZZY FAGGOT MUSIC COMING FROM?

Natty It's the lesbians above the poultry market. They like to dance.

Marcel There are DYKES in this neighbourhood?

Natty   Uh-huh. They're very cute. Serious types. I think they drink a lot.

Marcel   Well. Marcel says: this is BOYS' TOWN, honey. Marcel says: this is not the neighbourhood for LADIES' HOUR.

Natty   You've never seen them? Dragging groceries and laundry behind them? They do an awful lot of laundry.

Marcel   No fucking way. Marcel converses with MEN.

Natty   Marcel never talked to me. Marcel never talked to Jimmy.

Marcel   Listen here, Mister Sandman. Marcel can spot those who are worth conversing with. Marcel knows a dud when Marcel spots one. LISTEN UP MY LEZZIE SISTERS: CUT THE FUCKING MUSIC. DANCE TO YOUR OWN DIFFERENT FUCKING DRUMMER BUT LEAVE MARCEL OUT OF IT.

Music gets louder.

Marcel speaks and the whole world DOESN'T LISTEN. Marcel regrets that Marcel was forced to converse with unseen womanhood. But that is the way the cookie crumbles here in the meat market.

Natty   You never talked to me. You never talked to Jimmy while he was bleeding to death in your own backyard.

Music out.

Marcel   Sigh. Oh my ridiculous shrinking boy child. SIGH. Marcel sighs a big sigh as Marcel recalls the flight of this pathetic boy child one night not too long ago when there was blood on the cobblestones and on his chicken-little hands. Marcel saw all. Marcel speaks THE TRUTH. What were you doing, sweat pea? Where were *you* running to? Marcel says: end of fairy tale.

Natty   Courage. Courage in the face of adversity. Danger. Grab the danger by its horns and ride it. Ride it. I don't. I

don't. I don't wanna die. I am. I am. I am. . . . dangerous.
I am dangerous and I am . . . NATTY. I AM NATTY. So
you are, he said. So you are. He swept me off my
earthbound feet and it was many years later I betrayed
him.

Music in: 'You Make Me Feel (Mighty Real)', (Sylvester).

Jimmy *enters. He dances as if he's dancing in a crowd, all smiles
and sweat. He's doing poppers.* **Marcel** *is awe-struck by this
apparent apparition.*

Natty Then as now, I wouldn't dance with him. Old
habits die hard. But he danced for me. There's nothing
sexier than watching somebody dance for you. We were so
young and so happy. His body a dazzling intricacy of
muscle and smoothness. His hands yet unblemished by
stress, work, heartbreak. Jimmy. Your body was a testament
to youth and so was mine in its half-assed way. The
importance we attach to our bodies. They are ephemeral.
We are ephemeral and if I could have danced with you
that night I would have told you so. Bodies are
unimportant until we lose them.

Jimmy Natty Weldon. Watch me dance for you.

Natty I'm watching, Jimmy. I'm always watching.

Jimmy Let's grow up and become Senators. Diplomats.

Natty *approaches* **Jimmy**.

Natty Let's *not* grow up and avoid the mess.

Jimmy I like mess. The stuff of life. I'm a dancing fool.

Jimmy *continues to dance.* **Natty** *is motionless, close to him.*

Natty Beautiful people are allowed to be fools. They can
even dance. But the less beautiful are left running after
departing trains. Missed connections. You're beautiful,
Jimmy.

Jimmy Someday my prince will come and his name will

be Nathaniel. Someday we'll be seventy-five and rail at the indecency of the younger generation. At the old gay home, poppers will be fed to us intravenously and Bette Midler will do the New Year's Eve show.

Natty How old are you, Jimmy?

Jimmy I'm twenty years old and I am HOT. Come on. Let me take you on a fast train to meet my folks.

Natty I'm a coward.

Jimmy This is the seventies. There's no room for cowardice.

Natty I was never twenty years old. I'm tired. Jimmy. What if I told you that in fifteen years I will betray you. What if I told you that I will run from you when it counts most. What if I told you that in fifteen years I will watch you die. What then?

Jimmy *takes* **Natty** *into his arms.*

Jimmy There's always the hope that you won't run. The next time.

Natty There's never a next time, Jimmy.

Jimmy Everywhere you look there's a next time.

Boy *enters. Music out.*

Boy Are you a faggot?

Jimmy (*to* **Natty**) Tell me what you'll do. Next time.

Natty I ... I ...

Boy You. YOU. Ugly man. Jerkoff. Fuckface. I smell the fear on you. HATE YOURSELF FOR ME. Show me you know what I mean. WHO ARE YOU, BOY?

Natty I'm ... I'm ...

Jimmy Hold me close and tell me who you are. Take me places and show me that we will be legion, marching in rows as far as the eye can see and we are all telling each other who we are. Over and over.

Natty I'm ... I'm ...

Boy It doesn't matter how I get you. In the end I'll get you all. I'll crush you under my heel because YOU CAN'T TELL ME WHO YOU ARE.

Natty I'm Natty.

Jimmy So you are. So you are.

Jimmy *and* **Natty** *kiss.* **Boy** *pulls out a knife.* **Marcel** *drops to the ground, covering his head with his hands. Lights up on* **Tilly** *and* **Jaye***, who watch from their apartment.*

Tilly He's got a knife. He's gonna use it.

Jaye Get away from the window.

Marcel Pleasepleaseplease don't look at me. Don't look at me. Don't look at me.

Boy You think I'm pretty? How pretty am I? Tell me.

Natty You ought to be ashamed of yourself.

Boy But I'm not. I'm taller and prouder and PRETTIER than you.

Tilly Should we scream or something? I don't know, to chase him away?

Jaye Get away from the window.

Marcel I don't wanna be cut. No cuts. No bruises. NO CUTS. Go awaygoawayaway.

Natty Let's be reasonable. Talk sense.

Jimmy He's not reasonable, Natty.

Boy I'm not reasonable.

Natty You've got a future. It's bright. Put down the knife and talk to us.

Jimmy He's not reasonable, Natty.

Boy I'm not reasonable. I'm PRETTY.

Tilly Let's do something.

Jaye Why should we?

Marcel Marcel does not want to see this. Marcel says: NO.

Boy Faggot. You disgust me. You crowd my world.

Natty I'm . . . I'm . . .

Jimmy Hold me close. Hold on.

Boy GET OUTTA MY NEIGHBOURHOOD.

Natty I'm . . . I . . . CAN'T.

Boy *stabs* **Jimmy** *repeatedly.*

Boy WHO'S PRETTY NOW. WHO? WHO?

Natty *runs away.* **Boy** *runs away.* **Marcel** *rises to look at the carnage.* **Jaye** *joins* **Tilly** *at the window.*

Jaye Call the police.

Tilly Okay.

Jaye It's so . . . quiet.

Tilly Yeah. We better call the cops.

Jaye Okay.

A silence, as **Marcel**, **Jaye** *and* **Tilly** *look at* **Jimmy**.
Headlights beam at **Marcel**. *Lights down on all but* **Marcel**.

Marcel HEY. COME AND SIT WITH ME A WHILE. YOU DON'T EVEN GOT TO PAY. BE WITH ME. BE WITH ME.

Headlights disappear. Lights up on **Natty** *at the vanity. Throughout the following scene, he very carefully removes the postcards from the mirror, cuts them up into tiny pieces, and throws them to the wind.*

Natty We'll never forget, will we, Marcel?

Marcel   What are you talking about silly gay boy?
WHAT?

Natty   Where are you from, Marcel? Where is that place
that lets you forget?

Marcel   Marcel is a citizen of the universe. Marcel forgets
nothing. However, Marcel does employ considerable editing
skills. From time to time.

Natty   Sometimes I think I'll be fine in the end. That I'll
wake up in the morning and be able to get through the
day without telling myself even one lie. But you know, just
thinking that it's gonna be okay in the end is a lie. So.
Where does *that* leave us?

Tilly *and* **Jaye** *enter the street. They drag a shopping cart with
them. It's full of beer.*

Marcel   My, my. If it isn't the luscious lushes of Little
West 12th Street.

Jaye   Fuck off, freak.

Tilly   Jaye, *really*. (*To* **Marcel**.) Hi. I'm Tilly. This is Jaye.
And this is our beer. I think we almost met you at the
police station.

Jaye   Yeah. You were looking particularly Jayne
Mansfieldesque that morning.

Marcel   Marcel says: lesbians have no manners.

Natty   Hi. I'm Natty. I'm a liar.

Tilly   Oh, great. So are we.

Natty   Really.

Tilly   Sure. We lie all the time. About most everything.

Jaye   We steal, too. We stole this beer.

Marcel   Marcel wants nothing to do with petty thieves.

Jaye   Aren't you an anachronism?

Natty   This is Marcel. Marcel . . . hovers.

Jaye Why do you refer to yourself in the third person, Marcel?

Marcel Marcel IS the third person.

Jaye Heat-stroke. Transvestite clown succumbs to heat-stroke. Melted down in the prime of womanhood. A sad, sad story.

Natty Did you really steal that beer?

Tilly Yeah. You ought to see it out there. It's wild. Not a soul in the streets. Supermarkets deserted. Restaurants abandoned. But the cars. Wow. More cars than I've ever seen packed together like . . . like butane lighters waiting to explode.

Jaye We need the beer 'cause we ain't got air-conditioning.

Natty I'm trying to be courageous. And everyone's gone. Nobody to watch me spit at passers-by.

Tilly We're here. You want a beer? I think we almost met you at the police station, too.

Natty I was the one with the bag over my head, crouching in a corner. If you don't mind, I'll trade you some perfume for a beer.

Jaye Looks like we're having a block party.

Jaye *removes a small portable radio from the shopping cart.*

Marcel Marcel must return to work. Marcel has no time for parties.

Jaye Haven't you heard? They've cancelled work.

Marcel *Who* cancelled work?

Jaye The big deals. The men in suits. Though I doubt they're wearing suits at this moment.

Jaye *turns on the* **Radio**. *Static. More static. Then:*

Radio . . . schools, banks, post offices closed. Subway and

bus service has been suspended. Current Central Park
temperature a hundred and forty-three degrees. A rapid
increase in temperature expected by daybreak.

Radio *goes to static.*

Marcel   Marcel, for one, welcomes the heat because the
cars will die sooner. Marcel waits with arms spread wide as
the widest sea, for all Marcel's children to run back to
mamma.

Jaye   Uh-huh. Prostitution thrives in hard times.

Tilly (*to* **Natty**)   I'm afraid. Really.

Natty   What do you fear?

Tilly   Everything. I'm afraid of cars. Motorboats. Voting.

Marcel (*to* **Jaye**)   Why don't you go live in BROOKLYN
with the rest of your sisters? Why don't you leave Marcel
to Marcel's business?

Jaye   Looks to me like Marcel hasn't had any business in
a long time. Tilly. Look. He's got cobwebs sprouting from
his underarms. Lack of use.

Tilly   Mostly, though, I'm afraid I'll lose Jaye. And then I
would just crumple up and blow away. Like a panic
napkin. We insult each other a lot, but we like it that way.

Marcel (*to* **Jaye**)   I AM NOT A HE. I AM ...
MARCEL.

Natty   How would you lose her? Why? Well. I guess I'm
the last one to be asking those questions.

Tilly   I could lose her the way I met her. In an instant.

Marcel *takes a beer from the shopping cart.*

Marcel   Marcel requires retribution for your insult.

Tilly   I mean, isn't that always true? One minute you
know somebody, the next minute you don't. One day
you're in love, the next day you're not. You look a girl in
the eye and you make a snap judgement. Love makes

spontaneous decisions.

Natty   And so does hate. Cowardice.

Marcel   Oh my little ones. Welcome to Marcel's
PHILOSOPHY CORNER. Let's see. We've got one
horrifically skinny almost naked queer boy and . . . oh my
. . . one DRUNKEN DYKE . . . waxing poetic on the
nature of our hasty, hasty hearts.

Jaye   Have you got something better to say?

Tilly   I met Jaye at Kennedy Airport. She was to meet a
cousin from Los Angeles. I flew into New York looking for
a home. I was especially unattractive that day. As I
approached the ground transportation exit, I felt a hand
grab my arm. I whirled around and it was Jaye. She said –

Jaye   You're ugly, but you must be the one.

Tilly   I couldn't tell if this was a compliment. She took
my bags to her car, muttered something about an Uncle
Roger.

Jaye   I passed on regards from Aunt Ida.

Tilly   I wondered where we were headed. She said –

Jaye   The barbecue's at three.

Tilly   I mean, who could argue? I began to hallucinate.
Maybe I was destined to be in the back seat of a stranger's
Honda Civic with no idea of where I was being taken. All
I could think about was her eyes. Her funny hat. The way
she gripped the steering wheel.

Jaye   I stopped three times so she could vomit.

Tilly   Jesus, was I *sick*. But I couldn't help it. This was
completely unlike me, to be in a car with a sexy woman
who was wearing a funny hat. A hat with a musical *flower*
attached to its brim. Wow. And then, as I was about to
pass out from the thrill of it all, she said –

Jaye   I wish I'd known I had such a wacko cousin.

Tilly   I blurted out, but, hey, I'm not your cousin. Stop the car. There's been a mistake.

Jaye   I stopped the car.

Tilly   But there was no mistake. She turned to me. I was a mess. Drool dangling from the corners of my mouth. Acne grew spontaneously, like spores. She said –

Jaye   I know you're not my cousin. I was just testing the quality of your imagination.

Tilly   Oh, sure, I said. But I don't even *know* you.

Jaye   And why the fuck *don't* you know me? Said I.

Tilly   Well. So. Why not? It was true. She looked at me and there was a conspiracy of understanding.

Jaye   Don't believe her. She was squinting a lot. And she adores conspiracy theories.

Tilly   And every year on that day we go back to Kennedy. Sit in tacky bars and make passes at the flight attendants.

Jaye   I *love* flight attendants.

Natty   *begins to douse himself with cologne.*

Marcel   Oh nononono. Marcel says: please do not open Doctor Caligari's cabinet again.

Jaye   Why don't you ZIP IT and DRINK UP. Marcel. Or you'll miss the bus to HELL when it rounds the corner.

Tilly   Excuse me. Natty. That's your name, isn't it?

Natty   Jimmy liked airports. We meant to build our vacations around cities that had remarkable airports. But we never managed to get out of New York. There was always something to be done. Always something to do right under your own nose.

Tilly   Look, I didn't mean to make you feel bad. Jaye and me, we're really very fucked up. So don't use us as an example.

Natty   As an example of what?

Tilly   Well. You know. Whatever people use . . . other people . . . as examples of.

Jaye   Natty. Listen. You really shouldn't mix colognes like that. It'll have a bad effect.

Natty   Cologne sustains me. Rivers of cologne. I can't stand my own smell any more. I want to go to meetings. I want to learn how to *like* drugs. I want to visit all the places I've had people mail me postcards from. I want to PARTICIPATE. I WANT HIM BACK.

Natty *clears the vanity with one swipe of a fist. Bottles shatter on the streeet.*

Marcel   Marcel says: boys will be boys.

Natty   My skin is . . . bubbling. The heat. THE HEAT. LOOK. I'M DEVELOPING BOILS.

Jaye *touches* **Natty** *and jumps back.*

Jaye (*really much more interested in her hand than in* **Natty**)   Ouch.
Christ. Tilly. We need a towel. And some cold water. This boy's . . . really hot.

Natty (*to* **Jaye**)   I'm gonna burn in hell.

Jaye (*totally uninterested*)   Listen. We're gonna, you know, get some help.

Natty   My limbs are gonna drop off.

Tilly   It's our fault. I knew it. We let that night happen and in doing so, allowed the weather to take over.

Marcel   And why the fuck *shouldn't* the weather take over? I've already seen a ghost tonight. Nothing can compare.

Natty *grabs* **Jaye**.

Natty   You saw it, didn't you.

Jaye   Yes.

Natty   You watched him die.

Jaye (*she pulls away*) Not . . . exactly.

Tilly Yes. We did watch him die. The sky split open. The temperature rose. And nothing's been the same since.

Jaye Well. *That's* true enough. Lately, our lovemaking has come to resemble something out of Genet.

Marcel Mama said there'd be days like this. There'd be days like this, Marcel's mama said.

Natty What was it like? Tell me.

Jaye We called the police. That's what it was like.

Natty No. I mean. What was it like? To see him die. I didn't. See it. I should have.

Tilly Don't do this. It's not necessary.

Natty It is necessary. I've learned practically nothing, it's true. But I do know that. Tell me something. Anything.

Tilly We watched from above. We thought we were safe.

Jaye I drank beer and thought . . . how lucky I am not to be him.

Tilly We called the police. We did. But by that time, there was nothing left to protect us from.

Natty How could you. How could you . . . *watch*?

Jaye How could you run?

Tilly And you know, tell me something. What would you have done? If you were us, if you were a couple of girls holed up in a crappy apartment? Huh?

Natty I . . . I would have . . . run. Again. And again. I have no pride.

Natty *cries. A silence, as* **Tilly** *and* **Marcel** *busy themselves with anything but* **Natty**. **Jaye**, *forced to take action, pats* **Natty** *half-heartedly on his back.*

Jaye We saw you a lot, you and your lover. You shopped at all the food stores we couldn't afford. We envied your clothing. We fantasised about what art you'd collect. And each time we saw you we said, we really must invite them up for a drink.

Natty   I was thirty before I told anybody except Jimmy that I was gay. Nobody knew.

Jaye   That's what we all think. Nobody knows. We wear it like it's a medal of honour. We're sick to do it, but we do it anyway. And then one day, we get well. Shake the shame right outta our hair and wonder, well, why in the fuck did we ever let it get the best of us? The trick is to get rid of it. *Before* the point of implosion. Before it eats us to pieces.

Natty   I'm in so many pieces I don't remember what it's like to be whole.

Tilly   And so we said, we really must invite them up for a drink. But we didn't. What did we think would happen?

Headlights beam directly at **Marcel**.

Marcel   And once again, Marcel lifts Marcel's weary shell of a body and entertains the troops. Marcel wears a dress so Marcel can gather all of humankind underneath it. Oh my lonesome dove, are *you* going to help Marcel pass time? Let me tell you honey, this absolute COW of a dyke called Marcel an anachronism. What do you think of THAT? Well. At least I am recognizable. AT LEAST I AM THE LAST OF THE MOHICANS. I saw it, too. DO THEY THINK I DIDN'T SEE IT? That night, Marcel was collecting business like it was stardust. Marcel was BUSY. And Marcel saw the blade strike its target and Marcel hit the street so fast Marcel didn't notice that Marcel was lying in TRASH. Animal innards. Guts. COW BLOOD. Marcel sank in entrails for the better part of an hour before the cops came to drag Marcel off. Marcel sat in a precinct. Marcel sat in a straight-back chair whilst no gentlemanly police officer gave Marcel as much as a HANDY WIPE. Marcel stank. Marcel was humiliated and covered in debris. But still. Still. Marcel saw everything and in the end, all

Marcel saw was that cool steel blade. And Marcel realized.
MARCEL KNEW THAT ... I ... knew that. I was
wearing a dress and some bad falsies and every ounce of
self-preservation kicked in and and and ... there was me
and my dress and ... I could cut myself no slack. I sank. I
went way way down that night. DON'T THEY THINK I
KNOW THAT? Oh. My speedy traveller. Shut off your
engine and ignite my transmission. Teach me to DRIVE.
Take it all away. Take me HOME.

*A sudden explosion of blinding hot white light. Just for an instant,
and then it is gone. Radio static is heard.*

Radio   ... a hundred and sixty-seven degrees and rising.
Unconfirmed reports from Hoboken, Piscataway and
Edison, New Jersey of automobiles spontaneously
combusting. And this just in ... at Kennedy Airport, a
Delta seven-forty-seven exploded on takeoff. At Port
Authority, a Greyhound bus bound for Lincoln, Nebraska
melted within seconds of entering the Holland Tunnel.
Current Central Park temperature a hundred and sixty-
seven and RISING.

Radio *goes to static. A brief silence. Lights down on all but*
Marcel.

Marcel   Marcel Hughes. H-U-G-H-E-S. Yes. That is my
... actual ... name. I was born at 227–27 Horace
Harding Expressway in Queens, New York. My mother,
Sally Hughes, was a practical nurse. Or practically a nurse.
I can never remember which. My father, whose name I
cannot bring myself to utter, was a small businessman.
Very small. He owned a shed, took it to a corner, and
called it a newsstand.

Lights up on **Jaye**.

Jaye   My lover and I were watching television. Yeah.
That's right. She's my lover. You got a problem with that?
Okay. So we're watching television and we hear this noise
from the street. I hear somebody say: FAGGOT. I always
hear that word when it's said. Always.

Lights up on **Tilly**.

Tilly Jaye and I were watching television. Well, Jaye was watching. I was looking out the windows, as usual. Excuse me? No. I do not SPY on people in the street. Well. Actually, I do. But. Anyway. Jaye was watching a basketball game and cursing herself because, you know, it was such a dykey thing to be watching.

Marcel It was very dark. And I was observing this from quite some distance. Pardon moi? Oh. I was . . . walking. I was taking a walk. I often take walks in the neighbourhood. What? Yes. I LIKE to walk. So, I can tell you that he was definitely Hispanic. Or a light-skinned black. Pretty skin. Smooth. Gorgeous. A big guy. Don't you just LOVE big men?

Jaye I saw this guy stabbing this other guy. The guy with the knife was a fair-haired tall white guy. Maybe six foot three. Broad shoulders. Strawberry blond with freckles. Good-looking. Like the kind of jerk I used to date before I got wise. I remember thinking I hadn't seen hair that colour for a long time.

Tilly He must have been, oh I don't know, nineteen or twenty. Small. Delicate. Wiry. With devastating hands. I adore hands. And this kid had glorious hands. And he worked out. Great body. Little rippling muscles all over him. But those hands. Hmmm. Wondrous.

Marcel Oh yeah. He was a FAT motherfucker. And old. That sucker was OLD. Forty-five at least. But I think jolly old fat men are sexy.

Jaye Other than that, he was pretty nondescript. *You* know the type. Played some college football. Has a beer gut, but otherwise, you know, he's in pretty decent shape. He was attractive, and I couldn't understand how somebody who was kind of attractive could do such a shitty thing.

Tilly I can't tell you much about his face, but if you showed me his hands I'd know. You see somebody use his hands to kill and you don't forget it.

Lights up on **Natty**.

Natty   Do you know what I recall most vividly? That
Jimmy called me an asshole. Those were his final words to
me, I think. I think . . . why did we survive AIDS, Jimmy
and me, to come to *this*? There's no dignity left. I'd like to
go home now if I may. I can't tell you what he looked
like. I barely saw him. I've got a lot to bury.

Boy *enters. He stands before the group first in profile, then full face.
Then he holds out his hands to them. The group, in unison, with the
exception of* **Natty**, *point fingers at* **Boy**. **Natty** *bows his head,
unable to look.*

All except Natty   That's him.

Lights down on all but **Boy**.

Boy   Makes no difference to me *who* I kill. I could tell
you that it was a *personal* thing. I could tell you about how
goddamned pretty the blade is at night. Out in the open
air. But I'm not *going* to talk about *those* things. I'm gonna
let you put me on the news and I'm gonna nod my head
at a lot of stupid people talking about misunderstanding
and compassion and bad upbringings and I'm gonna
fucking laugh out loud. What? Who said something about
bias crimes? What the fuck is BIAS? This is about HATE.
And there isn't a lawyer or a doctor or any fucked up
fucking do-gooder alive who can do a damned thing about
it. You wanna fight me, you got to FIGHT me. Lock me
up. Come on. Do it. You can take away my blade, but I'm
still out there. There's more of me back where I come
from.

Lights down on **Boy**. *Lights up on the rest of the scene.*

Empty beer bottles and cans scattered everywhere. **Natty** *has taken to
cutting* **Marcel**'s *pantyhose into tiny pieces.* **Marcel** *sits in the
shopping cart. He drinks beer.* **Jaye** *spins him around in circles.*
Tilly *sits among the remnants of the broken cologne bottles. She takes
shards of glass and dabs them to her wrists, her neck, any pulse point*

she can find.

Tilly I've never smelled a Chanel perfume before. Hmmmm. It's not as . . . old smelling . . . as I imagined.

Natty That Number 19. An elusive scent. Not everyone can wear it.

Tilly Yeah, well. It suits the street. (*Dabs a shard of glass against her wrist.*) Shit. It cut me.

Marcel Oooooooweeeee. Marcel is a dizzy miss lizzie. Stop the world honey, 'cause Marcel wants to get OFF.

Jaye We're creating a breeze, Marcel. If we spin long and hard enough, we'll make a typhoon that will carry us to . . . who knows where.

Marcel Take me to the river.

Jaye (*stopping the cart*)   River's dried up. We could *walk* across to Jersey.

Tilly Jaye. The Chanel CUT me. I dabbed it on and it fucking CUT me.

Marcel Don't you bother about that my little Sapphist. Chanel is not an equal opportunity parfumière. Chanel knows which wrists it belongs on.

Tilly Oh God WHY did we choose to live in a neighbourhood full of gay men?

Jaye Because we think we *are* gay men.

Tilly Don't start in on me again, Jaye. We're snobs. That's why. We don't even have enough money to buy brand-name toilet paper and we think it's more refined to live with faggots. I swear. I feel like Eliza Doolittle in drag. AND THERE'S NO MORE BEER. WE DRANK TWENTY-SEVEN CASES AND WE'RE NOT DRUNK.

Jaye Look. There are no lights on in Jersey.

Radio static, very loud. Then:

Radio . . . supports have collapsed. Repeat: the George

Washington, Triborough, Brooklyn, Manhattan,
Williamsburgh and Queensboro bridges have collapsed.
Current Central Park temperature one hundred and eighty
degrees. Repeat one hundred and eighty and rising.

Marcel   Good. So much for the bridge and tunnel crowd.

Natty   The neighbourhood is ours again. You'd think I'd
be happy about that. But I'm not.

Tilly   I'm bleeding. It doesn't hurt, though. You always
think you have time. You know, to do certain things. Say
whatever needs to be said.

Jaye   You do say whatever needs to be said. You talk in
your sleep.

Tilly   What do I say?

Jaye   You talk about ... Melanie Griffith. Flight
attendants. Tarts.

Tilly   I've barely gotten used to the way you sleep. And
now it's gotten so hot we *can't* sleep. Shit. I can never
adjust to change.

Natty *collapses.*

Marcel   Girls. GIRLS. EMERGENCY.

Marcel *tries to push himself towards* **Natty**, *who sits bolt upright
and speaks with great urgency.*

Natty   Things I ought to have done but didn't: buy a
Jaguar adopt a puppy become an Episcopalian take
communion and I should have been promiscuous when
promiscuity was good should have called my dad before he
croaked should have gone to law school should have loved
him truer cleaner braver should have. Could have. Didn't.
BE HANDSOMER LOSE WEIGHT SPEAK MY MIND
FIGHT FIGHT FIGHT BACK.

Marcel   Marcel says: GET ME OUT OF THIS
FUCKING CART.

Tilly *helps* **Marcel** *out of the shopping cart.* **Jaye** *touches*

Natty, *tentatively, as if she's touching a bug.*

Jaye *He's* awfully hot.

Natty This is the way it happens. With strangers. One minute you know somebody. The next minute you're dead.

Sudden explosion of hot white light. Silence. **Marcel** *and* **Tilly** *hold each other. Headlight beam directly at* **Marcel**.

Marcel That's the biggest motherfucking car I've ever seen.

Tilly It's shimmering.

Marcel Oh my deep-pocketed traveller. Tell Marcel you are the richest man in the UNIVERSE. Oh my road warrior, the world is burning up and Marcel doesn't want to miss the FIRE.

Tilly It's glowing. Jaye. That car is GLOWING.

Marcel GLOW MY WAY OH DANNY BOY. BURN WITH ME.

A car horn is heard. Silence. The horn sounds again.

Tilly They're honking for you.

Marcel I'm not going.

Tilly Why not?

Marcel I played Mystery Date in high school. I know the bum's waiting for me behind the door. I KNOW IT.

Natty (*to* **Jaye**) Tell me why I ran away. Tell me why I'm still running.

Jaye There's no end to it. Never has been.

Natty I'm feverish.

Jaye Uh-huh.

Natty I like that. Feels like something's . . . happening.

Tilly Look Marcel. You've got a fucking CUSTOMER. When's the last time one of those rolled through?

Marcel   Marcel is very particular.

Tilly   Who do you think's gonna drive by? There aren't exactly limitless options at this point.

Marcel   I didn't think I'd live to see the day when a lesbian became my pimp.

Tilly   Times change.

Car horn sounds.

Natty   Is there . . . something happening?

Jaye   The city's falling apart. Nothing new there.

Natty   Something's ending. Something's busting up.

Jaye   Yeah. I feel that way every time I take the subway.

Car horn sounds.

Marcel (*considering this carefully*)   I like to travel. I like to FLY.

Tilly   Wow. That car is . . . LEVITATING.

Marcel   Oh mymymy. WAIT FOR ME, PETER PAN. Marcel's going to places where there is no slime to sink down into. Where the big girl's shop is always OPEN.

Marcel *tidies himself up, starts towards the headlights. An explosion of hot white light, and he's gone.*

Radio   . . . no longer registering. Temperature can no longer be measured. Two hundred degrees at last reading. Last reading. Last reading. Barometric pressure is at a standstill. Jones Beach has fallen into the Atlantic. We advise all residents to —

Radio *goes to static.*

Tilly *gathers up a pair of* **Marcel**'s *pantyhose and wraps them around her wrist.*

Tilly   I can't stop bleeding.

Natty   This is the way it happens. This way.

Tilly   But it's slow.

Natty   With strangers.

Tilly   And unpredictable. Shit. Now what. I'm turning into a SHRINE. I'll bleed for ever and people will kneel at my feet. They'll light candles. Make offerings.

Natty   I'm shivering. Sick. I'm paying for something.

Jaye   Bullshit. We never pay for anything. Be quiet.

Tilly *kneels at the ceramic basin. She submerges her head in it. While* **Natty** *speaks, she bangs her head into the basin. Slowly. Rhythmically.*

Natty (*a great realization*)   Something's busting up. I'm . . . imploding. A fluorescent bulb I am a bulb a light a sickness an arrested development an ember the world in my pocket and and and I WANT HIM BACK I WANT A CHANCE TO NOT DIE IN THIS HEAT I WANT I WANT –

Jaye   Shut up. SHUT UP. MY GIRLFRIEND'S GOT FUCKING STIGMATA. Shut. The fuck. Up.

Music in: Intro: 'Prelude to Love/Could This Be Magic' (Donna Summer). **Tilly** *snaps to attention. Her hair and face are soaked with water and bits of blood.* **Tilly** *and* **Natty** *bop along to the music. It fills them with an odd sense of determination and direction.*

Jaye   What the fuck . . .

Tilly   I'm melting. I'm bleeding and wet and God. I LOVE THIS SONG.

Natty   Dress me.

Jaye   It's too hot for clothes. Be quiet. Tilly. TILLY. LOOK AT ME.

Tilly   I can't. I'm too busy falling apart.

Jaye   Why won't you look at me?

Tilly   Don't know. Don't know.

Natty   Clothe me. In white.

Jaye   And where is this music coming from? WHERE?

Tilly   Nineteen seventy-something. Before we were mean.

Natty   Before we lost time. Please. Dress me up and take me to a DISCO.

Natty *and* **Tilly** *continue to dance.* **Tilly** *removes her blouse.*

Jaye   What are you doing?

Tilly   Melting. Moulting. Something.

Tilly *undresses completely. She rifles through the clothing rack. She finds a dazzling white suit.* **Natty** *begins to shake violently. He falls to his knees.* **Jaye** *cradles him.*

Jaye   I've never held a man in my arms like this. Never wanted to. Still not sure I want to.

Natty   So cold. So . . . fucking . . . cold. We're burning up.

Jaye   Have I always been this mean? Have I? God. If it's true I'll slit my throat.

Tilly *puts on the man's suit jacket. The pants. They are ridiculously large on her. She goes to* **Jaye** *and* **Natty**, *kneels beside them. Her hair, if possible, seems to get wetter.*

Jaye (*touching* **Tilly***'s face*)   Baby. You look . . . deranged. You're so wet.

Tilly   Hey. You never touch me in public.

Jaye   Things change.

Natty *continues to shiver, but he's happy, he's smiling. The music is loud and glorious.* **Jaye** *kisses* **Tilly**.

Tilly   Wow. You kissed me. And I'm not even drunk.

Natty   Take me to a disco and play this song over and over. Make it sweet. Make it pretty. Make it count. Help me. Clothe me. CLOTHE ME.

Tilly *and* **Jaye** *dress* **Natty** *in* **Tilly***'s clothing. Her blouse. Her slacks. Whatever. Strangely, they fit him rather well.*

Tilly   Water and blood pouring out of me. I feel so clean. I'm shedding myself.

Jaye   You're glorious. A mess, but glorious.

Natty   My heart is breaking it's busting up I'm fine I'm happy I need . . . contact . . . make contact. MAKE CONTACT. PLEASE. PLEASE. MAKE THEM UNDERSTAND. WE ARE NOT . . . WE ARE NOT COWARDS.

Jaye *removes* **Tilly***'s jacket. She then removes her own blouse.*

Natty   I can't stand all this. Beauty. I can't.

Jaye *grasps* **Natty***'s hand, tight. She bends to take* **Tilly***'s breast into her mouth.*

Tilly   Oh God. We're so close to the edge, we can't even see it coming.

Jaye *and* **Tilly** *begin to make love. The music continues, insistent.* **Natty** *holds on to* **Jaye***'s hand.* **Jimmy** *enters. He's dressed in white from head to toe. He holds a knife.*

Natty   Jimmy. Oh Jimmy where have you gone. Where are you going to.

Jimmy   I'm on my way. Be on my way with me.

Jimmy *pulls* **Natty** *to his feet.* **Jaye** *and* **Tilly** *continue to make love.*

Natty   Where are we going?

Jimmy   We're going to Ten West. We have a date.

Natty   But I lost my hair. I can't go anywhere.

Jimmy   We're going to make you well. Take this.

Jimmy *gives* **Natty** *the knife.*

Natty Jimmy. This is a knife. A weapon.

Jimmy It's a beginning. Tear up the world for me. Make your mark.

He leads **Natty** *to the enormous map of the meat-packing district. He takes* **Natty***'s hand, lightly tracing over the map with the knife.*

It's easy to get someplace if you know where you're going. Look. Look how we're gliding through.

Natty *slashes through the map with the knife. Again. And again.*

Jimmy Time to fly, Natty Weldon.

Natty Lift me.

Jimmy *lifts* **Natty** *into his arms. They step through the map. They're gone.* **Jaye** *and* **Tilly** *are a splendid sight amid the ruin. A glorious flash of white light and they disappear.*

The torn-up map begins to shake, violently.

Blackout.

Butterfly Kiss

Butterfly kiss: a caress given by winking one eye so that the lashes brush against the face of the receiver.

Crowell Dictionary of American Slang

Butterfly Kiss was first performed at the Almeida Theatre, London, on 7 April 1994. The cast was as follows:

Lily Ross	Elizabeth Berridge
Jenny Ross	Susan Brown
Sally Ramona	Mary Macleod
Sloan Ross	Oliver Cotton
Martha McKenzie	Debora Weston
Christine, the	
Countess Van Dyne	Sandra Dickinson
Teddy Roosevelt Hayes	Larry Lamb
Jackson Trouver	Andrew Woodall

Directed by Steven Pimlott
Designed by Mark Thompson
Lighting by Hugh Vanstone

Characters

Lily Ross, *a small, dark woman in her mid-to-late 20s with a splendidly dry and ironic sense of humour.*

Jenny Ross, *Lily's mother, mid-to-late 40s. A mild hypochondriac, lusty, rather beautiful and neurotically thin. She has a stunning singing voice.*

Sally Ramona, *Lily's grandmother, mid-to-late 60s. Meaner than she thinks she is, chiefly because she completely lacks sentimentality. Doesn't realise how funny she is.*

Sloan Ross, *Lily's father, mid-to-late 40s. An intriguing personality contradiction: sexy and handsome in a remote yet gentle way; academic yet un-professorial; cold yet sympathetic; imposing yet ineffectual. He will never let his working-class roots betray him.*

Martha McKenzie, *Lily's lover, 35ish. Crisp, no-nonsense approach to all things cannot hide a flirtatious and quite light aspect to her dealings with Lily. Sexy and rather feminine, with a highly developed sense of irony.*

Christine, the Countess Van Dyne, *Sloan's lover, late 40s. A born-and-bred New Yorker from Howard Beach, Queens, who, while very young, married a dubious European count and then deserted him. Faux elegant and naive in the most unassuming way. Speaks with a pronounced Queens accent.*

Teddy Roosevelt Hayes, *Lily's first lover, mid-to-late 40s. An ex-US Marine who's big, handsome, and somewhat slow on the uptake. Sweeter and more polite than one would expect.*

Jackson Trouver, *Lily's attorney, 35ish. A thoroughly charming and cynical raconteur.*

The Setting is a jail cell. Lily's memories of events transform the cell into many places: a lower-Manhattan kitchen; Jones Beach in November; a woman's bar; a waterfront house in Queens; a Manhattan hi-rise; a patio in Fort Lauderdale, Florida. It is not necessary to present the cell as strictly realistic; however, the *sense* of present place must be recognisable as a jail cell.

The Time is the present, the past, the imagined past and the imagined future. Although Lily's age ranges substantially during the course of the play, no attempt should be made to 'play' the younger ages.

Act One

Lily (*to the audience*) Of course, what's always been the *most* interesting to me is the Halls-Mills trial of 1926. Testifying from a portable hospital bed, Jane Gibson, also known as the pig woman, accused Mrs Halls and her brothers of murder.

Lights up on **Sally** *and* **Jenny**. **Jenny** *wears a slinky black cocktail dress. She sips at some Scotch. Wrapped tightly around her right arm is the sleeve of a blood pressure pump.* **Sally**, *while watching television, nonchalantly squeezes the little black air pump.*

Sally Look at this, Jenny. They got Jackie O's doctor on.

Jenny Imagine that.

Lily The defence counsel, however, proved Miss Gibson to be a most unreliable witness. She could not remember who or when and where she had married, or whether or not she had, indeed, been divorced.

Sally You was a pain in the ass when we took that drive out to the Boo-vee-ay mansion. Phil and crazy Figgy driving us in a storm. Out to some house we wasn't sure we could find. You was a real fucking pain.

Jenny My arm. Not so tight, Mother.

Sally Pregnant and screaming with the bulk of it, you were. I said – and I remember perfectly well saying this to you – I said: HEY. YOU STUPID ENOUGH TO KNOCK YOURSELF UP WITH TROUBLE, YOU BETTER BE SMART ENOUGH TO BITE THE BULLET OF MOTHERHOOD WITHOUT COMPLAINING. Yeah. Ruined my chance to catch a glimpse of some old rich lady at a window. Long yellow fingernail scratching against a· pane of glass.

Jenny   You're hurting my arm.

Sally   Yeah? Maybe I'll pop a vessel. Would you like that, Jenny?

Lily   The Halls-Mills case remained unsolved. Mrs Halls and her brothers were acquitted, courtesy of the pig woman. My name is Lily Ross. I may be less fortunate.

Jenny   My pressure's 140 over 90. You're probably making it go up 50, 60 points.

Sally   Bullshit. I'm pumping some life into your arm. Hey: wouldn't it be something if Lily married John-John Kennedy? They're Catholic, ain't they? What will you wear to the wedding?

Jenny   Black.

Sally   He's a *smart* guy. He's gonna get himself a university education. And money. Lily'd buy us a house in Florida. Big brick house with a portable patio.

Lily   Or consider the case of Bela Kiss, a Hungarian tinsmith who murdered his wife and her lover in 1912. Over the following fifteen years, Mr Kiss advertised for new wives. He killed twenty-one women, mostly by strangulation, and took the bodies to his cellar, where he kept them in drums. The bodies bloated in alcohol.

Jenny   I like New York. Sloan likes New York.

Sally   I'm *tired* of New York. What I need is SUNSHINE. If your husband don't like Florida, leave him here. Lily's gonna take care of us.

Jenny   Lily's not interested in buying houses. And how do you know John-John Kennedy will like the idea of Florida? Look: my pressure's up. I'm getting sick. Give me some more Scotch.

Lily   Mr Kiss's crimes were discovered at the outbreak of World War I, which proved to be a most welcome diversion for him. Bela Kiss vanished during the war.

Sally   Well. Then forget about Lily. Who needs her? She'll buy the house with the blue-blood's money. We'll live there.

Jenny   Have a drink with me, okay?

Sally   Not me. But you go ahead. Keeps you quiet.

Jenny   You could drink me under any table.

Lily   I work in a small gift shop at the South Street Seaport. The kind of place that attracts Canadian tourists. I'm interested in composition. Musical composition, that is.

Sally   I could leave you here, you know that. Let you rot in place. Shrivel up with a shot glass in one hand and a blood pressure kit in the other. I shrivel little by little myself, just thinking about how I could have given birth to something like you.

Jenny   I'm not so bad.

Sally   You're a vegetable in a party dress.

Jenny   Where's Lily?

Sally   She's probably reading something. Kid's got no sense.

Lily (*holding out her arms to* **Jenny**)   Mama.

Jenny   Lily-pie, come over here and brush your mama's hair.

Sally (*still watching TV*)   Goddamn. It's that good-looking Tony Tucci. He's real *old* now. Went berserk after his younger sister shot up the older sister. You remember Tony Tucci?

Lily (*approaching* **Jenny**)   Give me the brush, Mama.

Jenny   Hiya, Lily. Your grandma won't drink with me. But maybe you'd like to.

Sally   Phil and me went to her trial. She never would say why she did it. It was really *something*. Tina wore such nice clothes at her trial. Made a strong impression on the jury. I could tell. But not strong enough, 'cause they sent her to the chair, anyway. If only she woulda said why she did it. *I* understood. Her sister wasn't no joy to look at every day. Yeah. Nice looking fella, that Tony Tucci.

Lily   I'm not old enough to drink, Mama.

Jenny   Nonsense, Lily-pie. The females in our line got the booze gene. Your own grandma started hitting the bottle at age two. Pint after pint of Gordon's in her baby bottle. Why, from the moment I escaped from her womb, she breast-fed me gin.

Sally   So what if I did? Maybe I gave you the only thrill of your life. So what.

Lily   I don't believe you, Grandma. It's impossible to breast-feed a child on liquor.

Sally   Fancy talk. You read that in some book?

Jenny   You read all you like, Lily. If you're not born pretty you might as well read. Or drink.

Lily   I'm too young to drink.

Jenny   Don't you think I look like Tallulah Bankhead when I wear this dress?

Jackson Trouver *enters. He addresses the audience.*

Jackson   Consider the case of my client, ladies and gentlemen. Lily Ramona Ross. Aged . . . twenty-something and three months. Born under the sign of the scorpion. For those of you who are interested . . . in that sort of thing.

Jenny   Really, Lily. People tell me I look like her all the time. When I wear black, especially.

Lily   I'm too young to remember Tallulah Bankhead.

Jackson   Don't you think it's curious how people are always interested in analysing a murderer's motive by way of, oh, astrological data and such?

Sally   Tallulah Bankhead my ASS. Sam Jaffe's more like

it. Oh, Lily, Sam Jaffe was out of this WORLD. A very fine actor.

Lily I've never heard of him.

Sally Yeah. Well, he played mostly loonies. Played your mother once.

Jackson Got a call one morning from my college buddy, Martha McKenzie.

Martha *enters.*

Martha (*she, too, addresses the audience*) My lover is in trouble, Jackson.

Jackson She says to me, Jackson, my lover is in trouble.

Jenny Your father likes me in black. Don't you like me in black, Lily?

Lily You look . . . thinner.

Jenny I'm fat? You think I'm fat? I'm not fat.

Sally Nah, Lily. She's not fat. Sam Jaffe was *thin*. Forget about her, Lily. Think about *me*. Why don't you go on one of those game shows and make us a bunch of money?

Jackson Martha's a photographer. Mostly travel assignments. We went to school together. And when she told me of Lily Ross's . . . circumstances . . . I could not refuse. It's what is called a once-in-a-lifetime case.

Martha She's been arrested, Jackson. They say she's murdered her mother.

Jackson Jackson, she says, my lover's killed her mother.

Jenny I've lost a lot of weight, Lily. I have. My pressure rises and my weight drops. It's the damnedest thing. And your father says I have to wear something . . . presentable . . . to his lectures. I think I look elegant in black. To hell with the rest of you.

Sally Isn't it about time you took another pressure reading, Jenny? Who knows. Maybe you got real sick while you wasn't looking. What about it Lily? A game show to make a fast buck?

Lily (*to* **Jenny**)   I like you better in bright colours. Pastels. why don't you wear pink?

Jenny   What do *you* know, Lily? Your father likes me in black. Go on. Read up on Tallulah for me, baby.

Martha   It happens while I am in Africa. When I return to New York, I find a note from Sloan Ross. It says, simply: CALL ME. Lily's clothes were gone. Her bookcases filled only with dust. Darker white patches on the bright white walls where her paintings had hung. I didn't particularly want to speak with Sloan Ross. He was always a difficult man.

Jackson   Let us say that Sloan Ross is not fond of my photographer friend.

Sally   It's always other people's kids who are raking in the dough on TV. But I got a hunch about you, Lily-doll. And if you don't win a bundle on Hollywood Squares, I was thinking you could marry one of the Kennedys.

Jackson   Martha spends a quarter on a call to the noted professor, Sloan Ross.

Martha   Hello, Mr Ross. This is Martha McKenzie. Your note requests that I call.

Jackson   I pay a visit to the Ross residence. The place has been mobbed for hours, this normally quiet walk-up where people claim to keep to themselves and say their hellos at the mailboxes. In theory, people think it's best to keep to themselves. In practice, common sense prevails.

Martha   And he says, Miss McKenzie, it's very good of you to call. Like he's talking to one of his students. Said he was quite busy now, but that if I would call Lily at such-and-such a number, she'd be happy to explain. Then he hung up.

Lily   I don't think I can marry a Kennedy, Grandma.

They live in Boston.

Jenny   Lily. Lily-sweet. I'm feeling light-headed. My heart's beating real fast. Where's my chart? Give me my chart, honey.

Jackson   The Ross apartment is not large. Cops all over, blue abounding. Takes me a while to get through the crowd. When finally I'm inside, I'm overwhelmed by the presence of white things. White appliances, wallpaper, linoleum. Very clean. Almost antiseptic.

Martha   I call such-and-such a number to reach Lily. The line's busy. Once, a man answers and mumbles something about a precinct. I hang up. How am I supposed to know that Lily's been arrested?

Jackson   And there's this cluster of blue uniforms in the kitchen. This white kitchen. Upon closer inspection, one notices splotches of red on all that white. Blood. There's blood seeping out of every corner. But it's splattered in bits. So that it seems hidden. Or lost.

Sally   Here we go again, Lily. Your mama thinks you been paying your grandma too much attention. Go on. Take care of her.

Sally *gives* **Lily** *a small chalkboard. A piece of chalk is attached to the board with a string. On the board are neatly written rows of figures:* **Jenny**'s *charting of her own blood pressure.*

Lily   Mama . . . I don't . . . I'm afraid to do this.

Jenny   I need you now.

Sally   That's right, Lily. Your mama don't feel right if that thing ain't pumped against her arm every twenty minutes. You're a big girl, Lily. It's time you learned your function here.

Martha   I try again. The same officer answers and I know I haven't dialled wrong. It's a long time before I actually speak with Lily. I was transferred quite a bit, you see, and I could taste the distance between us through the

telephone lines. As if each transfer, each click of each
switchboard, took me deeper underground. Under
something I could not accept.

Jackson   I don't stay at the Ross apartment. It's too
much, you know, with Sally Ramona on her hands and
knees, scrubbing at non-existent blood stains. A homicide
detective told me she'd been at it for three days. Ever since
the body'd been removed. There was a woman wearing a
blue nightgown in the hallway outside of the apartment.

Lily   I might hurt her.

Sally   You won't. Don't you think I've tried? Listen to
me. She ain't got pain cells.

Lily *takes her mother's blood pressure.*

Jenny   That's it. More. I feel it makes me right.

Lily *pumps too hard.* **Jenny** *slaps her.*

Jackson   This lady in blue's slugging down a bottle of
Gordon's. She's doing a jig and singing that song about
Lizzie Borden and her axe.

Martha   When I get through to Lily, she is not hysterical.

Jenny (*to* **Lily**)   Don't come near me.

Sally *takes the blood pressure pump from* **Lily**.

Sally   Why don't you go read something, Lily? Guess I
was wrong about not being able to hurt her. You learn
something new about your kids every day.

Jackson   I don't know why, but watching that woman do
her grisly number in the hallway strikes me as the funniest
thing I've seen in years. Red, white and blue this place is.
Like a flag. And a drunken woman singing songs about a
suspected hatchet murderess. It's all very . . . American.

Martha   Her voice does not crack. She says –

Lily   Please, Mama. Please listen to me.

Martha   – Mama, please. That's all. She hangs up. Very

quietly. As if she is putting down a teacup. It occurs to me that it's the second time this day a member of the Ross family has cut me off.

Jenny Leave us be, sweetheart. Your grandma knows how to bring me up. Leave us alone.

Sally cradles Jenny's head in one arm, strokes her hair. She takes Jenny's blood pressure with her free hand.

Lights down on Sally and Jenny.

Jackson But that woman forgot one thing. Lizzie Borden was acquitted. Like I said, the Ross case seems to be a big one. So I take it. Martha's got substantial amounts of cash.

Jackson *exits.*

Martha Do you have what you need, Lily? Is it . . . I don't know . . . comfortable enough?

Lily I've been reading a lot lately. Sensational crime cases. Mostly murder cases. There's a vested interest, I'll admit.

Martha Would you like to talk with a doctor? Anybody?

Lily I thought I'd write an opera.

Martha It wouldn't be difficult to get somebody in here. Jackson could help.

Lily Last week I thought it might be a string quartet. A lovely piece of action for violins. But now I think it must be a vocal piece. In a minor key.

Martha You're serious.

Lily I am. Are you familiar with the Harvard microbiologist who killed her parents? She was very young, and very smart. She had a future.

Martha No, Lily. I don't know about her. Would you please talk to somebody? It doesn't have to be me. I just want to know that you're fine.

Lily Putting on some weight, aren't you?

Martha   I stay home and read newspaper articles about you. I eat fudge. I miss you. I *like* fudge.

Lily   So. This very smart microbiologist, armed with graduate degrees from the nation's most prestigious university, can't find a job. Can you believe it?

Martha   I can't tell you how painful it is to read those stories. Strangers speculating about your past. Men who sit behind computer terminals for a living, playing their hunches about what makes you tick.

Lily   Miss microbiologist returns home. Unemployed, fat and most unhappy. She eats peppermint twists while her mother works at an A & P. One day, she uses her impressive education to assemble her father's shotgun. She'd never before touched a gun.

Martha   Nobody has an answer, Lily. They say you're not insane. But no one wants to believe that. I'm not sure *what* I believe.

Lily   And then she waits for her mother to come home. Mom walks in and her hulk of a spawn blows her away. Turns out mommy's little girl is a crack shot. She gets her father soon after. He's napping and doesn't have a chance to contemplate what a monster he's created.

Martha   Lily, I've been thinking I should go away. I've been offered an assignment in Germany.

Lily   Our heroine is judged to be criminally insane and is packed off to a state institution. Ten uneventful years pass. Miss Harvard becomes the subject of a television interview. Mr Newsman asks her if she is prepared, ten years after the fact, to talk about her motives. Dear, he says, a soothing modulating baritone, can you tell us why you did it?

Martha   I could wait for you, Lily. We would go together. Heidelberg. Munich. The Rhine.

Lily   Well. She looks right past our baritoned reporter, smiles, like she's a dowager empress amused by the efforts

of her lady-in-waiting. There is no faraway look to her
eyes. No glazing over. Foam is not in evidence at the
corners of her mouth. She says, 'why, of course I can tell
you what happened. My mother had a habit of going out
every evening at the same time. She told me she'd be back
within an hour, but each time she left she wouldn't return
until the next morning.' You see, Martha, this poor soul
hadn't a clue as to where her mommy went. All she knew
was that mommy went out with the moon and came in
with the sun.

Martha Please think about it, Lily. I'm not sure I can be
here much longer.

Lily By this time, our TV interviewer is most
uncomfortable. He doesn't have the upper hand. She's not
crazy, after all. And even though she doesn't have a
weapon, this huge man is afraid of her. There's a look in
his eyes. She notices, of course, and concludes her
explanation by saying that she allows her mother to do this
for six successive evenings. On the seventh evening, she
shoots her. She figures while she has the shotgun handy,
she might as well take care of her pop. It was a perfectly
plausible motive, Martha. And no one believed her. Mr
Newsman, faced with the woman's most remarkable
candour, relaxes. He even slumps back in his chair. Sure,
he thinks, she's out of her mind after all. Nothing to fear
any more.

Martha I want you to write that opera, Lily. In a *major*
key. I'll bring you music paper.

Lily Bring me fudge.

Martha I don't suppose ... you'd talk to me about it.

Lily You make the best fudge.

Martha Well. I'm going home. I'll eat a lot. I'll read
newspapers and refuse to answer my phone. I'll wait a
while longer for you.

Martha *exits.*

Lights up on **Jenny**. *She wears her cocktail dress and armband, as before.*

Jenny   Lily, can you tell me what it is exactly a lepidopterist *does*? Honestly, when I met your daddy he was a soldier. He was just a regular guy. It was years later he took an interest in bugs. I was reading up on the subject of butterflies in an encyclopaedia yesterday. Really. I was. Sitting here in my old comfy chair while you were at school, reading, and listening to Billie Holiday, her sweet voice, and the telephone rings. Ring ring goes the telephone and you know, for a long time I think it's part of Billie's song. A ringing telephone is such an unfamiliar sound to me, honey. I can't get together the extra push, the rush of energy it takes to pull myself out of that chair. So I figure, why bother? It'll stop soon enough. But it doesn't stop. And so I throw all I've got into the act of getting up and I answer and the ringing stops and there's a voice. A female voice with an accent. The voice says to my telephone: *Bonjour.* May I *parler* with Sloan Ross? I say to myself, Jenny, who the hell is Sloan Ross? The female voice is . . . nervous. I can tell by the breathing. Very quick. In spurts. And then I remember. Well, *yeah.* Sloan Ross is the father of my baby. I try to answer the voice's question, but by that time it's gone. What's left for your mama to do but return to her chair? It's a funny thing, Lily. When I met your daddy, I was a switchboard operator. The telephone was my line to excitement. And I couldn't even keep a timid female voice on the line. Well. It's better to sit in the dark and remember nothing. If you sit in the dark long enough something scary's bound to happen.

Lily   I'm right here, Mama.

Jenny   Lily-pie, are you here? Did you say something about dancing? That's nice.

Lily   No, Mama. I was telling you . . . I was going to say that I really do think you look nice in black.

Jenny   You shouldn't fib. But thanks all the same.

Lily I found a picture of Tallulah Bankhead today. You do look like her. In a way.

Jenny Why don't you talk to me about dancing.

Lily I've never been dancing.

Jenny Don't be so *boring*, baby. That's what your daddy says to me. Why don't you talk to me about *dancing*, he says.

Lily Mama, it's Lily. I'm here. Not him.

Jenny It's not me any more, Jennifer. I'm not the fella you hitched up with. Why don't you wrap your arms around me and DANCE?

She wraps her arms around **Lily**. *She kisses* **Lily***'s neck. She begins to dance.*

Oh yeah. Yessss. Of course. So sweet, baby. So light on your feet. Teach me what you know.

Lily *pushes* **Jenny** *away.*

Lily I can't do this, Mama. It's not right.

Jenny What are you looking at? What? How come you're looking at me that way?

Lily I don't know. I . . . can't touch . . . you that way.

Jenny Whatsa matter, Lily-pie. Too old to hold your mama. Too smart.

Lily I'm not him, Mama.

Jenny Who loves you best. Who loves you more.

Lily I can't say.

Jenny WHO LOVES YOU BEST.

Lily You love me best.

Jenny Who loves you more.

Lily You. You, Mama.

Jenny And who's your sweetheart?

Lily You're my sweetheart.

Jenny And I'm the nicest person you know.

Lily Yes.

Jenny So. What have you got to tell me?

Lily (*hesitates, offers her hand to* **Jenny**) Would you ... why don't you dance with me. Just a little.

Jenny Yes, sugar. It's so nice of you to ask.

Jenny *and* **Lily** *dance in place. It's really more of an awkward and tentative hug, but they do try.*

Jackson *enters. He addresses the audience.*

Jackson I've seen the evidence, the remainder, really, of most imaginable crimes. Many of my colleagues will tell you that a lawyer's success depends on how relatively unaffected he remains by the circumstances of his job. In truth, there's little that pulls at us or horrifies us because we are inevitably several steps removed from an actual crime. We do not look on while perps pull triggers. What we deal with is the aftermath of crime. And that's always ... intellectually satisfying. Emotionally undemanding. And safe. Most of all it is safe, what we lawyers do. Of course, it is as it should be. We cannot risk emotional involvement with the crimes upon which our livelihood depends.

Jenny *exits.*

Jackson A perverse instinct, an instinct that verges on crime itself, propels our interest in lawbreakers. It's the desire to know what enables crime to exist, but not the naked crime, the knife in a back, that we court. Like a lust we're ashamed of but can't quite shake, we like to take crime into dark places with us. Not out into the sunlight. Everything looks better in the dark.

Lily *listens to* **Jackson**.

Jackson I've lost only one case. A fifty-year-old baritone

who had a Broadway credit a million years ago, gives
singing lessons to co-eds in Arizona. He has a favourite
student – don't they all, though – pretty blonde kid. Sweet
sixteen. Kind of girl who's accused of having *promise*. He
takes her to the top of a hill one sunny Arizona afternoon
and tells her that altitude is good for the vocal chords. He
presents her with a tape-recorder, a big red bow Scotch-
taped to its top. He gives her a tape of his Broadway show.
She listens. She laughs. Perhaps she's nervous. Perhaps
she's more sensitive to the sadness of this scene than he
understands. So he strangles her. Cops find the recorder
blasting Rodgers and Hammerstein at the scene of the
crime.

I stood at the top of that hill, much later in the day, first
cousin to crime, thrice removed. And the only remaining
evidence of horror, the only trace of human involvement,
was a chalk outline of that girl's body on grass. I lost the
baritone's case. Do you have an idea of how difficult it is
to lay down a chalk outline on grass?

Lily Mama. Mama, where'd you go. I meant no harm.

Jackson Whatcha doing there, Lily?

Lily I'm talking to the voices in my head.

Jackson All right. Perhaps you can convince those voices
to have a chat with me.

Lily Sorry, counsellor. They're shy. They don't like
strangers.

Jackson Let's take it from the beginning.

Lily I've been through the beginning. Let's get on to the
end.

Jackson Start with Teddy Hayes.

Lily What are my chances of springing this place?

Jackson None. Now. What about Teddy Hayes?

Lily Listen. Martha's going to Europe. I'd like to go with her. So see what you can do for me.

Jackson   I'd like to win this case.

Lily   I'd like you to win this case.

Jackson   Good. Do you understand that if you keep your secrets to yourself, I don't win. You don't go bye-bye with Martha and nobody gets a picture postcard of Paris By Night.

Lily   Munich.

Jackson   Uh-huh. Well. Tell me something about Teddy Hayes.

Lily   Teddy is the dumbest man I know. But I like him. He's sweet and uncomplicated.

Teddy Roosevelt Hayes *enters.*

Teddy (*to the audience*)   Fourteen years old and smoother than a shot of Scotch. Slim hips. Never looks you straight in the eye.

Jackson   If he's so dumb, why did you fuck him?

Lily   Because, Jackson, like the mountain, he was there.

Teddy   Jones Beach. Middle of November. Her daddy's fond of cold water. We have this reunion every year, same time and place, in celebration of our Marine days. Me and Sloan Ross go all the way back to Camp LeJeune. Before he went off to study butterflies. Bugs were a regular obsession with Sloanie.

Jackson   Where and when did you meet Mr Hayes?

Lily   I told you. I didn't exactly meet him. He was just . . . there.

Jackson   Where? Be specific.

Lily   In the sand, of course.

Teddy   So this one particular year Sloan brings his daughter with him 'cause his wife is having one of her

blood pressure attacks or something. His goddamned
daughter. I say, look Sloan, it's real easy to offend a
fourteen-year-old girl. Got one of my own. And like I said,
it's real easy to cross her.

Jackson   Where was the sand, Lily? In a playground?

Lily   I don't know. Somewhere. It doesn't matter. He rose
from the sand like a monster. Muscled and wet and
shivering. He reminded me of something from a Japanese
horror film. I used to call him Mothra.

Jackson   Did you seduce him?

Lily   Who can say, really? Sometimes I think my father
seduced Teddy for me.

Jackson   Why would he do that?

Lily   My father is a scientist. He likes to watch.

Lights down on **Jackson**.

Teddy   I'm doing push-ups on Jones Beach and believe
me, I'm trying to forget the cold. Up walks Sloan Ross and
his baby. I say to the baby, how do you do? I'm Teddy
Roosevelt Hayes and I'm an ex-Marine. She says, hi there,
Teddy, I'm Lily Ross. Do you think I'm fat? I'm staring at
this little girl with slim hips . . . but *real* slim . . . and all I
can picture is how she's gonna have one hell of a time in
childbirth with hips like those. I say to her, well, Lily,
seems to me you've got the slimmest hips this side of
heaven and she grins, leans in real close so I can see her
tits and says, well, Teddy, what do you think about
THAT? Sloanie's having a grand time embarrassing me in
front of his kid. I spend the whole day covering myself up
with a beach towel. Sloanie keeps asking, hey, Teddy,
what's the deal with the *towel?* Like he knows I'm hiding
something. And I *am*. Middle of November and this girl
child with slim hips is running around Jones Beach in a
bathing suit. She's collecting sea shells and wriggling her
tight little ass in my face. What was I supposed to do? I'm
a pretty normal guy. Never been arrested. Never taken

much more than a social drink. And I'd certainly never been moved to excitement by fourteen-year-old buns. But Lily Ross . . . well. She was . . . exciting to me. I tried to put it out of my mind. Sloanie knew what was going on. He probably planned it. Slim hips. My my my . . . Lily Ross was a sweetheart. Can't believe she went and popped her mommy off that way.

Lily Teddy. Teddy Roosevelt Hayes. Are you really named after the Rough Rider?

Teddy Could be.

Lily How come you don't know for sure?

Teddy Don't know. The subject never came up.

Lily It's strange, Teddy. I mean, not knowing about your name. You're an ex-Marine.

Teddy That's right.

Lily My father's an ex-Marine. Now he collects butterflies. Don't you think that's an interesting change of direction?

Teddy Your daddy's an interesting man.

Lily Are you an interesting man, Teddy? I'm making small talk.

Teddy Uh-huh. Your daddy'll be back soon. And you won't have to fret about small talk.

Lily No he won't. He's hunting specimens on the beach. When was the last time you found a butterfly on the beach?

Teddy I've never looked for one.

Lily You have a daughter.

Teddy Yes.

Lily What's her name?

Teddy Eleanor.

Lily Nice name. Don't hear it much. Some names are more common than others. Take mine, for example. Very common. There's one in every kindergarten. Is your daughter pretty?

Teddy She's . . . pretty.

Lily Is she prettier than me?

Teddy That's hard to say, Lily.

Lily I mean, for instance. Is she as pretty as, say, other girls of her age?

Teddy She measures up just fine.

Lily But she's not as pretty, say, as me?

Teddy She looks like my wife.

Lily I see. Wives, of course, are never as pretty as other women.

Teddy Who told you that?

Lily My mama told me that. And she should know. Does Eleanor shave her legs?

Teddy What kind of a question is that?

Lily I have to shave every week. My grandmother says when girls start shaving, that's the end of *that*.

Teddy What's 'that'?

Lily You're sweating, Teddy. Are you sick? Don't get sick on me because I'm in your trust. Have you ever watched your daughter take a bath?

Teddy Let's lay off the questions, Lily. I'm not feeling so hot.

Lily If you had watched her bathe, you'd have known if she shaved. I'm just asking a question, Teddy.

Teddy Why don't you tell me what it is you'd like to do when you grow up.

Lily   I want to be an ex-Marine.

Teddy   Don't josh me.

Lily   I like to fight. Marines get into some good scrapes, don't they?

Teddy   Depends on what Marine's involved.

Lily   I'm going to be a composer.

Teddy   So. Tell me about . . . musical meter.

Lily   *You* know my father best of all, Mr T. R. Hayes. You can tell me something I don't know about him.

Teddy   Sure I could. Tell me what you know about music.

Lily   Music is like . . . watching sex. Just watching it. Yeah. All your ex-Marine muscles bulging. And the sweat. You're sweating like a pig, Teddy. That sweat on your arms is like tiny notes jumping between the staves. *That's* what I know about music.

Teddy   I'm too cold to sweat.

Lily   I'd like to meet Eleanor some day. Being as I am prettier than her. I'd say to her, 'Eleanor, you've got the handsomest father on earth. Such a nice looking man, that Teddy Hayes.' That's what I'd say to Eleanor.

Teddy   Tell me some more about the sweat on my arms.

Lily *touches* **Teddy***'s arm.*

Lily   See? This sweat droplet . . . right here. It's an 'A' natural. And this one. You know what this one is?

Teddy   Tell me.

Lily   It's a diminished seventh. A mystery chord. Do you believe I know what I'm talking about?

Teddy   Ain't you just a little cold out here? We could go inside. I'll buy you a hot chocolate.

Lily   Nothing open, Teddy Hayes. Do you think I'm fat?

Teddy You're thin as a rail, Lily Ross. Why, you're positively . . . diminished.

Lily It was my birthday a couple of weeks ago. Maybe that's of interest to you. I'm fourteen, Teddy.

Teddy Eleanor is fifteen.

Lily Wish me a happy birthday, Teddy.

Teddy Happy birthday, Lily.

Teddy *touches* **Lily**'s *breasts.*

Lily It's not so cold today.

Teddy We can make more . . . small talk. We could.

Lily I don't know how to make small talk.

Teddy *removes* **Lily**'s *blouse.*

Lily Know who was born on my birthday, Teddy?

Teddy Lots of people. Tell me. I don't know.

Lily Albert Camus. Madame Curie. Billy Graham.

Teddy I'm impressed.

Lily Who was born on *your* birthday, Teddy?

Teddy I was, Lily. I was.

Teddy *draws* **Lily** *into a kiss. He unzips his fly.* **Sloan Ross** *enters. He wears a tuxedo. He sports a neatly trimmed moustache. He watches* **Teddy** *and* **Lily** *as lights fade from them.*

Jenny *enters. As usual, she wears her black cocktail dress.*

Jenny Hello, Sloan. You're early tonight.

Sloan I've won a research award.

Jenny That's nice.

Sally *and* **Lily** *enter. Unobserved, they watch* **Sloan** *and* **Jenny**.

Jenny You like me in black, don't you?

Sloan Do I?

Jenny   Yes. Black is . . . slimming. You like that.

Sloan   You look like a cocktail waitress. I'm going away for a few days.

Jenny *unzips her dress. It falls to the floor.*

Jenny   I'll wear pink. Lily thinks I should wear pink.

Sloan   Put your dress on.

Lily *turns away.*

Sally   You gotta watch this, Lily. They're getting to the good part.

Lily   No, Grandma. It's not right.

Sally *slaps her, forces her to watch.*

Sally   *I* decide what's right for you. Watch your mama, Lily. Watch and learn.

Jenny   Help me, Sloan. Help me clothe myself.

Sloan   I can't. I'm going away now.

Jenny   Where you going, honey?

Sloan   Someplace else.

Jenny   I'm cold, baby. My dress is on the floor. Can you help me with it, Sloan?

Sloan *picks up* **Jenny**'s *dress, pulls it up over her hips, her waist.* **Jenny** *takes his hands into her own hands.*

Jenny   Touch me.

Sloan   I am touching you.

Jenny (*places his hands on her breasts*)   Here.

Sloan   I'm going away.

Jenny (*places his hands between her legs*)   And here.

Sloan   Turn around.

Jenny *does.* **Sloan** *lifts up her slip, He forces her to bend over at* *the waist.* **Lily** *starts after them.*

Sally   Are you out of your FUCKING MIND?

Lily   I . . . I have to save her.

Sally   She don't know she has to be saved.

Lights down on **Sloan** *and* **Jenny***.* **Lily** *begins to cry.* **Sally** *cradles her.*

Sally   When you was little, your poppy Phil and me took you to the Copacabana. And you felt just like this, all rolled up in a tiny ball, huddling against me. We packed you up in an A & P shopping bag and took you right past the bouncer. You be careful of men with moustaches, Lily. They have secrets.

Sally *exits.*

Music in: a slow, sultry, instrumental bar tune.

Martha *enters. She carries a drink.*

Martha   You don't talk much, do you?

Lily *shrugs.*

Martha   Been four hours and fifteen minutes by my watch. What's it by yours?

Lily *shrugs.*

Martha   I like to think I can name any woman's drink on the spot. Yours would be . . . Scotch. Definitely Scotch. Chivas?

Lily *shakes her head, 'no.'*

Martha   Johnny Red? Black? Perhaps . . . Dewars? A little White Label for the lady? ·

Lily   Pinch.

Martha   Ah. Nice. Somewhat pretentious. But nice.

Lily   Actually, it's all the same to me. What's your drink?

Martha   Brandy Alexander. House brandy.

Lily   I've never had a Brandy Alexander. I understand it tastes like candy.

Martha   Want to try it?

Lily   Four hours and . . . thirteen minutes. Your watch is fast.

Martha   So. My watch is fast. You're very pretty. What next?

Lily   Of course, my watch might very well be slow.

Martha   Could be. You're nervous. And remarkably pretty. How old are you?

Lily   Then again, bar clocks are always set ten minutes fast. We both lose. I'm twenty-four. Or twenty-five.

Martha   Do I take my pick?

Lily   If you'd like. There's some mystery attached to the circumstances surrounding my birth. Or so they tell me.

Martha   Well. You don't drink Brandy Alexanders, you don't talk terribly much, and you don't know how old you are. What *do* you do?

Lily   I like to . . . watch. Sometimes.

Martha   And are you here to watch, or to participate?

Lily   That would depend upon whatever the participation calls for.

Martha   Well, I myself am a particularly adept observer.

Lily   Then I guess you're here to watch. And not to participate.

Martha   I can be persuaded to learn. To participate. That is, Miss −

Lily   Ramona. Ross. Miss Ramona-Ross.

Martha   I wish you were about . . . thirty-five. But I bet you really are twenty-five. They tell me I've a weakness for younger women.

Lily   Who are 'they'?

Martha   Oh ... the same people who claim the mysterious circumstances surrounding your birth. Is Ramona your first name?

Lily   No. It's a family name. My mother's maiden name. My name is Lily Ross. Although I've preferred it to be Ramona.

Martha   Names are easily changed, Miss Ross. Especially here. I'm afraid I've no such thoughts about my own name. Martha McKenzie, of obviously Anglican descent.

They shake hands.

Lily   Are you also able to judge a woman by her handshake?

Martha   I like to try.

Lily   And how does mine measure up?

Martha   Admirably. And I'd guess you are ... a singer?

Lily   Not likely, Miss McKenzie.

Martha   An ... architect? Spy? Young woman with a past? Well. I'm a photographer. For your information, that is.

Lily   I'm a ... university professor.

Martha   No kidding. And what is it that you teach?

Lily   Butterfly collecting. (*Brief pause.*) I work in a gift shop.

Martha   Good. I browse in gift shops.

Lily   They tell me I've a weakness for tourists. And for older women.

They kiss. **Sloan Ross** *enters. He is, as always, tuxedoed. He carries a podium and cuts between* **Lily** *and* **Martha** *on his entrance.*

Martha *exits.*

Lily   Wait a minute. WAIT A MINUTE.

Sloan *sets down his podium and faces the audience. He clears his throat.*

Sloan   Good evening, ladies and gentlemen.

Lily   I don't want to hear your voice, Daddy. Not now.

Sloan   There is, in existence at this very moment, well over 100,000 species of Lepidoptera. This is the second largest insect order in the world, exceeded only by Coleoptera, the beetles. As this is an audience comprised largely of laymen, I shall avoid the use of technical terminology.

Quite an amazing statistic, as I am sure you will agree. It is inevitable that any large group of plant eaters as the Lepidoptera should be eaten by a great variety of other animals. Small mammals eat them directly.

Many bacteria and viruses attack the Lepidoptera and this, certainly, causes vast mortality. The Lepidoptera are not able to resist attack with the strong jaws or hard shells of other insect orders. Instead, they make cases in which they live during critical periods. Extremely important are adaptations of colour and form which enable them to escape the notice of their enemies.

Christine, the Countess Van Dyne, *enters. She is elaborately and carefully dressed. She's the feather boa and white glove type. She speaks with a very pronounced Queens (New York) accent.*

Christine   *C'est bon*, Sloan. *Les bon mots.*

Sloan   Well ... I try to make my lectures as entertaining as possible.

Christine   You'll be a sensation, Sloanie.

Lily   Who is this woman?

Sloan   There's more, Christine: The Hairstreak. There are hundreds of Hairstreaks, found chiefly in temperate and tropical regions. A remarkable feature is a bright orange and black eyespot at the anal angle of the hindwing. You might be interested to know that Hairstreaks show a marked tendency toward cannibalism.

Christine I don't think I *comprend*, Sloan.

Sloan Well. They. They . . . um . . . eat. Each other. It's very simple.

Lily I want to know who this woman is and why you've taken me here.

Christine But Sloan, it is so . . . *degutant*. I would not being it up in *my* lecture.

Sloan I've worked particularly hard on this one, Christine.

Lily (*touches* **Sloan**) Daddy. Introduce me. Please.

Sloan Ah, Lily. I would like you to meet Christine.

Lily Who is she?

Sloan Why, Lily, she's my friend.

Christine Ahhhh . . . *ici, ma cherie.*

Sloan And she is also a friend of Teddy's.

Lily (*to* **Christine**) You know Teddy?

Christine Yes. I have heard so very much about you, Lily.

Lily What is your name?

Sloan Christine is a Countess, Lily.

Christine (*extending a gloved hand*) I am Christine, the Countess Van Dyne. A pleasure to meet you, Lily.

Lily I've never met a Countess.

Sloan Lily: don't be rude to the Countess. Kiss her hand.

Christine *Mais oui.* It is the official greeting of Countesses.

Lily *kisses* **Christine**'*s hand.*

Lily   Your glove is very . . . soft. Where do you live?

Christine   *J'habite* Queens.

Sloan   Christine has a boat and a house on the water.
Wouldn't you like to see the boat, Lily?

Lily   I've never been on a boat. Do you know my
mother?

Christine   Sloanie . . . ?

Sloan   Christine is *my* friend, Lily. She doesn't know your
mother. You understand.

Lily   Of course. What do you do for a living, Miss, um,
Countess?

Sloan   Christine is a dancer, Lily.

Lily   Oh. A ballerina.

Christine   Oh, nonono, *ma petite.* I dance *le Jazz.*

Sloan   She works in a . . . club. Near her home.

Lily   A waterfront dance club?

Christine   Something like that. *Oui.*

Lily   Why do you speak French like that?

Sloan   Lily. Don't be rude.

Christine   It's all right. Sloanie. She's got a right to ask.
All Countesses are required to speak *français.*

Lily   I see. How come Teddy never talks about you?

Christine   Because, *ma petite chou,* it seems he has more
urgent business with you. *Non?*

Lily   Possibly.

Sloan   Well. We're running late, Lily, and we really must
go if we're to make the lecture on time. I hope that you
and the Countess will meet again. Under less . . . hurried
circumstances.

Lily (*to* **Christine**)   You're beautiful.

Christine   Why . . . *merci*. Truly.

Sloan   Do you know how to get home from here, Lily?

Lily   Yes.

Sloan   Very well, then. Shall we, Christine?

Sloan *offers his arm to* **Christine**. *They begin to exit.*
Christine *stops to drape her feather boa around* **Lily***'s neck.*

Christine   *A bientot, ma pauvre.*

They exit.

Lily   There's a game that children play when they mean
to be especially cruel, and it goes like this: if you step on
the crack, you will break your mother's back.

Sloanie, my father, taught me this game when I was five
years old. We're on our way to Lenox Hill hospital. It's
visit the sick mommy day. Of course, she's not . . . really
sick. She's someplace between pretending and death. But
how could I have known that at the time? It's early April
and I am dressed in navy blue. A Sunday. My daddy's got
these . . . huge hands. Like bear paws. And he takes my
miniature Lily-hands in his paws, and we begin to run. I
can't keep up with him. For each step he takes, I take four
or five. I'm terrified of messing my new blue suit. I can't
breathe any more and I think I surely will die. Just as I
think I might fall to the sidewalk, daddy squeezes my hand
even tighter and he begins to sing: if you step on the crack,
you will break your mother's back.

Singsong. Extraordinarily rhythmical. So terrified is the
young Lily of tripping concrete cracks. I wish I might fly.
But faster, faster we go. And when, at the end of our
sadistic run, I do step on that crack, I know my breath will
come no more. I have killed my mother.

This father of mine will not allow me to hold him. No

contact is Lily permitted. 'Baby girl,' he says, 'my only girl, it's a game.'

Martha *enters. She carries music paper and fudge.*

Martha   I made you some fudge. And I bought you some music paper.

Lily   Martha, I'd like to take everything backwards. Run it in reverse. Just for a second.

Martha   Will you talk to me now? Please.

Lily   Yes. I'm ready.

Music in: Mozart's Twinkle, Twinkle Little Star . . . variations.

Jenny *and* **Sally** *enter.* **Jenny** *wears a wedding dress and carries a spray of delicate flowers.*

Sally   Never trust a man with a moustache, Jenny. They have secrets.

Jenny   I'd like my first child to be a boy. They're easier to care for, don't you think? But I don't really have a preference. I want a large family.

Lily   If I tell you . . . if I . . . can tell you what happened . . . you must believe me.

Martha   I want to believe you.

Martha *eats some fudge.*

Lily   May I have some?

Martha *gives* **Lily** *some fudge. They eat in silence.*

Sally   He's late. The bastard's late. Brides are late, Jenny. Not grooms.

Jenny   Think of it, Mother. Our children will be beautiful. When Sloan's tour of duty is up, we're going to move someplace exciting. Rome. Vienna. I'll resume my voice lessons.

Martha   Lily . . . talk to me.

Lily   Run, Mama. Run away. He's late.

Martha   Lily. Lily, what's going on?

Sloan *and* **Teddy** *enter. They are tuxedoed and beaming.*
Christine *trails in behind them. She carries a bottle of champagne.*

Sloan   Jennifer, darling. I'm sorry to be late. But it could not have been avoided.

Christine   *Bon! Bon!* I love weddings.

Sally   We could have gone, Jenny. Now it's too fucking late.

Lily   Too late.

Martha   What's too late?

Sloan   Good afternoon, Mrs Ramona. My apologies. Allow me to present my best man, Teddy Roosevelt Hayes.

Sally   Oh yeah? Why don't you marry this guy, Jenny. At least he's clean shaven.

Lily   Martha, do you understand that if there was a way to stop them I would?

Martha   I think so. But you must understand that it's never possible.

Jackson *enters. He carries a bible.*

Jackson   If there is one among you who objects to this union of kindred souls, let him speak now.

Lily   OBJECTION.

Martha   Lily. Baby, hold me. Let me hold you.

Sally   It's the end of your road, Jenny.

Sloan *and* **Jenny** *join hands.*

Jenny   Our children will grow to do great things.

Sloan   Well, I'm . . . not sure how I feel about children. Immediately, that is.

Jenny   What do you mean, Sloan?

Jackson   In the presence of these various . . . friends . . . and relatives, I now pronounce you –

Lily   OBJECTION.

Jackson   – man and wife. Objection overruled.

Christine *applauds, throws confetti.*

Sally   You shoulda married this guy with three names when you had the chance. What difference does it make?

Jenny *and* **Sloan** *kiss.*

Jenny   Do you really not want any children, Sloan?

Sloan   We'll . . . see. We have time.

Teddy   Awww. Sloanie's a softie, Jenny. He'll come around. I know how you feel. I love kids. Always have.

Jenny *throws her flowers to* **Lily**. *They land at* **Lily**'s *feet. She picks them up, gives them to* **Martha**.

Martha   They're very pretty, Lily. Where'd you get them?

Lily   Martha. Listen to me. My mother asked me to kill her.

Blackout.

The Mozart plays on, full volume.

Act Two

From the darkness, **Jenny** *sings.*

Jenny 'Come sweetheart mine
Don't sit and pine
Tell me of the cares that make you feel so blue.
What have I done
Answer me hon
Have I ever said an unkind word to you?'

Lights up on **Jenny** *and* **Sally**. **Jenny** *stands on a table and holds a knife to her lips as if it were a microphone.*

Jenny 'My love is true
And just for you
I'd do almost anything at any time.
Dear when you sigh
Or when you cry
Something seems to grip this very heart of mine.'

Lights up on **Lily** *and* **Jackson**. **Lily** *smokes a cigarette.*

Jackson Tell me what you know about the American Family, Lily.

Lily I know nothing. I'm not part of an American family.

Jenny Shit. I forget what comes next. What comes next, Mother?

Sally Forget it. You ain't no singer, baby.

Jackson I'm asking you to theorise, Lily. For instance, you are aware of the national averages, are you not? Two and a half kids, a mortgaged home approximately twenty miles from a major city. Something like that.

Lily Is that what you come from?

Jackson No. And neither do you. Nobody I know does.

Jenny   I remember the words. I do. Listen:

'Smile my honey dear
While I kiss away each tear
Or else I shall be melancholy, too.'

Sally   It's time for your feeding.

Jenny   I'm not hungry.

Sally   You're wasting away.

Jenny   I'm fat. I have to learn that song.

Jackson   See, Lily, what I find interesting is that for all the talk about means and averages, most folks I know don't fit the mould.

Lily   Do you think I smoke well, counsellor?

Jackson   Funny thing is, lots of people pretend to be in the ranks of the average. Yes, they'll tell you, I *do* have one and a half brothers. I *did* live in Massapequa Park. But when questions begin to roll, you learn that there was no Buick station wagon with wood-panelled doors. And the half-brother is retarded, stashed away with his grandma in Allentown, PA. Or else he's selling roses to motorists on the Brooklyn–Queens Expressway. Yes. You smoke exceptionally well. Most criminals do.

Lily   You think I'm a criminal.

Jackson   Of course I do. What would you call yourself?

Sally   Goddamn you, Jenny. You'll eat. You will.

She takes the knife away from **Jenny**.

Get down. Now.

Jenny   *does.* **Sally** *ties a gigantic bib around* **Jenny**'s *neck.*

Sally   Sit. (**Jenny** *does.*) Good girl.

Sally, *ladle in hand, feeds* **Jenny** *out of a pot. She has to force the food down.*

Jenny   (*spitting out food as she sings*)   'Come to me my melancholy baby ... what have I DONE ... answer me HON ...'

Sally *throws the pot of food onto* **Jenny**'s *lap.*

Sally   I was the singer. You understand? You stole the notes right out of my mouth.

Lily   I began to smoke after I moved in with Martha. I knew it would annoy her. It was nice to be in a situation where something I did actually upset somebody else.

Sally   I want to go to Florida.

Jenny *giggles.*

Sally   You think that's funny?

Jenny *laughs louder.*

Sally   I am OLD, Jenny. When people get old, their children are supposed to take care of them. I get old and I have to take care of YOU. You think that's funny?

Jenny   It's the best joke I've ever heard.

Jenny *laughs uncontrollably.*

Lights down on **Sally** *and* **Jenny**.

Jackson   What do you think about my theory?

Lily   About smoking? Or about families?

Jackson   Well. If nobody I know comes from an average American family, and if nobody *they* know comes from one, and so on, who compiled the data about national averages?

Lily   Whoever had the most to gain by the data.

Jackson   Where are all the folks with two and a half blonde and perfect children? Where do they hide?

Lily   I don't know. Maybe they all live in the same place. You tell me.

Jackson   Do you know who James Ruppert is?

Lily   Certainly. You're talking to a true-crime expert.

Jackson Eleven of his relatives, including his entire immediate family, were gathered at Mr Ruppert's modest two-storey house in suburban Hamilton, Ohio, on Easter Sunday, 1975. He led his family on an Easter egg hunt. Later, while his mother and wife were setting the table for a holiday dinner, James Ruppert loaded two .22 calibre pistols, a .357 magnum and an 18-shot rifle. Three hours later, he calmly called the police and informed them that a shooting had taken place.

Lily Yes. He needed . . . thirty-one shots. To dispose of eleven people.

Jackson By all accounts, Mr Ruppert was as average as they come.

Jackson *exits.*

Music in: a cha-cha. **Christine** *enters. She dances, rather badly.*

Christine *Un, deux*, cha-cha-cha. *Un . . . deux . . .*

Lily When will my father be back, Countess?

Christine Ah, my sweet, do not worry. *Attendez-vous.* Dance *le cha-cha.* A young woman needs prospects, Lily. *Le dance* is the key that unlocks many doors.

Lily Yes. Look what it's done for you.

Music out.

Christine *Oui.* Maybe you would like to sit outside. In the yard. You can wait for Sloan there. He won't be long.

Lily I'm sorry. I didn't mean . . . I'm supposed to be at Mass with my father. It's Easter Sunday, you know.

Christine Is it? I don't pay any attention to religion.

Lily What country is your husband . . . a Count . . . in?

Christine I've forgotten. It was a long time ago, Lily. We were young and . . . well. You know how it is.

Lily No. I don't.

Christine   You haven't any reason to dislike me, Lily.

Lily   Oh. Where are your children?

Christine   Victor – that was the Count's name – has the children, because, to be frank, I never much cared for them. And they were boys. How was I to deal with foreign-born boys? Isn't it funny how difficult it is to get used to foreigners?

Lily   My mother wanted boys.

Christine   Victor wasn't very bright. And the children had accents. I left them all behind in Zurich.

Lily   Did you keep pictures? Baby shoes? Any reminders?

Christine   I kept the title. It's been useful.

Lily   I do like you, Christine. I do.

Sloan *and* **Teddy** *enter.* **Teddy** *has a bunch of flowers.*

Sloan   Lily, I've brought Teddy along to help us celebrate the holiday.

Teddy   Hiya, Lily. You like flowers, don't you?

Lily (*to* **Christine**)   Teach me to dance.

Lights down on **Christine**, **Sloan** *and* **Teddy**.

Lily   My father kept a picture of Christine in his wallet. A dancer by virtue of one badly creased photograph that frames a woman who looks very much like Christine, but younger. So young. She wears a spangled bathing suit and fishnet stockings. In her hair is a gardenia. She wears tap shoes. Behind this picture in my father's wallet was hidden a photograph of five-year-old Lily: eyes unfocused, tiny red mouth fixed in an uncomfortable grin. I took Christine's picture from Sloan's wallet. He assumed he'd lost it, like most other things in his life. For daddy, I left the photo of young Lily, hidden, at last, by nothing.

Lights up on **Sally** *and* **Jenny**. **Sally** *is sterilising a knife with a lighter.* **Jenny** *holds out a bare arm to her mother.*

Sally   I shoulda thought of this before.

Jenny   Yeah. Hey, Lily-pie, you gonna come to Florida with us?

Lily   I want you to reconsider this, Mama.

Sally   Whatsa matter, Lily. Got a problem with sunny weather?

Lily   My mother's place is here.

Jenny   I lost my place.

Sally   We're gonna have a fine time in the sunshine. Give me your hand, Jenny.

Lily   What are you doing?

Sally   Ain't you never heard of blood sisters?

Lily   You're not sisters.

Jenny   It doesn't matter.

Sally *cuts* **Jenny**'s *thumb, then her own. They press their thumbs together.*

Sally   Swear it now, Jenny.

Jenny   I swear.

Sally   Say: I swear to God I'll go to Florida with my mother.

Jenny   I swear to God I'll go to Florida with my mother.

Sally   I swear to leave my husband and daughter behind.

Jenny   I . . . swear. To leave.

Lily   How will you get there? Where will you live? You haven't any money.

Sally   She'll find a job. and she'll take care of me.

Lily   She's incapable of working.

Jenny   I used to be a switchboard operator.

Lily She'll explode on impact. She'll get off the
Greyhound and explode, like a grenade.

Sally Listen, Lily. She made me a promise.

Jenny I made her a promise.

Lily I don't want you to leave.

Jenny You're old enough. Go out, Lily. Leave me. It's
supposed to happen. How old are you now? Twenty . . .
thirty.

Lily Twenty-five.

Sally Twenty-five, she works in a store that sells T-shirts.
Hot stuff. Star material.

Jenny Yeah. A big zero.

Sally A leech. She sucks us dry, Jenny. Come on. Swear
to me. Do it.

Jenny A major disappointment. How old did you say you
were, Lily? Forty-six? Twelve? Seventy-seven?

Sally A big nothing. I'm really gonna enjoy being taken
care of.

Lily I'm twenty-five. And I'm moving out.

Jenny She's moving out.

Sally You hear that? She's walking out on you, Jenny.
The nerve. You raise a kid, they eat your food, they walk
out on you. I wouldn't allow it.

Lily You *didn't* allow it, Grandma.

Jenny I . . . I . . . get my chart, Lily. My pressure.
Where's my chart?

Lily Yeah. I'm moving out. I met someone. A woman.

Sally You what? You met a *what?*

Lily A woman. She reminds me of daddy's girlfriend,
Christine. You know Christine, Mama, don't you?

Jenny   I swear, I swear, I swear, I swear . . .

Sally   You met a fucking *woman*?

Lily   I have a picture of Christine, Mama. She's awfully pretty. Would you like to see?

Jenny   I swear. I do swear. I'll go to Florida and leave my husband and daughters behind.

Martha *enters.*

Martha   Have you ever made love to a woman, Lily?

Lily   Here, Mama. A *bon voyage* gift. From me to you.

Lily *gives* **Jenny** *the picture of* **Christine**.

Martha   You seemed so . . . experienced. In the bar. Don't get me wrong. I don't mind.

Jenny (*looking at the photograph*)   Is she . . . some kind of athlete?

Lily   She's a dancer.

Sally   I've never seen anything like this. Your daughter's telling you she's a DYKE.

Jenny   Really? Well, she's entitled. She's . . . what? Fifty-five? She's old enough.

Lily   Goodbye, Mama.

Lily *goes to* **Martha**.

Martha   I thought you were the teacher.

Lily   No. I like to watch. Remember?

Jenny *shows* **Sally** *the picture of* **Christine**.

Jenny   Nice looking, isn't she?

Sally   When are we leaving? I gotta pack, you know.

Jenny   Soon. We'll leave soon.

Sally   When?

Jenny Later, Mother. Later.

Lights down on **Jenny** *and* **Sally**.

Martha It's easy.

Lily Show me.

Martha Take off your blouse.

Lily *does.* **Martha** *reaches out for her, and* **Lily** *turns, her back to* **Martha**.

Martha Interesting. Do you always make love with your back to your partner?

Lily Yes. Is there something wrong with that?

Martha Well . . . it's kind of odd.

Lily WHAT'S WRONG WITH IT.

Martha *touches* **Lily**. **Lily** *pulls away.*

Martha Hey . . . it's okay. I'm not going to hurt you.

Lily *puts on her blouse.*

Lily I guess you want me to leave.

Martha No. I don't. Stay a while.

Lily Why? What do you want?

Martha Nothing. You. Whatever.

Lily Do you dance?

Martha No. I . . . well, I never really have.

Lily Good.

Martha Is this a test?

Lily Yes.

Martha And did I supply the correct answer?

Lily Yes. You did. Do you like . . . sunshine?

Martha Sure. I guess I do. Don't you?

Lily   No. I like winter. I like to shiver. Builds character.

Martha   Lily, listen. I don't know . . . what to do now. I'm very attracted to you. I'd like to . . . touch you. Hold you. Something.

Lily   Wouldn't you like to know what I know about music? I know a lot about music, Martha.

Martha *kisses* **Lily**.

Martha   Let me take you to bed.

Lily   I had a lover once.

Martha   What happened?

Lily   The choice was me, or his friendship with my father. He chose my father. Everyone does.

Martha   I haven't. I don't even know your father.

Lily   Don't you find it strange? I've just told you something quite out of the ordinary.

Martha   Not really. There's always a story more bizarre than your own.

Jenny *enters. She carries a can of shaving cream and a razor.*

Lily   I'd like to show you how to dance.

Martha   All right.

Lights up on **Sloan**. *He's sleeping, slumped back in a chair. His tux is a mess.*

Lily *and* **Martha** *waltz. They are initially unsure of each other, unsure of each other's body.*

Jenny *approaches the sleeping form of* **Sloan**. *She caresses his face, touches his lips. She kisses his forehead.*

Lily *and* **Martha**'s *dance becomes more graceful, more steady. They are enjoying themselves.*

Jenny   Truth is, Sloan, I don't know *what* you do. Never have. My mother calls you the Bug Man. And maybe she's

right. You are so very handsome. Lily left today. Yes, she's
gone. Where? Oh, well, I don't know. I didn't think it
appropriate to ask. Do you really mean it, Sloan? We'll go
away? I know, darling. I know you don't love that woman.
Yes, I do look marvellous in black. You're absolutely right.

Jenny *applies shaving cream to* **Sloan***'s moustache. She shaves it
off.*

Martha *and* **Lily***'s dance becomes a passionate embrace.*
Martha*'s hands are all over* **Lily***'s body, exploring it, becoming
accustomed to it.*

Jenny   It had to come off, Sloan. My mother says it
contained secrets.

Blackout.

Slide display:

Lily *and* **Sloan***, holding hands on the beach.*

Jenny*, posing with her knife as a microphone.*

A black-and-white police photo of the Ross kitchen, blood everywhere.

The photo of **Christine** *in bathing suit and fishnet stockings.*

Lights up on **Jackson***.*

Jackson   Shortly thereafter, ladies and gentlemen, Sloan
Ross left his wife and set up house with the Countess. Sally
Ramona did not make it to Florida. Life at the walk-up
remained untouched by the world at large.

Lily *enters, wheeling a hospital table upon which lies* **Sally
Ramona***.* **Sally** *is hooked up to an i.v.*

Jackson   Ladies and gentlemen, allow me to present the
defendant's grandmother.

Sally *(with great difficulty)*   Butter . . . flies.

Jackson   Mrs Ramona refers to the second largest insect
order in the world.

Sally   Never. Trust a man. With a moustache.

Jackson Mrs Ramona refers to the defendant's father Sloan Ross.

Sally STIG ... MA ... TA ...

Jackson Mrs Ramona refers to the Ross's traditionally Catholic upbringing of their daughter, Lily.

Sally *very suddenly sits bolt upright and begins pulling the i.v. tubes away from her body. She addresses* **Lily** *directly.*

Sally MANSLAUGHTER ... MANSLAUGHTER ... MANSLAUGHTER.

Lily It's the pig woman. Come to claim me for her own.

Sally I ain't no pig woman. I came to clean your mother's blood.

Lily Jane Gibson. Also known as the pig woman.

Sally I AIN'T NO PIG WOMAN.

She crawls around the floor. She scrubs the floor with her palms.

I had to scrub Jenny's blood from the floor. Look. See that? I'm scrubbing this spot, see? And it up and disappears on me. The blood is jumping around the linoleum and I can't catch it and I think I'm going crazy but no. No. It's really happening. A blood vessel in my head pops. I hear it. Like it's mocking me. I'm having a fucking stroke. TAKE CARE OF ME.

Lights down on **Sally**.

Lily *tries to touch the projected image of* **Christine**, *but it disappears.*

Martha *enters.*

Martha Lily, what did you mean? What did you mean when you told me your mother asked you to kill her?

Sloan, *now clean shaven, and* **Christine** *enter.*

Sloan Lily, why did you wait so long to leave home?

Teddy *enters.*

Teddy Hey, Lily, what's the deal with your old dyke friend?

Martha I am not old.

Lily Jackson. What if?

Jackson What if . . . what?

Lily What if. This never happened.

Jackson Ah. Yes. Everybody wants to play that game, Lily. Trouble is, nobody knows how to make it work. Go ahead. Try. You're on your own, Lily.

Jackson *exits.*

Lights down on all but **Lily**.

Lily My father is a renowned lepidopterist. My mother attends each of his lectures and she understands everything he says. Of course, she's very busy herself, being as she's rather a good mezzo-soprano. Just a cut below super stardom, but she does well. She's in demand.

My grandmother, once a famous mezzo herself, has retired to Fort Lauderdale. And because she's very wealthy, men pursue her. She's dazzling.

Lights up on **Sally**. *She reclines in a beach chair. She wears a bathing suit.*

Sally Hiya, Lily. Why don't you come down here with your husband and sons? I've got a big brick house with a portable patio. And guess what? I've got the best fucking tan in the world.

Lights down on **Sally**.

Lily My dearest friend is the world-famous flamenco dancer, Christine. She and her husband, the Danish Count Victor Van Dyne, frequently host dinner parties for my parents. When they're in town, that is.

Lights up on **Christine**, *in flamenco costume.*

Christine *Merci. Merci, mes amis.* And now, for my

fifteenth encore, I shall dance a bolero.

Lights down on **Christine**.

Lily   I, of course, marry John-John Kennedy and I bear him five sons. He is busy with law school and fund-raisers, which leaves me time to be with Martha McKenzie, my one true love. Martha and I often travel.

Lights up on **Martha**. *She's surrounded by luggage and cameras.*

Martha   Lily, I've got our itinerary. We land in Rome, where we'll spend four days at the Hotel Flora. We train from Rome to Venice, where we spend three weeks at the Danieli. After that, of course, you've got to be in London for the premiere of your new opera.

Lights down on **Martha**.

Lily   Oh, yes. And in between my various engagements, I find the time to complete my sixth opera. It's the one I'm writing for my mother. She's really looking forward to it. Lastly, I have set up a trust fund for Eleanor Roosevelt Hayes, daughter of my father's friend and my godfather, Teddy Roosevelt Hayes. Eleanor wants to be a composer, too. Teddy's proud of the example I've set for her. He's such a nice man.

Lights up on **Teddy**. *He wears sweat clothes and lifts weights.*

Teddy   Thanks for the gym, Lily. A guy's got to stay in shape as he gets older. My wife really appreciates it, too.

Lights down on **Teddy**.

Lily   Who says you can't have everything?

Lights up on **Jenny**. *She looks older, greyer. Her hair's a mess. She wears an old hospital robe and fluffy slippers. She tries to brush her hair, but can't quite do it.*

Lights up on **Sloan**. *He carries a gun.*

Sloan   Hello, Lily. How've you been?

Lily   I manage. We manage.

Sloan How's the gift shop?

Lily How's Christine?

Sloan Fine. She's fine. She asks about you.

Lily Give her my best, Daddy. I'm going to see mama today.

Sloan Do you need money, Lily? Are you supporting yourself?

Lily Martha does okay.

Sloan I see. Well. How's the, uh, music?

Lily Can't complain. I have lots of blank music paper.

Sloan Give it time. It'll come.

Lily No. It won't. I don't really know how to read music, much less write it. I just know . . . tidbits. Interesting facts. Trivia.

Sloan I'd like to help you, Lily. But I'm a little short of cash. Christine, well, she has expensive habits.

Lily Does it bother you, Daddy?

Sloan What?

Lily Me. And Martha. Mama. Teddy. Pick one.

Sloan What's to be bothered by?

Lily I just wondered. What's that?

Sloan A Luger. It's very old and valuable. It's . . . I want to give it to you. It's worth quite a bit.

Lily *takes the gun.*

Lily A foreign gun.

Sloan Yes?

Lily Christine mustn't like it. It being a foreigner. You know.

Sloan *laughs.*

Sloan   Yes. Well. I must go now. I have a class.

Lily   Thanks, Daddy.

Sloan   Oh, it's nothing. Really.

Lily   I'm thanking you generally. I want to know what it feels like to thank your parent for something.

Sloan *exits.*

Lily (*to the audience*)   My father kept a Luger by his bedside. In case he ever felt like shooting a butterfy.

Jenny   Lily-pie, will you fix your mama's hair?

Lily   Yes, Mama. I will. I always have.

Jenny   It was your forty-fifth birthday yesterday, wasn't it? I'm sorry I didn't send a card.

Lily   No, Mama. My birthday is in November. It was your birthday yesterday.

Jenny   It was? That's funny. Your grandmother didn't mention it. How's your husband? What was his name? Martin?

Lily   He's fine, Mama.

Jenny   Are you pregnant yet?

Lily   No Mama, not yet.

Jenny   When?

Lily   Soon.

Jenny   I entered a contest, Lily. I saw it in the newspaper and had your grandma cut it out. I enter a lot of contests. Sweepstakes. Look-alike competitions.

Lily   That's nice, Mama. Good luck.

Jenny   Oh, I won't win, baby. I just like to enter for the recreation. I like to anticipate winning. Have you finished writing that song for me?

Lily   Oh, yes. I've written fifty songs for you, Mama.

Jenny   I'm real proud of you, Lily. When will I get to sing them? I'm a little out of practice, mind you.

Lily   Soon, Mama. Soon. There's time.

Jenny   Are you pregnant yet, honey?

Lily   Yes, Mama. I am.

Jenny   That's lovely, Lily. I hope it's a boy. They're easier to care for.

Lily   I have two boys already, Mama. Don't you remember? I'm hoping for a girl.

Jenny   That's right ... how stupid of me. You have two boys. I knit sweaters for them.

Lily   That's right, Mama. And we go for drives to the country in our Buick station wagon.

Jenny   You know, I've always liked your husband's car, Lily.

Lily   He likes it, too. We all like it.

Lily *puts the gun on a table between her and her mother.*

Jenny   What's that?

Lily   It's a gun, Mama.

Jenny   Are you afraid of something, Lily?

Lily   No, Mama. There's nothing to fear.

Jenny   Would you name your baby girl after me?

Lily   Of course I will.

Jenny   Listen to me. Are you listening to me, Lily?

Lily   I'm listening.

Jenny   Your daddy was a wrong number, Lily, who ought never have been answered.

Lily   I know. Why don't we take care of it so that you don't have to answer?

Jenny Will you brush your mama's hair, sweet-pea? I like to look nice for you.

Lily All right, Mama. It's time.

Lily *takes the brush from* **Jenny** *and begins to brush her mother's hair.*

Jenny What's that on the table, Lily-pie?

Lily I told you. It's a brush.

Jenny Oh. Would you sing one of the songs you wrote for me?

Lily Of course. (*She begins to sing:*)

'The night was mighty dark
So you could hardly see
For the moon refused to shine.'

Jenny I know this song, Lily. I know it.

Lily That's because I wrote it just for you, Mama. Help me sing it.

Jenny (*she sings*)

'Couple sitting underneath
A willow tree
For love they pine.'

Lily Go on, Mama. You're doing fine.

Lily *puts the brush on the table and picks up the gun. She brushes her mother's hair with the gun.*

Jenny 'Little maid was kinda 'fraid of dark
So she said, I guess I'll go . . .'

Lily 'The boy began to sigh
Looked up at the sky
Told the moon his little tale of woe.'

Jenny 'Shine on, shine on harvest moon
Up in the sky
I ain't had no lovin' since
January . . . February . . .'

Lily 'June or July.'

Jenny There are more words, Lily. Aren't there more words?

Lily There's always something left to be said, Mama. But it's fine. It's pretty this way.

Jenny When will you let me meet your husband?

Lily He'll come to your concert.

Jenny My concert? When is it?

Lily Next week. You're singing my songs.

Jenny That's soon, Lily. I have to look nice. Do you think I should wear black? It's slimming.

Lily Whatever you'd like, Mama. It's yours.

Jenny Will it be dark?

Lily Would you like it to be dark?

Jenny Oh sure, honey. Everything looks better in the dark. That's when people are their prettiest.

Lily It's dark now, Mama.

Jenny Lily, are you here with me?

Lily I'm here, Mama.

Jenny Don't let me go.

Lily I'm staying.

Jenny Don't you let me go, Lily.

Lily I'll never let you go.

Jenny I'm ready, baby. Hold me. It's dark. Are you singing with me, Lily? Are you ready?

Lily I'm ready, Mama. And I'm singing at the top of my lungs. Hold tight, Mama.

Lily *presses the gun against her mother's head.*

Jenny   I was always so interested in a family with a past. With some history.

Lily   There's nothing ahead of you but the future, Mama. The future.

Blackout, as **Lily** *pulls the trigger.*

Disappeared

In memory of Pat, with love and thanks

Disappeared was first produced by the Leicester Haymarket and Midnight Theatre Company, in association with Chapman Duncan Associates, at the Haymarket Studio, Leicester. It opened on 2 February 1995 with the following cast:

Sarah Casey	Alexandra Gilbreath
Elston Rupp	Kerry Shale
Jack Fallon	Thomas Craig
Ellen Casey	Anna Keaveney
Ted Mitchell	Richard Bremmer
Natalie	Melee Hutton
Timothy Creighton	Steven Elder
Anthony	Eric Loren

Directed by Phyllis Nagy
Designed by Tim Shortall
Lighting by Johanna Town

It was subsequently produced by Leicester Haymarket and Chapman Duncan Associates at the Royal Court Theatre Upstairs, London. It opened on 27 June 1995. The cast remained the same except that Andrew Woodall played Ted Mitchell and Sam Dale played Timothy Creighton.

Characters

Elston Rupp, *a small, nondescript man of indeterminate age. Impeccably groomed in a very odd way.*
Sarah Casey, *a 25-year-old travel agent who's never been anywhere.*
Jack Fallon, *a 26-year-old bartender who believes everything he reads in the tabloids.*
Ellen Casey, *Sarah's disappointed mother.*
Ted Mitchell, *a New York City homicide detective whose physical appearance and dry demeanour suggest he's something other than what he is.*
Anthony, *Sarah's boyfriend. An Italian-American hairdresser with a magnificent body and little else. Sweet and good-natured, he's the kind of man who doesn't understand hairdresser jokes.*
Natalie, *Elston's employer. She owns a thrift shop she doesn't want. She wears only brand-new clothes, and never wears anything more than once.*
Timothy Creighton, *42, an entertainment attorney. Painfully shy, for a lawyer.*

The Time
One Sunday evening in New York City, and at various times
preceding and following that evening.

The Place
A run-down bar in Hell's Kitchen; a railroad apartment in
Hell's Kitchen; an Upper East Side thrift shop; an Upper East
Side apartment; a midtown police station; a Lower East Side
travel agency.

The Setting
This is a barren landscape with touches of the otherworldly. It
should appear as if everything here, while maintaining certain
aspects of naturalism, appears from nowhere.

Note
The use of capitals in certain passages does not necessarily or
exclusively indicate a rise in speaking volume. However,
capitalization always suggests a shift in intensity or emphasis.
Similarly, the use of 'beats' does not suggest the use of pauses.
Rather, the beats indicate shifts in thought, sometimes quite
abrupt shifts. The punctuation often does not conform to
standard punctuation as sentences are sometimes broken
where one might not expect them to be broken, and often
what might naturally be written as a question is written as a
statement. Strict attention should therefore be paid to the
punctuation pattern as it does create the text's rhythm.
Blackouts should not be used at all as the action from scene to
scene should proceed with fluidity. The music selected for the
play is not random. It relates very specifically to the text;
therefore, no substitutions should be made.

Act One

One

Music in: 'Elenore' (The Turtles). **Elston** *and* **Sarah** *at a seedy dive of a bar.* **Jack** *tends bar.* **Elston** *wears an ill-fitting tuxedo. His hair is slicked back. He looks ridiculously out of place. He watches* **Sarah** *dance. She's having a great time dancing by herself.* **Jack** *also watches her dance. Eventually,* **Sarah** *winds her way over to* **Elston**. *She performs for him, lip-synching to the tune. She runs her hands over the lapels of his tux. She's playful and not at all sexually suggestive.* **Elston** *pays her no mind. It's as if she isn't there. Unable to get a response from* **Elston**, **Sarah** *gives up. She sits at the bar and smokes.*

Sarah They wrote that song about me. Did you know that, Jack?

Jack *shrugs.*

Sarah I wasn't even born at the time. But it's about me, anyway. The guy who wrote it, he had a dream of the most fantastic woman he'd ever meet and it was me. How I look now. Did anybody ever write a song about you, Jack?

Jack *shrugs.*

Sarah Yeah. So. This guy, he's a Brit and he breaks out in sweats over his dream and so he writes this song. And his buddies in the band, they say, well bloody great, kid. But what's her name? So he says, dunno. Eleanor. Maybe. Then my mother fucks the whole deal and names me Sarah. Right? So. Ten years ago maybe, I'm listening to the radio and I hear this song and I know it's all about me. And I'm freaking out because, Jesus, I know it's the song I'm born to hear. I write the guy a letter, you know, send him a picture. I write, hey, I'm Eleanor but my

name's Sarah and I hope you'll understand. The bastard
never wrote back. I heard he was dead. Serves him right.
But you know, then it gets really creepy. You know what
happened then, Jack?

Jack *shrugs.*

Sarah   I'm at this Springsteen concert, I don't know, five
years back, right? And this geezer comes up to me. I
mean, this guy's so old his skin is yellow and he wheezes.
Got real long hair. Yellow-white. And he grabs me, you
know? Strong. For an old bag. And his breath, oh man, it
was like . . . dirt. Heavy. Like overwhelming . . . grime. I
think he wants to touch me or, I don't know, something.
And he leans in real close and whispers, 'Eleanor. How
lovely to see you again.' Creepy, right? Well. What do you
think of that, Jack?

Jack *shrugs.*

Sarah   I'm thinking maybe I should write it up for a
magazine.

Elston   Jack be nimble. Jack be quick.

Jack *and* **Sarah** *consider this.*

Jack   You wanna drink, mister?

Elston (*to* **Sarah**)   Jack be nimble. Jack be quick. It's
from a song. 'The Limbo Rock.'

Sarah   Uh-huh. Yeah. So?

Elston   A lyric. (*He sings.*) Jack be nimble, Jack be quick.
Jack jump . . . I don't remember the rest of it exactly. But
it's a song. About Jack. It's fate.

Sarah   Wait. Are you saying that somebody wrote a song
about Jack? And that it's fate?

Elston   No. I'm saying that your meeting with the geezer
was fate.

Jack   I've never heard this song you're talking about.

Elston I'm saying that the geezer was affirming your belief. Fate.

Sarah Yeah. Well. Maybe he thought I was his long lost granddaughter, too.

Elston It's possible. But not likely. Consider the statistics. In a group of one hundred women, what are the odds that even one of them will be called Eleanor?

Sarah I don't really know. What do you think, Jack?

Jack Dunno. Unless you was sitting in a room full of Roosevelts, I'd have to say the odds would be pretty low.

Elston Exactly.

Sarah Course, maybe there was a run on the name after the song came out. There's lots of Eleanors. Eleanor Parker. Eleanor Rigby.

Jack Eleanor Connolly. (*Beat.*) My ex.

Elston Jack, if I am remembering correctly, and I am not at all sure that I am, Chubby Checker sang 'The Limbo Rock'.

Sarah So what are you saying? Some old creep with bad breath calls me Eleanor and this means there's UFOs hiding out in a barn in Nebraska?

Elston I'm saying you believe. In fate. In the notion that nothing is random.

Sarah Right. And we're getting looped in some shit-hole on the West Side highway 'cause we knew we were gonna do it and so that's why we're here.

Elston You believe the song was written about you. Fact?

Sarah Yeah. It was.

Elston And you said that your meeting with the geezer was . . . creepy? Is that what you called it?

Sarah Yeah. Creepy. Like you.

Elston   In my book, Sarah, creepiness is a synonym for what we are afraid to recognize as our own. The very things we ought to embrace but will not. Embrace it. Sarah.

Sarah   Uh-huh. Well. What do you think this guy does, Jack?

Jack   Dunno. Suit don't fit him.

Sarah   Yeah. Like he got lost on his way to a New Year's Eve party a billion years ago. You a fan of *The Twilight Zone*, Jack?

Jack   Oh sure. Love the one where that kid wishes everybody into a cornfield. I like that.

Sarah   Oh God I wish I could do that. Wish people into cornfields. My boyfriend. My mother. This . . . creepy . . . guy.

Elston   Don't you like my clothing? I wore it for you.

Sarah   You hear that, Jack? This fuck wore a monkey-suit for me.

Elston   I usually don't talk this much. You must be special.

Sarah   Your technique's a little creaky. Try again.

Jack   Mister. You wanna buy Sarah a drink?

Elston   No. She drinks too much. I've noticed.

Jack   You wanna buy me a drink? 'Cause if you don't buy somebody a drink I'm gonna have to ask you to leave.

Elston   I'm sorry. I mean no disrespect. I'll drink whatever you give me. Please.

Jack   You wanna beer?

Elston   Whatever you'd like.

Jack   Jack Daniels?

Elston   It doesn't matter.

Jack   Come on, guy. What? Whiskey sour? Gin tonic? Decide.

Elston   I trust you, Jack.

Jack   Oh fuck me. I get one customer and he's a wacko faggot.

Elston   There's no need to get touchy, Jack.

Sarah   Don't mind Jack. He calls everybody a faggot. It's a term of endearment. Some kinda Irish thing. I know. My mother's the same way.

Elston   Are you Irish, Sarah?

Sarah   Yeah. What are you?

Elston   I'm an entertainment attorney.

Jack   Look. I don't care what you are. Just order.

Elston   All right. A Stoly Martini. Olives.

Sarah   A real lawyer drink. A real . . . creepy . . . lawyer drink.

Elston   Why do you say that, Sarah?

Sarah   What's an entertainment attorney doing in a dive?

Elston   A little bird told me you'd be here.

Sarah   You're so full of shit it's coming through your shoes. What are you really? Pimp? Truck driver? Atomic scientist?

Elston   I'm an entertainment attorney. Got lots of clients. You ever been to Ireland, Sarah?

Sarah   Who are your clients? Name them.

Elston   Ireland is beautiful, Sarah. I've been there fifteen times. On business.

Sarah   Your client list. Give it to me.

Elston   Business takes a man places. Do you know what

it's like to be in business, Sarah? Do you know what it's like to travel? (*Beat.*) I have many clients. The Turtles. For instance.

Sarah   You're lying.

Elston (*he sings*)   Eleanor, gee I think you're swell . . . coincidence? Or fate?

Jack   You manage turtles?

Sarah   Shut up, Jack. (*To* **Elston**.) Go on. I'm listening.

Elston   There's nothing more to say. I'll finish my drink and be gone. If you'd like, I'll send you a couple of tickets to their next concert.

Sarah   Nah. I'm kinda busy. And I have a fear of flying. But thanks, you know, for asking.

Elston   I'll leave you my card. If you change your mind.

Elston *gives* **Sarah** *a business card.*

Sarah   Timothy J. Creighton. Entertainment attorney. Yeah. Sure.

Elston   You shouldn't doubt me, Sarah. Sarah Casey.

Sarah   How'd you know that?

Elston   Coincidence. Or fate.

Sarah   Yeah. Well. That's not my name. So much for conspiracy theories.

Jack   Who said something about conspiracies?

Sarah   SHUT UP, JACK. (*To* **Elston**.) All right. Out with it. What do you want?

Elston   They call this Hell's Kitchen.

Sarah   Great. A tourist.

Elston   No. I . . . I live on the East Side. I was walking. I like to walk. At night. I like the river. I was thirsty. I stopped.

Sarah   You like to drink.

Elston   I like to drink.

Sarah   And you don't really like to talk. But you talk to me because I'm special.

Elston   Yes. And you have kind eyes.

Sarah   And I bet you think I have a big heart, right?

Elston   Yes.

Sarah   A big-hearted hooker. Is that what you think? Guess what. I'm not. Do you understand that? Do you think he understands that, Jack?

Jack *shrugs.*

Elston   I don't think you're a hooker. I think you're kind.

Sarah   This is where I live, okay? I have a job. You think there's nobody decent living on this side of town? Is that it? Because you are wrong. I'm not some lonely piece of ass losing myself in a booze-bag joint. I'm not.

Elston   I'm sorry you're so defensive.

Sarah   And I am not impressed by your business card Mr Timothy J. Creighton. Are you, Jack?

Jack   Nah. See lots of his type. Skinny. Lip sores.

Sarah   Creepy-looking bastard liar who looks as much like a lawyer as I do a brain surgeon.

Elston   All right. I'll tell you what I really do. I kill people.

Jack   No shit. For a living?

Elston   No. I just kill.

Jack   You don't get paid for it?

Elston   No. I do it. That's all.

Jack   Sonofabitch. How many people you pop?

Elston   Six. Maybe seven.

Jack   You're not sure?

Elston   I'm not certain that one died. She might have lived.

Jack   Yeah? Where you been doing this killing?

Elston   Here. Upstate. Different places. I like here best.

Jack   Yeah. More of a selection, right?

Elston   That's right. And anonymity. It's important.

Jack   Sure it is. Where do you do them? In the street? Just like that?

Elston   No. I take them home. And then I do them. In my apartment. I tend to keep them alive a few days. Before.

Jack   Oh. I get it. Like you're fattening them up and stuff. Yeah.

Elston   No. I don't feed them. I talk to them. For a while. Before.

Jack   Okay. And then. Then what? You . . . shoot them?

Elston   I drown them. In my bathtub. They put up terrific struggles. I love to watch them fight. You ever drown anyone, Jack?

Jack   I drowned a mouse once. Took a fuck of a long time.

Elston   Yes. And people take a fuck of a long time, too.

Jack   Uh-huh. And I guess this entertainment lawyer shit, I guess you just made that up.

Elston   No. There is a Timothy J. Creighton and he is an entertainment attorney. Although I'm quite certain he doesn't represent the Turtles.

Jack So this, uh, suit. It ain't yours?

Elston No. It's his.

Jack And you just took it, right?

Elston I borrowed it. I manage a thrift shop. Many people dropping off many clothes and other ... belongings. I have regular customers.

Jack Okay. I get it. You put on some other guy's old gear and then you go out and whack girls. Makes sense.

Elston Exactly my point, Jack. I am Mr Creighton when I wear his clothing. I am exceedingly wealthy and I live on East Seventy-Fifth Street. My wife is called Rachel and we are fond of making trips to the Cape. But Mr Creighton is compelled to kill people. Coincidence. Or fate?

A tense silence. **Elston** *breaks out into a broad smile.* **Jack** *laughs.*

So. How about another Stoly Martini, Jack. And whatever our friend Sarah would like.

Jack I gotta hand it to you, mister. You had me going there right at the end. Jeez, that part about the clothes. You know, it's like, it's –

Elston Creepy?

Jack Bet your ass. Jeez. Wow. I'm a fucking sucker.

Elston Fucking faggot sucker.

Jack (*laughs*) Yeah. Fucking fag sucker. *Salut.*

Sarah So what's your name. Really.

A beat before **Elston** *answers.*

Elston Tim. Tim Creighton.

Sarah Okay. Tim Creighton or whoever you really are. I gotta be up real early tomorrow and I'm so mad at my boyfriend I'm gonna take a hatchet to his face. I'll leave you here with Jack. You can trade stupid jokes and then maybe you can make him your first male victim. As for me, I got to get some sleep. Some of us work day jobs.

Elston   What do you do, Sarah?

Sarah   I'm a linebacker for the Giants. Satisfied?

Elston   No, really. I'm interested in the way you live.

Sarah   I bet you are. How about if I told you I'm a prison guard at Rikers Island? While I'm beating the inmates I have fantasies about replacing Sybil Danning in films like . . . PRISON DAMES IN HEAT. Yeah. Sarah Casey, muscles of steel, stars in BABES BEHIND BARS.

Elston   So your name is Casey. Sarah Casey. I guessed your name. Fate.

Sarah   So what. Some creeps are lucky.

Jack   She works in a travel agency.

Sarah   Shut up, Jack.

Jack   It's her uncle's shop. Down on East Seventh Street. Sells Warsaw package deals to old Polacks.

Sarah   You're disgusting, Jack.

Elston   That must be nice for you, Sarah. Working as a travel agent.

Sarah   Yeah. I'm thrilled.

Elston   Your boyfriend. What's his name?

Sarah   Who knows. I used to go with Jack, here. But then I discovered he was an idiot savant. His talent is pouring beer. He's real good at it. But I figure, see, there's no future in it. Jesus. I gotta get out of this city. I'll be brain-dead, I keep hanging with crap like you two.

Elston   You're a smart girl, Sarah. You'd like to travel. You dream of fame. Fortune. It's out there.

Sarah   Listen, asshole. I can play the tough broad with a minimal amount of brains as well as the next girl. And that's fine. That's just . . . fine. For people like you.

Elston   And why is that fine?

Sarah   It's what you expect. Young tart parks her ass on
a barstool on Forty-Eighth and the highway. You think,
sure, she's fair game. Nice girl. Not too much upstairs. Has
a way with men and hairspray. I play along because there's
no investment in you. I tell you nothing. You get . . .
nothing. I remain intact. Yes. I work in my uncle's travel
agency while I attend night classes at some second-rate city
college. Yes. I dream of many things and no, I am not
deluded by unreasonable expectations of a future dazzling
life.

Elston   And yet you believe that a man who lived several
thousand miles away wrote a song about you before you
were even born.

Sarah   Yeah. And you drown women in your bathtub.
We're a couple of charmers, aren't we?

Elston   You have kindness. You do. Sarah Casey.

Sarah   Thank you. Thanks for the booze, Jack. I'm outta
here.

Elston   Do you really think I look ridiculous?

Sarah (*considers this*)   Absolutely.

Elston   I know I do. I dress this way because it's the only
way people pay attention to me. Normally, I recede. Like
Jack's hairline.

Sarah   You're a pretty funny guy, Mr Timothy J.
Creighton.

Elston   You're the only woman who's talked to me.

Sarah   You're a sad man, right?

Elston   Lonely.

Sarah   Oh. That, too. And I'd guess you collect things.
What? What do you collect?

Elston   Stickpins. Gloves. Spectacles. Accessories. The trappings of things. (*Beat.*) And you don't collect anything. You go to the movies.

Sarah   Romantic comedies are my specialty.

Elston   Boy gets girl. Boy loses girl.

Sarah   Boy cries. Those are my favourites.

Elston   And then?

Sarah   And then. One night at a shitty rock concert, a dirty old maniac mistakes the girl for somebody he once fucked in a brothel. He calls her Eleanor. She finds it all very creepy. She goes home and passes out. She gets up the next morning. And the next. And maybe the next. That's all. The end.

Jack   I never saw a movie like that.

Elston   Shut up, Jack.

Jack   Hey. Fuckface. Don't you dare tell me to shut up.

Sarah   Jack was a Golden Gloves champ.

Jack   Fuck me, yes. Light-heavyweight. Won twice. Subnovice and Open classes.

Sarah   He could have been a contender.

Jack   Fuck me, yes. I was a contender.

Sarah   Of course, Jack was going to be a cop. But. It didn't quite work out. He lost his hair, instead. We're old friends.

Jack   Family friends.

Elston   You have a large family, Jack?

Jack   The largest. Yeah.

Elston   I'm an orphan. I was raised in a void.

Sarah   Weren't we all. It's late, boys.

Elston   But it's not too late for you to talk with me. Sit a while.

Sarah   Nope. The early bird gets the worm, et cetera.

Elston   You're an early bird. A kind bird.

Sarah   I'm really not so kind. I'm not.

Elston   I know. That's why I like you. Sit with me. Call me Tim. And I'll call you Eleanor.

Sarah   Why?

Elston   Because you deserve it. (*Beat.*) I'll tell you stories.

Sarah   What kind of stories?

Elston   True stories.

Sarah   And will they be sad stories?

Elston   If you'd like.

Sarah   Do you know any UFO stories?

Jack   There's this UFO that landed in somebody's backyard in Maine. It lands in the backyard and gets caught up in a clothes-line. And all the clothes get caught up, you know, overalls and stuff, 'cause it's the backyard of farmers, so there's lots of denim.

Sarah   This is not a true story, Jack.

Jack   I swear it's true. And these people, these farmers, they come running out and all their clothes are like, electrified. Electric current's running through their overalls and underwear and it's like watching a moving neon beer sign, you know, a blue one? 'Oh Jesus,' says this one farmer, 'we got to *do* something about this shit.' And while he's scratching his head wondering what he's gonna do, the electricity eases off and this farmer notices that all his clothes have turned white. The UFO's sucked all the colour from his clothes. Then, he hears music. Violins and shit coming from the UFO.

Sarah   Who told you this?

Jack Wait. So. This little fat guy smoking a cigar comes out of the UFO and he says to the farmer, he says: 'Upon this rock you will build my church.' Then, the fat guy blows smoke at the farmer and disappears. Poof. Just like that. So. The farmer uses the UFO as a church, builds an altar and some pews inside, like, 'cause he goes inside and it's completely empty. No controls. No gears. No nothing. And there it sits until this day. He kept the clothes-line up, the one with all the white clothes, as proof. The farmer's got a cable TV show, too.

Sarah You're an asshole, Jack.

Jack It's the truth. State police even found the fat guy's cigar stub. They keep it at the local station-house. Framed in glass. It's evidence.

Elston We like evidence, don't we, Jack?

Jack Sure. It's like . . . proof. That stuff happened.

Sarah Stuff happens all the time to you, Jack. And you couldn't prove it. Stupid fuck. If somebody walked in here and levitated you'd probably claim he was Saint Anthony.

Jack I'm religious. It ain't natural for men to walk on air.

Sarah They don't.

Elston Some men walk on air.

Sarah Yeah? Tell me about it. Tim. Tell me a story about a man who walks on air.

Elston I shall. Sit a while. Sit.

Two

Jack*'s press conference. He speaks to the audience. He squints, as if he's under hot bright lights.*

Jack Okay. You guys ready with the light? Right. So

where was we? Oh. Yeah. So there we was, the perp and
me. Eyeball to eyeball. Me and the perpetrator of the
alleged aforementioned crime. And I told Sarah, I said,
look woman: this guy ain't kosher. He's like some weirdo
in a waiter's outfit trying to pass himself off as a
representative of the legal profession. But she was real big
on him. Impressed by his clothes and his business card,
which, the perp had told us, was borrowed. I knew right
off. I knew this guy was a killer. He told us he was. And I
take people at their word. I'm a smart guy. And he wasn't
pulling nothing over my eyes. But Sarah, well, she always
had a weakness for little men. Not me. Like I said, I knew
right off. Let me tell you something. This guy had these
like . . . little sprouts of hair growing out of his lip. And
you gotta figure that's bad news. You figure, a guy around,
what is he? Thirty, forty? And he can't grow facial hair?
What is that? That's like . . . bad hormones. It's shit. It's
. . . perverted. Also, I gotta tell you about his ears. This
friend of mine, he's seen a lot of weird stuff in certain
areas of the Northeast Corridor, and he told me about
killer ears. I swear, yes, there is such a thing. All killers got
the same ears. A German doctor did a study on thirty or
forty of them. Guys like Speck, who popped off the nurses
in Chicago. And Berkowitz. You know, the wacko who
killed at the command of a dog? Oh man, whattya gonna
say about a guy who takes orders from a fucking Labrador?
So. They got these little tiny ears. No lobes. Like that
Nimoy guy from *Star Trek*. Well, they all got ears like that,
only less pointy. And this German doctor proved that all
killers have these ears. Look it up. It's evidence. It's all . . .
fucked up. This Creighton character, he had those ears. I
noticed straight off. But I didn't say nothing 'cause, well,
maybe he wasn't. A killer. But was I afraid of him? Nah.
Not me. I warned Sarah. I told her. And now it's her own
fault she's up and disappeared. Women don't listen.
Women don't wait. Sarah and me, we go way back. I'm all
broke up, but whattya gonna do? Life proceeds. I won two
Golden Gloves. Did I tell you that? I won. Twice.

Three

Ellen *at home in Hell's Kitchen, with* **Ted Mitchell**.

Ellen   Or some ice cream. I got that. Wouldja like some vanilla, officer?

Ted   No, ma'am. I'm here to ask you things.

Ellen   Which things?

Ted   Things. About Sarah.

Ellen   I told you what I know. She didn't say much. Not a talkative type. Worked downtown in my brother's travel agency. Talked about getting her own place. Never got around to it. She was twenty-five. We had our problems. I can show you pictures of her when she was little.

Ted   Mrs Casey. Did Sarah mention any friends, male friends? Was she . . . did she have lots of boyfriends.

Ellen   What are you implying? Just what are you saying about my Sarah?

Ted   Nothing. I want some background is all.

Ellen   Sarah had a fella. Skinny little guinea bastard. Anthony. I hated him. She did, too. You talk to him? Go ahead. My Sarah, she had shitty taste but she was faithful. My daughter was no slut.

Ted   I never implied she was. Your daughter is missing, Mrs Casey, and it is my obligation to uncover every lead, no matter how trivial or unpleasant.

Ellen   She's dead.

Ted   We don't know that.

Ellen   You have kids, officer? You got girls?

Ted   I have sons.

Ellen   You don't worry about boys. Girls, well, they're easier to talk to but you worry. Not that Sarah and me talked. We hardly talked at all. She was moody. She went

to night-school. What could I say to her? You think about
all these things and you don't say any of them and then
your kid dies.

Ted There is no evidence that your daughter is dead,
ma'am. Please. Talk to me. The contents of her room, was
there anything missing? A scrap of paper with a telephone
number. Anything.

Ellen There's a single bed with an extra firm mattress
and a burnt sienna crocheted blanket which I made for
Sarah when she was twelve and a half. She asked for burnt
sienna because she thought it was the saddest colour in the
whole Crayola box. It looked good on that *Eyewitness News*
telecast, didn't it? Are you sure you don't want some ice
cream?

Ted I'm sure. Thank you.

Ellen Well, that's it. For her room, I mean. Oh yeah.
There's a desk with nothing in it. And the record.

Ted What kind of record?

Ellen You saw it when you looked around with your
friends. The one that's nailed to the wall. She bought it
years ago. Wore out the grooves from playing it so much
so she broke it in half. Then she felt so guilty about
breaking it, she taped the damned thing back together and
nailed it to the wall. Over her bed. She actually thought it
was alive, that record. Told me some foreigner wrote the
song for her. You think that's a nice thing for a mother to
hear? She didn't do no drugs, but she was crazy. If they'da
had therapy when she was a kid, I woulda sent her.

Ted I have two sons, Mrs Casey. And I do worry about
them. I know how you feel. And I'd be alarmed, too, if
this had happened to either of them. I'm a parent. I
sympathize.

Ellen I'm not alarmed. I'm grieving.

Ted That's ... perfectly reasonable given the
circumstances, but we haven't the facts –

Ellen   Facts? I don't give a shit about facts. I know what
I know. And I know things. In my gut. Like I know my
Sarah is gone. Lost to me and to this fucking life she
coulda had. I hear her calling. Calling to me. But it's from
someplace far away enough so you can hear but you
cannot touch. You know what I feel like? I feel like
bowling. Heaving a big ball down an alley and having a
bunch of big guys throwing their big balls down the alley
next to mine. I wanna make a bunch of noise. Lots of
noise so I can drown out the sound of my kid calling out
to me.

Ted   We're doing what we can.

Ellen   You know what she's saying to me? She says, Ma,
why'd you have to be such a fucking lousy parent. Over
and over. Just that one thing. Well. She wasn't much of
talker. (*Beat.*) Maybe you'll be wanting some of that ice
cream now, huh?

Four

Sarah *and* **Elston** *at the travel agency.* **Elston** *wears glasses and
sports a moustache.*

Sarah   I'm sorry Mister . . .

Elston   Jonas. Mister Paul Jonas.

Sarah   Yes. Mister Jonas. There really aren't any junkets
to Siberia.

Elston   I didn't think there would be. But I figured, hey,
it's worth a try. It's a hard place to get to. By yourself. I
thought maybe a group, maybe there'd be a group of
people who shared my curiosity about the place. I'm very
curious about Siberia. Aren't you?

Sarah   I guess I am. Curious. About different places.

Elston   But not about Siberia?

Sarah   No. Not really. I'm sorry.

Elston   That's okay. You're honest. I like that in a travel agent. So many agents trying to sell you so many packages. So many bad packages. They'll sell you anything for a commission. And with so many people travelling these days. So many Americans travelling.

Sarah   Uhm. Yes.

Elston   Business must be good for you.

Sarah   Fairly good. Yes. So. You've got, let me see if this is right. You've got four weeks and you would like to go –

Elston   Someplace cold. And distant.

Sarah   Cold and distant. I see.

Elston   Well, because of heat-stroke.

Sarah   You don't do well in heat. I understand.

Elston   Oh, no. No, no, no. It's not me I'm worried about. I'm very healthy. It's others who worry me. I can't bear seeing people succumbing to the effects of heat. I'm queasy. You go someplace cold, you don't have to put up with that sort of thing.

Sarah   That's true. Perhaps Europe. It's off-season. Rates are very low. Austria's beautiful.

Elston   Really? Have you ever been there?

Sarah   Well, actually, no. I myself, I have never been to Austria. But my clients have told me. And of course, I've seen photographs.

Elston   There'd be skiing accidents. Broken bones. You'd have to consider that.

Sarah   I'm not following you, Mister Jonas.

Elston   In Austria. Mountains. Skiing.

Sarah   But you wouldn't have to ski. Not necessarily.

Elston   Good point. Chances are, though, that I'd *see* an accident. Mountains everywhere. I'd be surrounded.

Sarah   Well. There are cities. Vienna, for instance. I don't think there are any mountains in Vienna. Not within city limits.

Elston   It's intensely clean there, isn't it?

Sarah   I think I've heard that.

Elston   You can't trust a place that clean. You live in a filthy place, you can't ever really get used to a sparkling clean place, can you?

Sarah   I guess not.

Elston   Have you ever tried? To live in a clean place?

Sarah   I've lived in New York all my life. I suppose that means I've lived in filth and filth alone.

Elston   Well, I tried. Once I moved to Utah. The Salt Lake's out there. But Utah was religious. And I don't trust that, either. Religious peoples harbour the strangest notions, don't you think? Especially Mormons. And Catholics. Are you Catholic?

Sarah   Yes. As a matter of fact.

Elston   I could tell by your name. Casey. Good Catholic name. My wife says I snoop. I'm sorry. Tell me if I snoop. My wife, she would like to go someplace warm that has a casino. She likes to gamble. But me, I like to sit and shiver.

Sarah   How about if I could find you someplace cold. With a casino. Best of both worlds, no?

Elston   My wife's name is Natasha. She's not Russian. But she has a Russian name. I find that odd. Her father's favourite writer was Dostoevsky and he believed he was naming her after a character. I have a joke with Natasha. If we ever have a kid, we promise to call it Raskolnikov.

He laughs. **Sarah** *doesn't.*

Raskolnikov. Get it? *Crime and Punishment.* The book.

Sarah I've heard of it.

Elston Dostoevsky wrote it, see? It's about . . . well, here I go babbling. Babble, babble. That's what I do. I'm so limited in what I can say to other people at my own job that I just . . . go overboard with anybody else I meet. Sorry. I'm a bankruptcy trustee.

Sarah That's . . . really interesting.

Elston Oh, but it's not. It's heart-breaking. I take things away from people in order to provide them with a false sense of renewal. When you take something from somebody, it stays took. They don't understand that. I do. (*Beat.*) How about Alaska? You been there?

Sarah No. I haven't. However . . . it is cold. And there might be gambling.

Elston Bingo halls. Of course. Eskimo bingo parlours. Or perhaps I'm thinking of the Indians. (*Beat.*) You're very well-spoken. For a travel agent.

Sarah Thanks. I guess.

Elston It's a gift. Take me, for example. Here I am, chirp chirp chirping away at you, and I don't consider myself to be particularly adept at the gift of gab.

Sarah It's . . . I'm in a people job.

Elston Hmmm. But then, so am I. Difference being that in your people job, you give them things. Information, accommodation. The potential for snapshots. Me, I remove things from people. Information, accommodation. Cash.

Sarah Mister Jonas. Have you decided on a European vacation this year?

Elston Oh. Oh, I am sorry. I think I'm being gracious but what I really am is a fool.

Sarah I didn't mean that. Time. That's all. Time's a-wasting.

Elston Oh, yes. I understand. Tick tock. Miss Casey.

The most well-spoken travel agent I've ever met. But you're not well-travelled, are you?

Sarah   Well. No. I'm not . . . well-travelled.

Elston   Gosh. That's really strange. I mean, how can you sell airline tickets if you've never been on an airplane?

Sarah   I've been on airplanes. I have. But. It's true, I've never been abroad.

Elston   Would you like to go abroad?

Sarah   Yes. Very much. I'd like to see . . . Winchester.

Elston   An odd place for a young person to choose.

Sarah   Well, you know, there's that song. You know. (*She sings.*) Winchester Cathedral, you're bringing me –

Elston   You have a lovely singing voice, Miss Casey.

Sarah   Oh God, no. I don't. But thanks.

Elston   Do you sing in the shower?

Sarah   Pardon?

Elston   I do. Secret singers. Singing in showers. I sing Yma Sumac in the shower. Who do you sing?

Sarah   I . . . sing along. To different songs. There's this bar I go to. You know, a neighbourhood place in the Forties, near the highway and –

Elston   East or West?

Sarah   What?

Elston   Direction. Direction is important in travel. Precision. So. There's a neighbourhood bar in the Forties. East or West?

Sarah   West. *On* the highway, actually.

Elston   Of course. Sorry. Don't mind me. I'm an interrupter. By nature.

Sarah   Yeah. So. That's where I sing. In this bar.

Sometimes I think it's open only for me to wander in and
sing. Hardly anybody else goes there. Just me and Jack,
he's the owner. I mean, sometimes a bum'll wander in and
I give him a candy bar. Or something.

Elston   You're a kind soul.

Sarah   Nah. I just like to see people once in a while.
People I don't know.

Elston   But in your job, you see people you don't know
all the time.

Sarah   It's different. Here I talk about departures and
arrivals. At the bar, I talk about . . . singing. Drinking. You
know.

Elston   I do know. It must be sad having a job where
there's no psychic stability. Always coming or going. Never
staying put. The travel motif.

Sarah   Oh, sure. And you know what? When I'm in the
bar with Jack and I listen to the tunes – he's got a really
nice old Wurlitzer, only plays sixties tunes? Sixties tunes are
the best, 'cause I know I was meant to be my age now,
except I was meant to be my age in the sixties. Once, I
woke up and I knew all lyrics to all songs written in the
1960s. Creepy.

Elston   Yes. I see.

Sarah   And I think, hey Sarah, whatcha doing being alive
in the nineties? You missed the boat, girl. There's no going
back. And then I get sad.

Elston   I find it interesting, metaphorical perhaps, that
you work here. If you're around travellers enough, you'll
become one yourself. And travel right back into the 1960s.

Sarah   Well. Not exactly. Christ, no. Don't get me
wrong. I'm basically a happy person. I got a job. I gotta
boy. Anthony. He's sweet but he's dumb. Big hearted. A
hairdresser.

Elston   Got a.

Sarah   What?

Elston   Got a. Not gotta. Enunciation, Miss Sarah Casey. (*Beat.*) I like that phrase. Its implications. Christ, no.

Sarah   Yeah. Whatever. (*Beat.*) It's time. We picked a place. For you and your wife.

Elston   I hope you don't mind me correcting you.

Sarah   No. No, you're right.

Elston   It's just that you're so well-spoken. Generally.

Sarah   Absolutely. I should . . . pay attention. To things. Like that.

Elston   So. Let's see. Where to go? You pick.

Sarah   I can't do that. It's your vacation.

Elston   But you've been such a help already. And I don't especially care where I go. What's important is the travel itself. Here. I've brought this.

Elston *gives* **Sarah** *a map.*

Sarah   It's a map of the New York metropolitan area. New Jersey. Connecticut.

Elston   Well. There is the theory that the closer one stays to home, the further one actually travels. Emily Dickinson.

Sarah   What about her?

Elston   She proves the theory. She never left home. But she travelled. Frequently. (*Beat. He points to the map.*) Pick a place. Go on. Close your eyes and let your fingers do the walking.

Sarah   You know, if I do that, you might wind up in some truly awful place.

Elston   A vacation is what you make of it. A snapshot of a landfill can be just as rewarding as a snapshot of the Eiffel Tower.

A long beat, then **Sarah** *closes her eyes and picks a place on the* *map. She opens her eyes, and she and* **Elston** *ponder her choice.*

Elston   Seems I'm to spend my vacation in the Holland Tunnel.

Sarah   I could pick again.

Elston   Please don't. I believe in fate. And not in coincidence. Don't you?

Five

Elston *at* **Natalie**'s *apartment.* **Elston** *holds out a box of chocolates to* **Natalie**. *He's dressed as he was in Scene One.*

Elston   It's Fannie Farmer. Sorry. I meant to bring something else. But things weren't open. This being Sunday.

Natalie   I love chocolate, Elston. Thank you.

Elston   It's embarrassing, though. Even I know it's cheap chocolate.

Natalie   Well. It's the thought that counts.

Elston *(doesn't give her the chocolate; she clocks this)*   Yes.

Natalie   How's the shop? I know I haven't been around lately but . . . this cold. Can't seem to shake it.

Elston   It's the time of year. For colds.

Natalie   Yes. Yes, it is. *(Beat.)* So. The shop. It's doing well?

Elston   It's heavy on donations. Will you allow me to take you to dinner?

Natalie   No. Thank you. I have plans.

Elston   You're the kind of person who has plans. I'm not.

Natalie   Oh, I don't have too many plans. I go with the flow.

Elston   I wish I could go with the flow. But I can't. I read too much.

Natalie   Well. Reading's . . . a good thing. To do.

Elston   I mean, I'm not criticizing my job. You were kind to give me work. But it's not a fast-paced environment. I don't mind. I have time to read. Magazines. Trade magazines. You would not believe the number of different professions out there, Natalie. And each profession has a trade magazine. Why do you suppose they're called trade magazines?

Natalie   Look. I really don't know.

Elston   There's no barter system involved. It's not like, I trade you money for clothes. It's all about taking. Not trading. Don't you think?

Natalie   You're absolutely right, Elston. It's all about taking. So. How about I take the week's receipts from you?

Elston   Laura sends her best.

Natalie   Great. Send her mine.

Elston   Wouldn't you like to meet her? I mean, she knows how much you've done for me. She admires you.

Natalie   Meeting Laura would be . . . nice. Sometime.

Elston   We're going to be married. In the fall. I saw a travel agent two weeks ago and arranged the trip. We're going through the Holland Tunnel. By car. I wish we could take a train, though. I love trains. And people who travel. Don't you?

Natalie   When you work, it's hard to travel.

Elston   But you don't work. You own.

Natalie   Still. I've got to keep an eye on things, don't I?

Elston   Do you feel you've got to keep an eye on me?

Natalie   No. That is not what I meant. I mean to say that ownership is a great responsibility.

Elston   I see what you mean. Like the slaves. That was a great responsibility, keeping an eye on so many people.

Natalie   The receipts. Give me the receipts, Elston.

Elston   Laura's on tour this week. That's why I have a free night and why I thought you might . . . she's a tennis player. Did I tell you that?

Natalie   You might have. I don't really remember.

Elston   She's never won a tournament but she's in constant motion. I love athletes, don't you? Such grace under pressure. Such skill. I am completely unskilled. Have you ever noticed that about me?

Natalie   Yes. Yes, I – no. I didn't mean to suggest –

Elston   Laura's a pretty girl. Tall. Taller than me. A redhead. Freckles. Thin ankles. I like that in a woman. The kind of ankle that looks like it would break if you so much as blow on it. We were high-school sweethearts. In Idaho. She was the prom queen. I wasn't the king. But she preferred me to all the others. I was in science club. I looked at things. Under slides. Glass makes things look better. If people walked around pressed between two gigantic slides of glass, they'd look better, too.

Natalie   ELSTON. (*Beat.*) Please. The receipts. I need the receipts.

Elston *gives* **Natalie** *a large envelope.* **Natalie** *looks through it.*

Natalie   This is good, Elston. Very neat. You've done well this week. Thank you.

Elston   Natalie is a beautiful name.

Natalie   Well, yes. It is. Thank you.

Elston   A real spy name. My wife Natasha has a spy name and I'm forever telling her –

Natalie   What? What did you say?

Elston   I was saying. I was. My sister. She's . . . never mind.

Natalie   You said your wife. Natasha.

Elston   Did I? I'm thinking of Laura. Would you possibly travel with me?

Natalie   I think you should leave now. I do have plans.

Elston   I feel the urge to have plans. Let's travel to dinner. I don't know much about you, Natalie, but I would like to know. Everything.

Natalie   Our relationship prohibits. It.

Elston   Do we have a relationship?

Natalie   Yes. I'm your employer. I employ you.

Elston   I like that. I work for you. I belong to you.

Natalie   I wouldn't go that far.

Elston   I meant it figuratively. I love language. Don't you? I'm all dressed up with no place to go. Won't you let me buy you dinner? Let me spend money on you.

A telephone rings. It rings again. A beat.

Natalie   Excuse me, Elston. Don't touch – just stay put. All right?

Natalie *exits. Telephone rings again. And again. A silence.*

Elston (*as if* **Natalie***'s still there*)   I'm a magician. Really. Me and a girl named Blue, we do the New England carnival circuit. Did I tell you that? I have a special trick that nobody else does. Let me show you.

He takes a box of matches out of his pocket. He lights one, holds it between his thumb and forefinger. It burns down to his fingers. He doesn't flinch.

People faint when they see this trick. It doesn't hurt. It never hurts. It never hurts. (*Beat.*) I love fire. The way it travels. Don't you? Let me show you another trick.

He unwraps the box of chocolates. He eats them at a rapid pace, stuffing them into his mouth.

Excess. Excess is my encore. It's astonishing.

Natalie *enters. She watches* **Elston** *eating chocolates.*

Elston (*notices* **Natalie**)   I was hungry.

Natalie   I'm running late. You'll have to go.

Elston   How can you go out on a date if you have a cold you can't shake?

Natalie   Watch me and see.

Elston   When will you go to dinner with Laura and me?

Natalie   Some other time, Ellie. When I don't have any plans.

Elston   But you always have plans.

Natalie   Yes. I do.

Elston   So that means you don't go with the flow. You said you did. Could I ask you for a raise?

Natalie   Ask me some other time.

Elston   When? When shall I ask you?

Natalie   Soon. We'll talk.

Elston   We will? Good. Because there are some things I'd like to ask you. For instance, why is it called a thrift shop? Seems to me it ought to be called a generosity shop. You know?

Natalie   I'll have to think about that one. Later.

Elston   Have you ever been to New Jersey?

Natalie   No. And I don't ever want to go. Leave now. Please. I really have to get out --

Elston   Isn't it funny how you can live in a place for years and there's this other place right over a river yet you never seem to get there? (*Beat.*) You called me Ellie. Before. Why'd you do that?

Six

Jack *and* **Ellen** *at their press conference.* **Ted Mitchell** *and* **Timothy Creighton** *watch them.*

Ellen (*tapping her microphone*)   Is this on? Hello, hello. One small step for man, one giant leap for mankind. Testing. One. Two. Three. Hello. Ladies and gentlemen of the press: this is the press conference. With me is Jack Fallon, the bartender who, as far as we know, is the last person to have seen my Sarah before she . . . went away. What's that? Well. No. We don't know that she exactly went away.

Jack   We sure don't.

Ellen   Mister Fallon will *now* make his statement.

Jack   This is my statement: listen, buddy. We want her back. Come back, Sarah. (*Beat.*) That's all.

Ellen   What's that, miss? Nope. Haven't heard a thing. No ransom notes. And it's a good thing, too, 'cause I ain't got any money. I'm ordinary. YOU HEAR ME, YOU SKINNY CREEP? I GOT NO MONEY. (*Beat.*) I have some pictures of Sarah from happier times.

She displays baby photos.

See? All smiles. And to think she might be, at this very moment, stuffed in a trunk or bound and gagged and forced to – well. A mother's private grief is best not spread over the airwaves.

Jack   Mrs Casey ain't feeling well, fellas. What? No. No, I can't talk to you about that night on the advice of the New York City Police Department. Can't give away details of what you might call the perp's *modus operandi*. Huh? No. I ain't got no book deals out of this. And the bar's open, guys. Round the clock. I got my mother working days. Just in case, you know, the asshole's stupid enough to come back. I'm offering my Golden Gloves trophies to anybody who comes into the bar with information leading to the arrest of the perp. How's that?

Ellen I just wanna say: honey, come home. I'm keeping
a candle in the window so you can see our satellite
antenna guiding your way. Your room is untouched by
human hands. Except, you know, mine. I boughtcha a new
record. See?

She holds up a 45 r.p.m. record.

Cost a bundle, so you better come back and listen to it. I
hoped you was gonna be a nurse so you could patch up
the mess I – I can't. I can't go on. The stress. The
sleepless nights. What's that? No. I don't got no current
pictures of Sarah. We stopped taking pictures when the
Polaroid broke. No. No graduation photos. I wasn't there.
Look. It wasn't a big deal.

Ted Mitchell *steps forward.*

Ted Thank you, Mrs Casey. At this time, we'd like to
announce that we have located Timothy Creighton, who
had been identified as the man with whom Sarah Casey
left O'Malley's Saloon on the evening of the thirteenth. Mr
Creighton, would you please step forward?

Timothy Creighton *inches forward.* **Ellen** *and* **Jack** *watch
him.*

Jack That ain't him.

Ted We know.

Timothy (*at a microphone*) My name is Timothy
Creighton. I was not in O'Malley's Saloon on the night of
the thirteenth. I've never been to O'Malley's Saloon. In
fact, I've never been west of Fifth Avenue. Nor do I plan
an excursion west of Fifth Avenue in the foreseeable future.
I am an entertainment attorney. I am forty-three years old.
My wife, a research biologist, and my three sons are my
pride and joy. I have been, from time to time, a Little
League coach. I have never met Sarah Casey and really, I
don't plan to meet her. In the foreseeable future. Though,
of course, I and my entire family, wish her well and expect
that she will return to her ... mother ... soon. I am – I

am disturbed. By the incessant media crush I've been subjected to. My doorman, regrettably, has fallen prey to the temptation of easy cash and so several of you have been permitted to camp inside my building's lobby. And my wife swears that some of you have watched her doing laundry in our basement. Thus, Detective Mitchell and I have decided the time is right. For me to come forward. I am not involved in any way in this case. Nor do I know who might be. Please. Leave us alone. Contrary to published reports, I am not part of a satanic ritual abuse cult. I do not make human sacrifices. My wife was never involved in a day-care scandal and yes, my children are my own. Let me repeat: I am not a criminal. I'm just ... tired of getting funny looks from my greengrocer. I'm afraid to go to my barber. Please. Understand this. Thank you.

Timothy *exits.*

Ted (*to* **Ellen** *and* **Jack**)   He's given us a name.

Jack   What name?

Ted   A name. Of a man. There might be a connection.

Ellen   *He* seems like such a nice man.

Ted   Mrs Casey. We have a lead. A good one.

Ellen   Lead? What lead? My daughter's dead. (*Beat, then back to the press corps.*) I'm crotcheting a new blanket for Sarah so it's ready for her. When she comes home.

Seven

Music in: 'Paper Doll' (The Mills Brothers). **Sarah** *and* **Anthony** *dance.* **Sarah** *tries to teach* **Anthony** *to waltz, but it's really the wrong song to be using.* **Sarah** *is dressed as she was in Scene One.* **Ellen** *reads a tabloid.*

Anthony   Hey. Gimme a break, Sarah. This music sucks for dancing.

Sarah   It's not so bad. It's old. I like old things.

Anthony   Yeah. Like your mother.

Ellen   Hey. Shit for brains. Watchya mouth.

Anthony   Mrs Casey, you ever dance to this stuff?

Ellen   Leave me alone. I'm reading. I'm learning things.

Anthony   Yeah? What things?

Ellen   Important things.

Sarah   Ma. You don't learn anything by reading stuff like that. Read a book. A newspaper.

Ellen   I watch TV for my news. I like the colour commentary.

Anthony   Mrs Casey, you know how to waltz?

Ellen   Sure. Sarah's pig of a father taught me when he was drunk. He thought he was Christopher Plummer and I was Julie Andrews in *The Sound of Music*. He tried to re-enact the gazebo scene. It didn't work. But wouldn't that be nice? A gazebo. I've always wanted one.

Sarah   You can't have a gazebo in the city, Ma.

Ellen   Why not? People got shrines, don't they? I want a gazebo. Hey Anthony: you gonna buy me a gazebo?

Anthony   Yeah. When your daughter marries me.

Sarah   Great. Like I'm some fucking dowry for a gazebo.

Ellen   Marry him already. Get it over with.

Sarah   I'd rather he learned to waltz.

Ellen   What? So you can dance at the wedding?

Sarah   No. That's not why.

Ellen   What the fuck are you talking about? Nobody dances once they're married.

Anthony   Hey, Mrs Casey. Watchya mouth.

Ellen   You big asshole. Shut up. Cut my hair. Ain't that what you do? Cut hair?

Anthony You want a haircut now?

Ellen Fucking right. Come over here and make me beautiful.

Anthony *tends to* **Ellen***'s hair throughout the remainder of the scene.*

Sarah I can't believe this, Anthony. You promised.

Anthony I kept my promise. We danced.

Sarah Don't cut her hair. Let's go out.

Anthony You wanna go to the movies?

Sarah No. I just . . . wanna go. Downtown. To the Village. I want a double espresso.

Anthony I can make you a double espresso. Besides, you know I don't feel right in those café places. Lotsa guys, you know, talking about foreign films and stuff.

Sarah What's wrong with that?

Anthony Nothing. If you're a foreigner.

Sarah I hate you sometimes, Anthony. I really do.

Ellen A perfect way to enter marriage. With rage. Go on. Do it. I waited until my rage at your father was gone before I married him. And look at what an uninteresting life we led. May he rest in peace.

Sarah I don't want to get married. I want to travel.

Anthony Fine. We'll go to Sicily on our honeymoon. My grandma's got a big house with those French windows.

Sarah I don't want to visit your grandmother. I want to visit Italy.

Anthony Sicily's Italy. I speak the language. Don't worry.

Sarah I DON'T LIKE YOUR GRANDMOTHER.

Ellen I'll go with you, Anthony. We get there, you sit me in a garden, give me a jug of red wine, you go off and do your business. I need a vacation.

Sarah   Anthony. Come out with me. Now.

Anthony   Say you'll marry me and I'll come out with you.

Sarah   I don't want to marry you.

Ellen   And just who does she think she's gonna marry?

Anthony   She's playing hard to get.

Ellen   I played hard to get once. And what did it get me? Got me a man who thought he was a member of the Von Trapp family singers. Take a hint from your mother, girlie. Marry this guy. He's got his own business.

Anthony (*to* **Sarah**)   I love you, babe.

Sarah   Jesus. Fuck you all. I'm too young to get married.

Ellen   You know, Anthony, she's been this way since she's been taking night classes at Pace.

Anthony   Yeah? I didn't notice no changes.

Ellen   Oh, I notice the changes. She speaks in tongues. You oughtta hear it.

Sarah   I'm studying Greek, Ma.

Ellen   Yeah, well. Whatever it is, I can't read it. And if I can't read it, cook it or hit it, I don't trust it. Do me a favour, Sarah. Just *say* you'll marry him.

Anthony   We're gonna have a great reception. My brother's band is gonna play. We'll have it at this place out in Flatbush.

Sarah   I won't get married in Flatbush.

Ellen   What? You'd rather get married here? See, Anthony? I think Sarah has this hunch she's gonna marry some Hollywood type. Kinda guy she can speak in tongues to. But look. Look at what I'm reading. It says that everybody in California is dying from cancer. See? So it don't do you no good to leave home.

Anthony   I hadda uncle who went to California. San Diego. There's some kinda really big aquarium and it was his lifelong dream to go there and see the whales. So he saves and saves his money – which he was doing for a long time, 'cause he was a hot-dog vendor at Yankee Stadium – and finally he gets the cash together for the trip. He don't tell nobody he's going, 'cause it's like something he's been dreaming of his whole life and you don't share that stuff with anybody. So one night, he just disappears to San Diego. Turns up at Sea World. And what happens is, the place is closed. The first time in its history the place is closed for renovations. My uncle's, like, booked this two-week trip. So what does he do? Every day for two weeks he leaves his motel and drives to the gates. Stands there all day long. Fucking old guy trying to glimpse a whale through gates.

Sarah   I don't want to hear any more stories about life's little disappointments, Anthony.

Ellen   Be quiet, you. Go on, Anthony. I like this story. It's soothing.

Anthony   You're not gonna believe what happens to him.

Ellen   What? Don't tell me. The whale, using an animal's ESP, senses your uncle's presence and swims up to the gates?

Sarah   You're sick.

Anthony   No, wait. Wait. So. On his last night, he's frantic. He's gotta leave the next morning. And he knows he ain't ever gonna be able to afford the trip again, 'cause, like he's seventy-seven goddamned years old. So. On that last night he starts climbing the gate. Scales it, like he's a teenager or something. He gets to the top and for a single second, I guess he can see the whales. Then, like that: ba-bing. He slips at the edge, impales himself on the top of the gate. Ba-boom. Clean shot. Right through the heart.

Poor fuck. (**Ellen** *and* **Anthony** *laugh.*)

Ellen   At least he didn't stay in California long enough to catch the cancer.

Sarah   You two are pathetic. That's a really charming story, Anthony. I guess there's some lesson attached to it? A moral?

Anthony   Lesson? Who said anything about a lesson? I'm asking you to marry me, Sarah.

Ellen   The lesson is this: don't go nowhere without calling ahead to see if it's open. That means you, Sarah.

Sarah   I'm not calling nobody. Europe's always open, Ma. Countries don't close.

Ellen   Yes they do. Fucking Russians closed their country.

Sarah   Guess what? IT'S OPEN AGAIN. Read something. LEARN SOMETHING.

Ellen   Look you little bitch: I know more than you're ever gonna know. You got your father's attitude oh miss high and mighty stuck up bastard daughter of a mick NO GOOD FUCK. I know all I need to know about how to get through THINGS.

Anthony   Hey hey – chill out, Mrs Casey. I got the scissors right here. Don't wanna hurt you.

Ellen   Go ahead. Hurt me. I won't notice. I got a daughter who uses me for a doormat. Wipes her feet all over my GUTS. I'M SORRY I DON'T GOT THE KEYS TO FUCKING PARIS FRANCE IN MY POCKET.

Sarah   Anthony, you wanna know what I did in school on Friday?

Ellen   GO ON. HURT ME. SUE ME.

Sarah   Answer me, Anthony.

Anthony   Yeah, yeah babe. I do. If I listen to what you did at college, wouldja marry me? Wouldja?

Sarah   I'm going out.

Ellen   Yeah? Whereya going on a Sunday night?

Sarah   I'm going to Russia. There's a train leaving Grand Central any minute. (*Beat.*) I'll be at O'Malley's.

Ellen   Oh. Little booze-bag.

Sarah   Bitch. You make me wanna give up. You hear that? I sit here with the two of you, and you make me want to GIVE UP. I sit here too long and it's like tendrils grow up my legs, like I'm being rooted here.

Ellen   That's because you can't communicate. That's because you're moody.

Sarah   It's in my genes.

Anthony   What's in your jeans, babe? You restless?

Sarah   Yeah. I'm restless. I wanna talk to Jack. He always listens.

Ellen   And I don't?

Sarah   I'll be at O'Malley's. (*Beat.*) Don't wait up.

Eight

Elston *at the thrift shop. He wears boxer shorts. He's surrounded by clothes, which he sorts through. There's a full-length mirror nearby.*

Elston (*holds up a pair of trousers*)   Thank you, Mister Harris. Thank you for the wool. When it's cold, wool's best. Unless you have cashmere. But who can afford it? Mister Harris, I hope you and your wife are warm tonight. I hope you are huddled together and sipping champagne by candlelight. I hope you have a fireplace. I hope your children are asleep and dreaming of a time when they'll be free to travel. I hope they're never ill. I hope you remember me.

He puts on the trousers. He holds up a shirt.

And thank you, Mister Chester Ingalls, for this cotton. It's a very fine English shirt. I hope you're in London now. I hope you're relaxing in a five-star hotel in Knightsbridge. I hope you're not afraid of leaving your home after dark. I hope you never tire of giving away your old clothes. I hope you remember me.

He puts on the shirt. He holds up a jacket.

And where would I be without you, Mister Holloway? This jacket is a magnificent piece of tailoring. The very finest silk and linen. The mixture is exquisite. I fear you're full of rage. I hope you don't beat your girlfriend. I hope she agrees to the house in Westbury. I hope that one day you will hop a commuter train to that house and there she'll be. Waiting for you at the station in a red Volvo. I hope you never declare bankruptcy. I hope you remember me.

He puts on the jacket. He examines himself in the mirror.

For what is a man without his friends?

Ted Mitchell *enters.*

Ted Elston Rupp?

Elston Yes.

Ted The door was open. The front door.

Elston Yes.

Ted I'm Ted Mitchell. NYPD. Homicide division.

Elston Yes.

Ted I'm like to ask you some questions. Would you . . . come with me?

Elston Yes.

Ted Shall we go?

Elston Do you have a car?

Ted Yes. The car's outside. Out front.

Elston I love cars. (*Beat.*) Take me someplace.

Elston *holds his hands out in front of his body, as if to be handcuffed.*

Blackout.

Act Two

Nine

Ted Mitchell *interviews* **Elston**.

Elston Is this the place where you question criminals?

Ted Sometimes.

Elston It looks like that kind of place. I've never been to one of those places. But. This has the feel of a place where people experience fear.

Ted Are you experiencing fear?

Elston Oh, no. No. I trust you. You took me someplace.

Ted You like to travel.

Elston Yes, I do. But I don't often get the chance. Work. Family obligations.

Ted You told me you don't have a family.

Elston That doesn't mean I don't have obligations. To family. We carry obligation with us, Ted. Regardless.

Ted You had family. Once. Tell me about them.

Elston Am I under arrest?

Ted No.

Elston Do you have a family?

Ted Everybody does.

Elston And do you feel obligated to them?

Ted Tell me some more about Sarah Casey.

Elston A lovely girl. A travel agent. Do you know she never went anywhere?

Ted   No. I didn't. How do you know that?

Elston   She told me.

Ted   When? When did she tell you that?

Elston   When did you become a detective?

Ted   Did Sarah Casey tell you she never travelled before or after you left O'Malley's? (*Beat.*) I became a detective six years ago.

Elston   Did you have to shoot somebody to become a detective?

Ted   No, Elston. It doesn't work that way.

Elston   Did you have to go to a special school?

Ted   No. No special school. Tell me more about Sarah Casey.

Elston   Sarah Casey went to school. But she didn't need any particular skills to become a travel agent. Just like you don't need particular skills to be a detective.

Ted   I answered some questions for you. Now, you answer some for me.

Elston   Give and take. I give, you take. Am I under arrest?

Ted   No. Should you be?

Elston   I have many friends. Natalie's my best friend.

Ted   I know. She told me that.

Elston   When did she tell you that?

Ted   Oh, about the same time Sarah Casey was telling you about her lack of travel skills.

A silence.

Elston   Natalie has nice ankles. Did she show you them?

Ted   She showed me her ledgers. Said you kept them up well. Said you're a good worker. Solid. Honest. Are you honest?

Elston I'm taking Natalie to dinner next week. She's very busy. But she made time for me.

Ted Did you have dinner with Sarah Casey?

Elston When? When are we talking? I need times. I do better. With a little direction. That's why I'm such a good worker.

Ted That Sunday.

Elston That Sunday. (*Beat.*) No. No dinner with Sarah Casey.

Ted But you did leave O'Malley's with her.

Elston Yes. Yes, I did.

Ted And then?

Elston I went home.

Ted And what about Sarah?

Elston She's lovely. A travel agent. I love to travel. Am I under arrest?

Ted No. (*Beat.*) I love to travel.

Elston Do you? You must drive a lot. Being a detective.

Ted Did you know that the average detective logs more miles per annum than the average cabbie?

Elston Yes. I do know that. Maps. You must have lots of maps.

Ted Oh, sure. I had a special glove compartment built to accommodate all my maps. I like roads.

Elston Yes. And there are many, many roads in this country. Aren't there?

Ted Yup. Roads are necessary for travel. And for what else?

Elston Sightseeing. Speedy exits.

Ted   That's the interesting part. Speedy exits.

Elston   You sound like you know what I'm talking about, Ted.

Ted   Yes. Fast cars. Starless nights. Blind alleys. Places to hide. Speedy exits.

Elston   If you drive so much, you should know what I'm talking about. That's not what I'm talking about.

Ted   Educate me, Elston. Please.

Elston   I observe speed limits. Actually, I always drive in the right lane. With the old people. Except for the exits. On exit ramps, I accelerate. Fifty, sixty, seventy. Someday I'd like to take an exit ramp at eighty.

Ted   Isn't that dangerous?

Elston   I don't know. Maybe.

Ted   If you think it might be dangerous, then why do you do it?

Elston   I get excited when I anticipate arriving. At a destination. Having a family is dangerous, too.

Ted   Maybe.

Elston   Well. If you think it might be dangerous, then why do you do it?

Ted   Do you own a car, Elston? Did you maybe take Sarah Casey for a ride?

Elston   I take cabs. Do you know, I won't take a cab unless it has a plexiglass barrier inside to separate passenger and driver? (*Beat.*) I used to drive. But I've never owned a car, Ted.

Ted   We've been at this for two hours. Did you know that?

Elston   Yes. It's been very pleasant. Did Natalie tell you she didn't like me? Because I wouldn't like to spend money on a woman who doesn't like me.

Ted   You like money.

Elston   No. I don't. That's why I spend it.

Ted   Did you spend any money on Sarah Casey?

Elston   Oh, no. I barely know her. Though she likes me. I would spend money on her. She's kind. Are you kind, Ted?

Ted   All right, Elston. These are the things I know about you: You like to travel. You won't ride in certain taxis. You're a good worker who keeps on honest ledger. You met Sarah Casey at O'Malley's last Sunday evening. You left the bar with her. You're taking Natalie to dinner. Give me something else. Sarah Casey has disappeared.

Elston   Good for her. She deserves to go. Away. She's never been anywhere.

Ted   Did you take her anywhere?

Elston   Well. I told her that there was the possibility. Of going away.

Ted   You have a fiancée named Laura.

Elston   Laura is a tennis player.

Ted   I know. She's never won a match.

Elston   She's never won a tournament.

Ted   There's one thing, though, Elston. About Laura. We can't find her.

Elston   Perhaps she went away.

Ted   We can find no evidence that she actually exists.

Elston   You know, Ted, when I was a boy, people went away a lot. And they never came back.

Ted   People who go away generally leave a trail.

Elston   Are you going to arrest me?

Ted   Tell me why you posed as Tim Creighton last Sunday night.

Elston   Because I wore his clothes.

Ted   You told Jack Fallon and Sarah Casey that you were a killer.

Elston   I also told them I was Timothy J. Creighton. Ted. Why won't you arrest me?

Ted   I will ask you once more. Why. Why did you tell those people you were a killer?

Elston   Because they believed me. Because. Haven't you ever wanted to be anybody else, Ted?

Ted   Never. Why do you want to be somebody else?

Elston   Because I'm more honest than you. I know. Who I actually am. Do you? (*Beat.*) Arrest me. Please.

Ted   Are you a killer?

Elston   Have you ever shot anyone on the job?

Ted   Not yet.

Elston   But don't you want to? Don't you? If you don't have an urge to use your gun, why do you carry it? Shoot me.

Ted   That's enough. That's – look. I'll tell you something. I admit it. I don't like my job. I don't especially like the company I'm keeping lately. I don't like you. I might be doing other things. I might have swum the English Channel. I might have been a priest.

Elston   I wish you were a priest, Ted. I wish I had something to confess.

Ted   I really couldn't care less for a confession. I want to believe that you are just another sad bastard who's got a thing for wearing other people's cast-offs. I want to believe that you lead the same fucking boring life I lead. That the worst thing you've ever done is short-change Natalie a few bucks on the week's take. Tell me you're dull, Elston. Tell me what I want to hear. Help me see this through.

Elston   You're an unhappy man, Ted. You need a vacation. You need to travel.

Ted   If you've got nothing to do with that girl's disappearance, why didn't you contact us?

Elston   I didn't know you were looking for me.

Ted   It's been all over the news.

Elston   I don't have a TV. Or a radio. I don't read newspapers.

Ted   You know an awful lot of trivia for somebody who doesn't pay attention to the media.

Elston   I said I don't read newspapers. I do pay attention. I do.

Ted   Did you kill Sarah Casey?

Elston   No. Did you? Is that why you're so unhappy?

Ted *grabs* **Elston**.

Ted   Listen you little sonofabitch: HELP ME.

Elston   You don't want me to be guilty. I can tell.

Ted   I don't give a good goddamn if you're guilty. GIVE ME SOME ANSWERS.

Elston   You're kind, Ted. Like Sarah Casey. Why are you so unhappy?

Ted   I HATE MY JOB I WISH I WAS ON THE TAKE MY WIFE'S ABOUT TO LEAVE ME I REALLY DON'T CARE AND I. CANNOT STAND. MY CHILDREN.

Ted *releases* **Elston**. *A silence as* **Ted** *composes himself.*

Elston   On that night. That Sunday night. I close the shop early. I don't know why. I decide to do inventory. I come across Timothy Creighton's tuxedo. Mrs Creighton had been in earlier that week. She always dry-cleans her

donations. She's one of the few to observe that rule. And it
is a rule, you see. Sometimes, I break the rule and accept
unwashed clothing from customers I like. I don't know
why. Mrs Creighton makes regular donations. I know her
first name. She doesn't know mine. She never did. I
wonder if that bothers her now. I've never met Mr
Creighton. I find a business card in the left breast-pocket of
his tuxedo jacket. It's stained. Red wine, I think. I feel
sorry for Mr Creighton. I don't know why. But in that
moment, I like him very much. I have to like a person to
wear his clothes. Don't you? I put on the tux. I leave the
shop. It is six thirty. I go to Natalie's. I drop off the week's
receipts on Sunday nights. She hadn't felt well that week. I
had hoped she would allow me to take her to dinner. She
wouldn't. Allow me. I don't know why. I leave Natalie's. I
head home. I get to my front door and I find I can't insert
my key in its lock. It occurs to me that I should go to
Timothy Creighton's house. But I don't. I don't know why.
I go to O'Malley's. I don't go to bars, but I go there. Men
in bars laugh at me. Because I'm so small. Because they're
glad they're not that small. Because I allow them to laugh.
I am O'Malley's only customer that night. I take an
immediate liking to Jack Fallon. I begin to wish that he
could be my brother. And then. Sarah Casey enters the
bar. I recognize her instantly as the woman who had
helped me plan a vacation two weeks earlier. You didn't
know that, did you, Ted? I went to her travel agency. I do
that frequently. Drop by. At different travel agencies. I talk
to women who work in travel agencies. It's the only time
women are happy to speak to me. When there's the
possibility that I'll spend money in their business
establishments. I often offer to spend money on women I
know. And they never let me. I don't know why. Sarah
Casey was the last travel agent I spoke to. Of course, at
the time, I was wearing the clothing of a Paul Jonas. Poor
Mister Jonas died on the QE2 while he and his wife
celebrated their diamond jubilee. He never did get to wear
his new suit. So. Wearing the clothes of Paul Jonas, I, with

the aid of Sarah Casey, plan a vacation I never intend to take. Sarah is very kind. I pay in cash. I buy two packet trips, via Greyhound buses, to Atlantic City. I leave the travel agency and mean to rip up the tickets. But I don't. I don't know why. When I see Sarah at O'Malley's I feel it is fate. We talk. Sarah confesses a desire to travel. I'm certain she doesn't recognize me. I entertain her by proposing the possibility of differing scenarios. For her life. Overall, I'm sure I present a very attractive portrait of Timothy J. Creighton. And while I like Sarah, I know she will not allow me to spend money on her. She will not suggest a ride on the Circle Line. She will not. Take a trip. With me. She tires. She wants to go home. I open the door for her. She steps outside. I show her the bright, full moon. I point her in the direction of the Holland Tunnel. There is a moment when our continuing in the same direction is possible. She takes a step. I hesitate. It makes all the difference. I watch her walk downtown. I watch her take steps. I stand perfectly still. I call out to her. Sarah, I say, Sarah Casey: where are you going? And then she disappears.

Ted (*after a silence*)   Thank you. (*Beat.*) Would you like . . . a cup of coffee?

Elston   Will you arrest me now?

Ted   Would you prefer, I don't know, tea?

Elston   Will I make you famous, Ted?

Ted   Well. I'd rather you made me rich.

Elston   I'm sorry about your wife. And your kids.

Ted   Are you?

Elston   Don't leave.

Ted   I need some coffee.

Elston   I like you, Ted. Why'd you let go of me? I liked it when you held me. I liked it.

Ten

Natalie *and* **Timothy** *at the police station. It's clear each knows who the other is, but neither wants to commit to conversation.*

Timothy How could you hire somebody like that? There. I've said it. I had to say it.

Natalie I'm sure I don't understand what you're talking about.

Timothy I've never even met this man. Do you realize that? I'm here to identify a tuxedo.

Natalie He sells old clothing for me. That's all I know. And I don't think we're supposed to be chatting right now.

Timothy I'll probably lose my job over this.

Natalie Well. I'm sorry.

Timothy No. You're not sorry. You're mortified. Mortified that you're involved in this at all.

Natalie But I'm not involved. (*Beat.*) You're the lawyer, aren't you.

Timothy Yeah. Lucky me. Personally, I think you're the guiltiest party in this mess.

Natalie You're much more handsome than you appear to be on television. I've seen clips of your statement. You're actually very handsome.

Timothy Well. Thank you. (*Beat.*) I've got to ask you this. I really do. Don't you screen applications for employment? Don't you ask for references?

Natalie This is the situation, Tim. May I call you that? May I call you Tim?

Timothy Timothy. I prefer Timothy. Actually.

Natalie Well then, Timothy. This is the situation. I inherit a ridiculous business from a dear but preposterous spinster aunt. I have no wish to sort through dirty old clothes. Now I ask you: Is this an unreasonable position to take? It's a charity business. How is anybody supposed to make anything of it? Nevertheless, I respect my aunt's wishes and take over this – thrift place. And who do you think I can hire for the overwhelmingly tedious job of running the hovel on a daily basis? Would you do it, Timothy? No. I thought not. Furthermore, what do you suppose I can afford to pay the lucky recipient of this position? I can hardly be picky when we're talking a minimum wage type situation. Don't you agree? Yes. I thought you would. And so. How can you fault me for hiring a thoroughly agreeable – if somewhat odd – young man? He told me he was from Nebraska. He told me he was the child of farmers. He's polite. He's well-spoken. He's never stolen anything from me and he's not likely to leave his job and decide to become an artist. He took a polygraph. He passed. He's mine for life if I want him. What else should I have done? So he embellishes from time to time. He seems to have several wives and fiancées, all of whom he really can't keep straight from one conversation to the next, but . . . who am I to judge? I think he's honest. And I believe he is telling the truth about the Casey girl's disappearance. He's always on time. He makes the customers laugh. And while it's true I would not choose to be his friend, I don't think that counts as proof of anything other than that he – he makes me nervous. In fact, he makes my skin crawl. He's not the kind of man I ordinarily talk to. He's small.

Timothy You hired a man who makes your skin crawl. You hired a man who wears other people's clothing.

Natalie Well. Coming from a thrift shop perspective, I don't find that at all unusual.

Timothy You don't.

Natalie Of course not. Look, he sells other people's clothing to other people all the time. Lots of people wear other people's clothing. I had no idea he was doing . . . whatever he was doing . . . and I thoroughly object to the practice but –

Timothy   You support him anyway.

Natalie   I didn't say I support him.

Timothy   You'll stick by him on this.

Natalie   I didn't say that, either.

Timothy   Most of the people I work with think I have something to do with this woman's disappearance.

Natalie   Did you?

Timothy   I said I didn't. The bartender said I didn't.

Natalie   People lie. People are paid to lie.

Timothy   You don't actually believe –

Natalie   I read it. In the *Post*. It's one theory.

Timothy   Oh. I missed that one.

Natalie   It's very interesting. You see, the theory is that you and the bartender are in it together.

Timothy   I think I've heard a variation on this.

Natalie   You take attractive young girls and sell them into the white slave-trade. In California. Evidently, it's running rampant out there. And, the theory continues, you framed Elston. You know. Made it look like he did it. Or at least raised the serious possibility that he did it.

Timothy   Did what? (*Beat.*) Look. Is it just a coincidence he was wearing my suit? Or maybe – maybe the bartender and I hit him over the head, dressed him up in my suit, dragged him to the bar, sat him on a stool and waited until he woke up? And, naturally, he'd have no memory of such an event.

Natalie   The *Post* didn't offer any details. It just made a couple of suppositions.

Timothy   I could make a couple of suppositions about you.

Natalie No. You couldn't. My name is not being associated with, well, the more unsavoury aspects of this case.

Timothy Like you said. People accept money. To lie.

Natalie Meaning just what. Exactly.

Timothy Meaning. If I lose my job, I'd maybe take some money to say a few things about you.

Natalie Really, Tim, don't be ridiculous. You're being ridiculous.

Timothy People stare at me when I walk my dog.

Natalie I should be so lucky, Tim.

Timothy I'm angry. And CALL ME TIMOTHY, GODDAMNIT.

An awkward silence.

Natalie After this blows over, you can probably get a job anywhere. You'll be a celebrity. Who wouldn't want to hire somebody like you? The office gossip would be extraordinary. But what about me? All I'm left with is the same no-win business situation. What do you think I can do? Hang a sign outside: THIS IS THE PLACE WHERE IT MIGHT HAVE HAPPENED?

Timothy My privacy has been violated.

Natalie Whose hasn't? Sell your story. Beat them to the punch.

Timothy He was wearing my clothes. He might have killed a woman while he wore my tuxedo.

Natalie And she might have simply walked away. You know, this is not exactly the Lindbergh case. Grown corpses really are hard to conceal. Not to mention there's been no evidence, none whatever, to connect Elston to anything other than having worn a tuxedo that didn't fit him.

Timothy People look at me and they see a criminal.

And I cannot stop feeling guilty for something that somebody else did while I was holding my wife in my arms.

Natalie   I just thought of something funny. You're here to identify a tuxedo. It's like identifying a body, except it's not. Isn't that funny?

Timothy   Why are you here?

Natalie   Oh. Well, Elston. He had nobody else to pick him up.

Timothy   He's here? He's in this building now?

Natalie   Yes. I think I'll do something nice for him this evening. Like take him to dinner. (*Beat.*) Unless of course you'd rather come out to dinner with me. After you identify the tuxedo.

Timothy   No. Thank you. I have . . . reading. To catch up on. (*Beat.*) Would you do me a favour? Would you . . . tell me you don't believe I have anything to do with this? Because I'm beginning to doubt myself. Sometimes. Sometimes I think, well, what if. What if my wife hadn't cleaned out our closets that day. What if I had been home to stop her from giving away that tux. It didn't fit me any more. But I liked it. You hold on to things that mean something to you.

Natalie   I'm afraid I can't sympathize. I try not to wear anything more than once if I can help it.

Timothy   Somebody's daughter is missing and possibly dead. And I can't escape the feeling that she, well, that she saw me that night. Or a part of me. I can't . . . say anything else. About it.

Natalie   Okay. I don't believe you had anything to do with this. (*Beat.*) Now. Why don't you come out with me for a drink? You really are a good-looking man. Much better looking than you appear to be. On television, I mean.

Eleven

Ted, **Ellen** *and* **Anthony** *at* **Ellen***'s apartment.* **Ellen** *holds a half-crotcheted blanket.*

Ted It's an empty room on the highway between Forty-Fourth and Forty-Fifth. Not a bed. Not a chair. Not one stick of furniture. Just . . . globes. Of every conceivable size and description. A globe of the moon. Of Mars. A geopolitical globe. A population density globe. And one file cabinet. Full of five-by-seven unlined white notepads. And on these notepads, neat rows of dates and times. No names. Just descriptions. Physical descriptions of people. Quite detailed. Like a diary which contains essentially the skeleton of information. The first entry reads: 'Tall chestnut-haired man on south-west corner of Fifty-Seventh and Sixth. I thought he smiled at me. Was probably wiping a speck of dirt from the corner of his mouth.' The last entry: 'Pretty redhead, five-three, in elevator at Chrysler Building. I sneezed. She didn't notice.' (*Beat.*) I have never seen anything like his closet. An enormous walk-in inside which was all the furniture. An EZ chair. A captain's chair. A chipped maple bureau. An oak schoolboy's desk. An Army issue wool blanket. Three goose-down pillows. And framed family photographs. Except on closer inspection, we discover they are the photographs that came with the frames. One frame still carried its price sticker. And there are very few articles of clothing. Almost none. (*Beat.*) The bathroom is spotless. So is the kitchen. We find nothing. No hair. No fingerprints. Certainly, most certainly, we find no blood. In the medicine cabinet there's a four-year-old empty prescription bottle of Tylenol with codeine. On the fridge is taped a postcard of Napoleon's tomb. Postmarked at the GPO on Thirty-Third and Eighth. It's addressed to Elston and carries no message. Inside the fridge, one mouldy grapefruit. One unopened box of Devil Dogs. An eight-ounce can of Campbell's V-8 juice. An airline-sized bottle of Stolichnaya vodka. (*Beat.*) The only eating utensils are plastic. Four knives, two forks, seven spoons, neatly stacked in a plastic cutlery tray. Two plastic dinner plates.

One ceramic coffee mug. One soup bowl, badly chipped. A broken two-slice toaster. A roulette wheel ashtray from Resorts International, Atlantic City. A Manhattan residential telephone directory in which are circled in red felt pen the numbers of well-known people. He has no telephone, but he has written a listing for himself in the directory. He wrote it in black ink.

An uncomfortable silence.

Ellen So, officer, this is very interesting and all, but I don't see why you gotta tell us the contents of this creep's refrigerator. My baby girl is dead and you're telling me about tomato juice?

Ted In going over the details, there is the possibility of finding clues.

Anthony Where's this guy now? He's out on the street? You let him go?

Ted He's co-operated. He *asked* us to examine his apartment. He's told us his version of events, which does not differ significantly form Jack Fallon's version of events. Except, of course, that Elston Rupp does not recall Jack Fallon's self-confessed heroics.

Anthony So this guy, this little fuck, he's out and walking around?

Ted Would you like me to arrest him for impersonating an entertainment attorney?

Ellen HE MURDERED MY DAUGHTER. DROWNED HER IN A BATHTUB.

Ted We have nothing to substantiate that.

Ellen Yeah, well, you got nothing that *doesn't* prove it, do you?

Ted I don't know what to tell you.

Anthony You believe this guy?

Ted I am tending toward it, yes.

Ellen   You believe this faggot psycho who walks around in dirty clothes but you don't believe normal people like us?

Ted   You weren't there. He was. Listen to me. I would bet that if you rounded up, at random, two or three dozen guys who live in a ten-block radius, you'd find that they'd all tell more or less the same sad story. The exact same story of their lives, Mrs Casey. The details would not significantly differ from man to man.

Anthony   I got a friend, this guy I grew up with in Bay Ridge? Since he was a kid, he's been collecting his girlfriends' toe-nail clippings. Can you imagine? Puts them in a shoebox.

Ellen   Whatsa matter with you, Anthony? You taking his side? You taking the side of a pervert?

Anthony   Mrs Casey, no offence. You know, it's just – some guys, they're weird.

Ted   Yes. Some guys are weird.

Ellen   I'm sitting here with a couple of professional fucking Freuds and neither of them can tell me what's happened to my daughter.

Ted   Perhaps she did simply leave. Go away. Escape.

Ellen   My daughter would never ESCAPE. She wasn't the type. Besides, she was gonna get married. She was gonna go to Sicily on her honeymoon. We was all gonna go. Personally, I wasn't big on the idea of Italy. But at my age, I'd take anything. Right, Anthony?

Anthony   Mrs Casey, she didn't wanna marry me. I mean, we gotta give her some due. The girl said she did not want to marry me.

Ted   Is that true, Mrs Casey?

Ellen   What does he know? What? He cuts hair for a living. That's not normal. My daughter, she – oh what's the point. She was fucked up. That's the point. I don't care. I don't. Whether she's dead or gone to New Jersey or if she's camped out on the ROOF. I DON'T CARE.

Another uncomfortable silence.

Ted   There won't be an arrest. I'm sorry. I think that Sarah is alive. I hope . . . you get a phone call or a note that says, hi Mom. I've decided to become a Shaker and I'm making furniture in Pennsylvania. (*Beat.*) I have nothing else to offer at the moment.

Ellen   Hey, hey – WAIT. You can't go. Where's my satisfaction? Huh? WHAT AM I LEFT WITH?

Ted   I don't know. Another blanket?

Ted *exits.* **Ellen** *holds up the unfinished blanket.*

Ellen   I called my daughter a booze-bag. That's the last thing I said to her.

Ellen *throws down the blanket. She lets out a single cry of frustration and rage.*

Twelve

Elston *and* **Natalie** *at the police station.*

Elston   Thank you for coming. Are you mad at me?

Natalie   Why would I be mad at you?

Elston   A day's revenue. Lost.

Natalie   Well. You'll make it up to me.

Elston   How?

Natalie   Elston. Is everything, well, is it all okay now? Did you – fix it?

Elston   I'm not arrested. If that's what you mean.

Natalie   Good. I'm glad it's over.

Elston   It's not over. There's the girl.

Natalie   Of course. The girl. (*Beat.*) We can't help that,

Elston. We don't know where she is.

Elston   Yes, we do.

Natalie   We do?

Elston   Yes. She's elsewhere. (*Beat.*) Are you going to fire me?

Natalie   Probably not.

Elston   Are you going to give me a raise?

Natalie   No. Well. Eventually.

Elston   That's okay. I don't need money.

Natalie   Elston, everybody needs money.

Elston   I used to think so. (*Beat.*) I had some people over at my apartment this morning.

Natalie   I wasn't aware you had any friends.

Elston   I don't. They were detectives. Men with magnifying glasses.

Natalie   Oh. That must have been exciting. Or something.

Elston   I invited them. But I shouldn't have.

Natalie   I imagine they would have invited themselves into your apartment if you hadn't extended the courtesy.

Elston   That's an odd concept. Extending courtesy. Like extending a hand. (*Beat.*) Do you know where I live?

Natalie   Uhm. No. Yes, yes – I mean, I read about it. In the *Post.* But your address wasn't given out. Not exactly.

Elston   Too bad.

Natalie   Why would you want a bunch of strangers knowing your address?

Elston   You're not a stranger. (*Beat.*) I live on the highway. Well. Above the highway. In a room. I can see the traffic.

Natalie   That's . . . pleasant.

Elston   I watch the traffic and think, where are you all going? Why don't you stop a while? Slow down. And then I realize I shouldn't be concerned about speeding cars when I don't even know who my neighbours are. Or if I even have any neighbours. My building might very well be deserted. Except for me.

Natalie   People make noise. They cook. You'd know if they were there.

Elston   I don't cook.

Natalie   Well. Neither do I. So. There you go.

Elston   Let me take you to dinner.

Natalie   No. I can't. I have . . . a friend. From out of town. Visiting.

Elston   Oh. A traveller.

Natalie   Why don't you see a movie?

Elston   I don't see movies.

Natalie   Oh, come on. An insignificant little comedy, something to take your mind off –

Elston   Nothing is insignificant. (*Beat.*) What an interesting phrase: take one's mind off. Have you ever noticed how most of the language we use to suggest mental activity conjures up a violent physical action? Take one's mind off. Off his rocker. (*Beat.*) I have to go home now. I have to watch traffic.

Natalie   Elston, I've got to ask you a really big favour. I know you've got a load on your – what I mean is. Well, would you please not wear the customers' clothes any more? I don't want to be a bitch, but. It's probably unsanitary.

Elston   Give and take.

Natalie   If it was up to me, I would let you borrow . . .

whatever . . . you know.

Elston   It is up to you.

Natalie   The customers are horrified.

Elston   How do you know? You're never there. (*Beat.*) The favour. What's the favour you want?

Natalie   That. I just asked you. About the clothes.

Elston   Don't you want me to buy you groceries? Or flowers?

Natalie   I hate flowers. And I don't cook. Remember?

Elston   I might move to New Jersey.

Natalie   Why would you do that? It's across the river.

Elston   Well. You won't allow me to offer you any courtesy. But I can offer you my hand.

Elston *extends his hand to* **Natalie**.

Natalie   Elston. This is a little weird, isn't it?

Elston   We're friends.

Natalie   We . . . know each other. A bit. Yes.

Elston   Shake my hand. Please.

Natalie   I'll see you tomorrow. At the shop. Don't be ridiculous.

Elston *drops his hand.*

Elston   You've been very kind. I think. I – I'll open the shop early tomorrow. I'll make it up to you. I think. I think – good night. Natalie.

Natalie   Yes. Uhm. Ciao.

Elston *exits.* **Natalie** *lights a cigarette. She doesn't smoke it.* **Ted** *enters.*

Natalie   I meant to be nice to him. Take him to dinner.

Buy him a drink. Something. But I couldn't. He. He makes my skin crawl.

Thirteen

Jack *and* **Timothy** *at O'Malley's Saloon.*

Timothy   I had to see it. For myself. I hope you don't mind.

Jack   No skin off my back, bud.

Timothy   It's hard to believe, but I've never been this far west.

Jack   Yeah? Do you like it?

Timothy   I've lived in New York eighteen years and I've never seen this part of town. I imagined, I don't know, something different.

Jack   Yeah. I know. People think all sorts of things. Tough things.

Timothy   Show me where she sat.

Jack   Huh?

Timothy   Sarah Casey. That night. Where did she sit?

Jack *(indicating the barstool)*   It ain't a shrine, mister.

Timothy *(sits on the barstool)*   Did she sit like this?

Jack   Yeah. I guess. To tell you the truth, it's kinda fuzzy to me now.

Timothy   And Rupp. Where did he sit?

Jack   Someplace else. I don't know. Funny how your memory goes, real quick like.

Timothy   They walked out that door together. And Sarah Casey was never seen again. Rupp touched that doorknob. The night appeared. And she was gone. *(Beat.)* I dream about this.

Jack   Lemme give you some advice, pal. Forget it. You wasn't even here. Me, now I was here. And I can't even remember where the fuck they sat. It's better that way.

Timothy   Better for whom?

Jack   You got to grab your bull by its horns. Like me. Take me, right? I'm buying a new sign, some of that fancy neon. I call the bar Sarah Casey's now. Didya know that?

Timothy   Well. Congratulations.

Jack   I figure, Sarah, she was a tough kid. She woulda appreciated my business sense. She's gone, it don't matter. She comes back, she'll be honoured to have the place named after her.

Timothy   A beacon on the highway.

Jack   Huh?

Timothy   A candle in the window.

Jack   Yeah, sure. Candles in windows. That's good. I might do that. Like I said, you gotta figure your angle on every situation. What's your angle on this, mister?

Timothy   I'm in therapy.

Jack   Whoa, buddy. Heavy shit.

Timothy   Don't you think your life has been altered in some way? I mean, I might be having dinner with my kids now. But I'm not. You might be shooting the shit with Sarah Casey now. If not for this.

Jack   Nope. I think . . . we're doing exactly what we're meant to be doing. And I think there's reasons for what we're doing but fuck me if I know what they are.

Timothy   Has business picked up since – since the, uh, name change?

Jack   Nah. But it could. I betcha it could.

Timothy   Elston Rupp. That's one of those names. A name from another universe.

Jack   Yeah. A real . . . farmer name.

Timothy (*after a pause*)   I'd like a drink.

Jack   Sure. Listen, it's on me. What'll you have?

Timothy   Stoly Martini. Olives. (*Beat.*) Did you really make Rupp for a killer when he walked through that door.

Jack   Personally, between me and you – this is between me and you, right?

Timothy   Right.

Jack   Look, I couldn't tell a killer from a fucking priest. But Rupp's not talking and she's not here, right?

Timothy   Right.

Jack   But I did win the Golden Gloves. I swear.

Fourteen

Elston *and* **Ted** *at the thrift shop.* **Ted** *carries a box of clothing.*

Ted   I've brought some things.

Elston   Are they clean?

Ted   I washed them myself. Ironed everything. Even the socks.

Elston   Why?

Ted   Why not?

Elston   I mean, why here? Don't you have local thrift shop?

Ted   I want to keep in touch.

Elston   You feel you know me.

Ted   I don't know you.

Elston   You've dusted my apartment for fingerprints. You feel you're entitled.

Ted   Look. I'm just donating some clothes. I'm sorry.

Elston   I'm sorry for you. Are you sorry for me?

Ted   I'm troubled by you.

Elston   I burned my notepads. You read them.

Ted   I browsed through them.

Elston   Why didn't you read them?

Ted   It wasn't necessary.

Elston   It was necessary. If you wanted to know me. But you don't. So.

Ted   There are unresolved questions. I'd like to ask you. But.

Elston   I won't answer your questions any more, Ted. Because if I answered them, you wouldn't come back here.

Ted   If you answer me, I won't bother you again.

Elston   Bother me, Ted. (*Beat.*) I hope Sarah Casey's in Winchester.

Ted   So do I.

Elston   People from all over the city come in here just to look at me. Do you think they're afraid of me?

Ted   Do they look you in the eye?

Elston   Never. I had this thought yesterday: before Sarah Casey disappeared, I probably stood a better chance of making eye contact with a person, even though I was anonymous. Now. Well. I couldn't tell you the eye colour of anybody who's been here in the last week. (*Beat.*) You don't look me in the eye, Ted.

Ted   Maybe you should get another job.

Elston   Do you think I could be a detective?

Ted   Well, if you can't stand people fearing you, then police work is not ideal.

Elston   I didn't say I couldn't stand it. You can't stand it, though. (*Beat.*) I don't see Natalie any more. She has a messenger pick up the week's receipts on Sunday nights. The messenger brings me my paycheck. There's a different messenger each week. So there's some variety. I see more people that way.

Ted   You watched that woman walk away. Tell me you watched her walk away.

Elston   Last week, the messenger asked me for my autograph. It was thrilling. But he thought I was the lawyer. He thought I was Timothy Creighton.

Ted   Verify it for me. Please.

Elston   There's some irony in this, Ted.

Ted   People just don't disappear.

Elston   I know that. (*Beat.*) You'll need a receipt. For the clothes.

Ted   Maybe you're right. I should bring them someplace closer to home.

Elston   I knew you weren't the type to give away your old clothes. You hoard things. People. Faces. You can't stand the thought of other people in your pants.

Ted   I'll go now.

Elston   I thrive on all things second-hand.

Ted   Well. I guess that's why you like me. (*Beat.*) Goodbye, Elston.

Elston   You'll come back.

Ted   Anything's possible.

Elston   You're mine.

Ted *exits, leaving his clothes behind.* **Elston** *begins to undress.*

Elston   I can't wear clothes at all any more. I'm doing this favour for Natalie.

Fifteen

At O'Malley's. **Elston**, **Sarah** *and* **Jack**, *as in Scene One. Music in: 'Happy Together' (The Turtles).*

Elston The fascinating thing about being an entertainment attorney is that you meet people who have problems you couldn't begin to imagine. It makes one feel better about one's own problems.

Sarah I don't guess you have many problems. You have money.

Elston I carry the burden of all my clients' sadness.

Sarah That is such bullshit. You hear this guy, Jack? He's talking about carrying burdens.

Jack Burdens are what animals carry.

Elston I'm an animal. Aren't you an animal, Jack?

Jack Hey, I like animals. But I ain't no animal.

Elston It would be simpler. To be an animal.

Jack You couldn't protect yourself. You'd be at the mercy of other animals. Bigger animals.

Elston What if you had teeth? And say you were seven feet tall. You couldn't think, certainly. But you could protect yourself. Seeking protection is a primary animal instinct.

Sarah I wanna be a fish. Then I could swim. A lot.

Elston You could swim away. The earth, Sarah Casey, is seventy-five per cent water. And so are we.

Sarah Yeah, but I'd wanna be a slim fish. A pretty fish. And that way, I wouldn't last long. I'd get eaten up in a hurry. Or else end up in some sadistic kid's fish tank.

Elston Why does the kid have to be sadistic?

Sarah Well. Let's just say it's my burden.

Jack   I hadda mute parrot when I was a kid. Christ. I wish I'd tortured it.

Sarah   Oh, man. I really really wanna get out of here.

Elston   People always say 'I wanna get out'. And they rarely mean it. They rarely walk away. We stay. We don't take steps.

Sarah   That's easy for you to say, Mister-Entertainment-Attorney-to-the-Stars.

Elston   What if I told you that I live in one room. That I use no furniture. That I sleep in a closet. Would you believe me?

Sarah   Whaddya think, Jack? You believe this guy sleeps in a closet?

Jack   No way. This guy, he sleeps on a fucking king-sized waterbed.

Sarah   Yeah. And he's got some obnoxious bitch wife who spends all his money. And he loves it.

Elston   I like the bit about the money. Go on.

Jack   He's got a Swiss bank account. And he . . . collects. Yeah, he collects like, mink stoles. Sells them to the Japs.

Elston   Ermine. It would have to be ermine.

Sarah   He's got a castle in Germany. On the Rhine. That's a river, Jack. And he wants to teach his wife how to waltz, but she's too pigheaded to learn. It frustrates him. A lot.

Elston   That's perfect. So far.

Sarah   So. He likes to dance and he would love to learn Greek, but his fucking mother is always criticizing him about it. Constant ridicule. He doesn't have any close friends. And he's trapped in this loveless marriage he doesn't have a clue how to get out of.

Elston   And what does he do about this?

Sarah He ... doesn't know. He feels like a fake, like he's not entitled to something different because he doesn't have any money.

Elston But he has a castle on the Rhine.

Sarah Right. But it's ... it's his mother's castle. she's evil and she won't give him NOTHING. And he he he – lives in one room with a a a single bed and a desk with nothing in it and her only hope the only piece of comfort she has is a stupid old record nailed to her stupid old wall which is painted pink 'cause her bitch of a mother says pink is for GIRLS and she clings to this delusion that the record was written for her and she thinks that means she's entitled to GO SOMEWHERE SHE'S NEVER BEEN. (*Beat.*) Which, for her, is just about everywhere. She knows the name of practically every shit hole in this wide wide world but she's only seen the names on maps. She'll probably marry a good-natured man who she won't love, because at least then she can take a vacation. But basically, she thinks she'll drink until she drops.

Elston And then?

Sarah Something endless and black. She'll have a kid 'cause she's got nothing better to do. She'll be tempted to drown the kid, but she won't. Because she is not an animal, even though maybe she would like to be a fish. But she can't swim. 'Cause she never learned.

Elston And then, having no other option, she will walk on air.

Sarah He's talking shit again, Jack. Just when I was beginning to like him a little.

Elston I'm talking about miracles, Sarah. Our capacity to accept the impossible increases exponentially when we are at the ends of our ropes. (*Beat.*) Are you really beginning to like me?

Sarah I got a soft spot for religious fanatics.

Elston Have you ever been at the end of your rope, Sarah?

Sarah   Sure. Can't you see my rope burns?

Elston   I have them, too.

Sarah   Yeah. Well. We can march in a parade some day and reminisce about our war wounds.

Elston   I can walk on air.

Sarah   God. I wish that was true. I do.

Elston   If I could walk on air, it would be the most strange and wondrous sight, no?

Jack   The strangest thing I ever seen was my mother burying this mouse she killed in a trap. She breaks the thing's neck, right? And then she goes all soft and wants to bury it in the fucking backyard. And get this, like, she wants to dress it up in something nice. And the only nice thing she's got is my christening robe. I say, Ma, whaddya wacko or something? And she says, Jack, it'd be a sin not to bury this mouse in a soft white robe and since you're just too dumb to have kids, I don't expect you'll be needing it. (*Beat.*) And I had to agree with her.

Sarah   Thank you, Jack. You've proved once and for all that it's possible for men to walk on air. Thank you.

Elston   What's the strangest thing you've ever seen, Sarah?

Sarah   Well. Aside from the sight of me in my mother's house? Let's see. I'd have to say . . . this guy. He comes into the travel shop a couple of weeks ago. He's got this map in his pocket. The map's so old and so worn it looks like it's come outta the womb with this guy. He asks me to close my eyes and pick a vacation destination for him off this map. But it's a map of the tri-state metropolitan area. He insists I choose. And so. I close my eyes and I pick the Holland Tunnel. This guy is so . . . so grateful. His desire to go anywhere – just to go – is so strong. So well-defined. He has such trust. In me. And suddenly I feel the desire to kiss him, full on the lips, for a very long time. Because really, he has as little idea of where to go or what to do as I have. I don't kiss him. I don't take him by his hand and lead him into the world. I am eyeball to eyeball with a man who's the only person I'm likely to meet who fully understands the desire to simply . . . vanish. And I send him into a tunnel.

Elston That's the saddest story I've ever heard.

Sarah I know. Don't you think I know that?

Elston Maybe you'll meet that man again. And you'll walk on air. Together.

Sarah I wouldn't know him if he bit me in the ass.

Elston You can make the choice to remember. I do. You can take steps. What do you think, Jack? Can you take steps?

Jack Yeah, sure. I step outta my apartment, I step outta my car, I step in my bar, I step back out to my car, I step back into my apartment. Lotta steps, I'm taking.

Sarah Look. It's been nice, guys. But. Time to face the music. Time for beddie-bye. Time to imagine myself falling asleep to something other than the sounds of hookers getting pissed on the highway.

Elston The waves lapping gently past your castle on the Rhine.

Sarah Sure. Fairy tales do come true it can happen to you. If you're deluded at heart. (*Beat.*) I'm so . . . something . . . I can't even push myself to walk. I gotta stop drinking and start walking.

Elston Let me help you to the door. I have a long walk ahead of me. It's time I started off.

Jack That's a fuck of a long walk, mister, to the East Side.

Elston Not if you walk on air.

Sarah   Whaddya think, Jack? Am I stepping out with a lawyer or with some maniac who drowns women in his bathtub?

Jack *shrugs.*

Elston (*as he opens the door*)   Does it matter, Sarah Casey?

Sarah (*a beat, as she considers this*)   Makes no difference to me. But I sure hope you do walk on air. 'Cause it would be something to see.

Elston   Our potential to walk on air is infinite. Shall we?

Elston *bows to* **Sarah** *as he holds the door open for her.* **Sarah** *exits. A beat, then* **Elston** *follows her out, the door remaining open behind him.*

Blackout.

The Strip

As always, for Mel

The Strip was first performed at the Royal Court Theatre, London, on 23 February 1995. The cast was as follows:

Ava Coo	Deirdre Harrison
Tina	Amanda Boxer
Lester	Nicholas Farrell
Loretta	Cheryl Campbell
Kate Buck	Nancy Crane
Otto Mink	Nicholas le Prevost
Calvin	William Osborne
Martin	Patrick O'Kane
Tom Warner	John Padden
Suzy	Caroline Harker

Director Steven Pimlott
Designer Tobias Hoheisel
Design Assistant Patrick Watkinson
Lighting Designer Peter Mumford
Sound Paul Arditti

Characters

The Americans
Ava Coo, *mid-to-late 20s.*
Tina Coo, *45ish.*
Lester Marquette, *40s.*
Loretta Marquette, *30s.*
Kate Buck, *mid-30s.*

The English
Otto Mink, *alias Murphy Greene, of indeterminate age.*
Calvin Higgins, *late 20s.*
Martin Higgins, *30ish.*
Tom Warner, *early 20s.*
Suzy Bradfield, *30ish.*

The Time
The present, shortly before a total solar eclipse.

The Setting
A fluid, non-naturalistic landscape dominated by an enormous three-dimensional re-creation of Sphinx and pyramid which represents the exterior of the Luxor Hotel, Las Vegas, Nevada. It never leaves the stage.

Note
Scenes should begin and end in overlap; that is, except where indicated, there is never a blackout and the action of those on stage is continuous. It is possible that the physical action of any scene begins before its preceeding scene ends, and so on.

Act One

Darkness. Music in: 'Rescue Me' (Madonna). Lights up on tableaux, a slow unravelling of scenes:

Martin *and* **Tom** *in their Earls Court flat.* **Martin** *wears scanty workout clothes. He performs an impressive aerobics routine.* **Tom** *eats chocolate and times* **Martin** *with a stop watch.*

Ava, **Calvin** *and* **Otto** *at the Chateau L'Amour, Jericho (Long Island).* **Ava** *tries to look like Madonna. She doesn't. She lip-synchs to the song.* **Otto** *and* **Calvin** *are reticent.*

Suzy *in her Earls Court flat watching telly, eating crisps and masturbating simultaneously.*

Kate *at her desk in Arlington, Virginia. She wears Walkman headphones. She cleans a 9mm. automatic pistol.*

Lester *and* **Loretta** *in their Earls Court hotel. Their room directly overlooks* **Martin** *and* **Tom**'s *flat.* **Lester** *watches* **Martin** *and* **Tom**. *He polishes a pair of cowboy boots.* **Loretta** *bottle-feeds her infant son,* **Ray**. **Ray** *wears a white miniature Ku Klux Klan hooded robe.*

Tina *in Vegas at a one-arm bandit. She drops coin after coin into the slot without results. She swigs big shots from a bottle of tequila. She's fairly bored with all of this.*

The music fades into the sudden sound of a progressive slot machine jackpot being hit. Bells and sirens. A river of coins dropping out of slots. The sound is overwhelming.

Everybody listens to the phantom jackpot hit.

Abrupt shift in focus to **Otto**, **Ava** *and* **Calvin** *at the Chateau L'Amour.* **Otto** *speaks in a deep, wonderfully resonant English voice.* **Ava**'s *a native New Yorker.*

Otto   Female impersonation is a rather curious career

choice for a woman, Miss Coo.

Ava   You could tell? I saw you could tell. I practise too much. Or maybe not enough.

Otto   I shouldn't have thought rehearsal an issue.

Ava   You're English.

Otto   Am I?

Ava   I could tell. Hey. We're even. You could tell I was a woman. I could tell you weren't American.

Otto   But I am American, Miss Coo. I have a passport.

Otto *displays his passport for* **Ava**.

Ava   Otto Mink. Is that an English name?

Otto   No. It's not.

Ava   I always wanted a passport because they're glamorous things to have. Well. Not that I have anywhere glamorous to go. I mean, you don't need a passport to get to the city.

Otto   Which city?

Ava   You know. *The* city.

Otto   Yes. I see your point.

Ava   Anyway, my mother used to say, Ava darling, tits are the only passport a girl will ever need.

Otto *puts away his passport.*

Otto   Miss Coo. I will be frank. Your act is not appropriate for the Chateau L'Amour.

Ava   Okay, well, fair's fair.

Otto   You are talentless.

Ava   Oh. Do you – I mean – is there, like a reason you carry your passport with you? Because I never met anybody else who did that and I was just wondering, well, do you think I could ever be –

Otto Citizenship is precious, Miss Coo.

Ava Maybe I'm mediocre? Is that what you mean?

Otto No.

Ava Your passport picture is good, Mr Mink. Usually they cut off the top of your head or they catch you drooling and your hair looks like Little Richard's. I know about hair. I've got a certificate from the Wilfred Academy of Beauty. Two years, it took me. Turns out I'm allergic to hair spray. Two fucking years.

Otto Many of us take decades before finding our vocations.

Ava I don't really look like a girl. I'm too . . . something. I got big tits, but they look fake, or so this guy from Hoboken told me. I went to beauty school with this drag queen, Tina, and I think I kind of look like her so . . . so. It was this or Star Search. I figure, the TV camera doesn't lie but maybe a smoky scuzzy club full of drunken queens will. That's my mother's name. Tina. Funny, ain't it?

Otto Perhaps if your mother was a drag queen.

Ava I have performed my act in public. I want you to know that. People paid to see me.

Otto The Chateau L'Amour is not a smoky scuzzy club, Miss Coo.

Ava Hey, wait, I didn't mean – I'm sorry. I speak just total . . . shit. Oh God. Why can't I just want to be a typist or an actress like normal women?

Otto Because you're idiosyncratic. Special.

Ava Yeah. Talentless jerkoff me. Real special.

Otto Talent is a liability in the most important jobs.

Ava Oh sure. Tell that to, you know, Steven fucking Spielberg.

Otto I speak of true importance. Relevance. Resonance.

For instance: are saints talented?

Ava   What – you mean, like the chick who went crazy
and ate clay or or – the guy who talked to birds? My
mother has this gigantic book of saints, with pictures and –
you know who my favourite one is? Veronica. What a
fantastic name. And her picture. Terrific make up. She
wore the most beautiful shade of blue eye shadow.

Otto   Exactly. Do you think Saint Veronica had any
talent? Or Saints Theresa, Bernadette and Anthony, for
that matter?

Ava   Sure. Of course they had talent. They did things like
. . . shit. They did miracles.

Otto   No, Miss Coo. They had a calling. A common
vocation. The hand of God provided their direction. They
were empty vessels waiting to be filled with relevance.

Ava   Jesus. Well. That's depressing.

Otto   Just as you are an empty vessel waiting for me to
fill you.

Ava   Uh-huh. Okay. I'm . . . open. To suggestion.

Otto   I own another club. The club is located in another
part of this country. I will write its name down on this slip
of paper. You will take the slip of paper.

*He produces, as if from nowhere, a pad and pen. He scribbles on a
piece of paper. He holds it out to* **Ava**.

Take it.

Ava *takes the piece of paper. She stares at it.*

Ava   Tumbleweed Junction. Okay. So.

Otto   Find it and sing, Miss Coo. Good luck.

Otto *prepares to leave.*

Ava   Hey, wait. Is there something you're forgetting to tell
me, like, where this club is and maybe how I'm supposed
to get there? I mean, I got a car but where the hell am I

supposed to be driving it? And – correct me if I'm wrong here – but are you offering me a job, Mr Mink?

Otto All the information you need is written on that slip of paper.

Ava Oh great. Two words, two fucking words. Tumbleweed Junction. Hey – this ain't in Jersey, is it? I'm not singing in Jersey. (*Referring to* **Calvin**.) Maybe your friend here knows the directions?

Otto I've never seen this man before.

Otto *exits.*

Ava Find it and sing. My ass.

Calvin (*he's English, but he's lived in America for a long time and has no perceptible English accent*) I loved your act. It made me cry.

Ava You cried? Nah. You didn't cry. Did you?

Calvin Yes. I did. I cry at odd times.

Ava Hey. If he don't know you, you don't work here. Right.

Calvin Right. I don't work here.

Ava You ever hear of a club called Tumbleweed Junction? I bet it's some dive in Secaucus. I just know it.

Calvin Sorry. No. I don't go to clubs much. But I . . . I think you are talented. And I couldn't tell that you were a woman.

Ava That's . . . really nice of you to say.

Calvin My brother's gay.

Ava Oh. Really.

Calvin It sounds strange to tell you, I know, but I have been to clubs with him where female impersonators have performed. So I know. A little something. About it. (*Beat.*) That was long ago, of course.

Ava   Sure. Uhm . . . I gotta get a map of America, 'cause it looks like I'm taking a trip. You don't by any chance have a road map? Or a twenty for some gas? I'm broke.

Calvin   I do. Have a map, that is. Would you like it?

Calvin takes a map out of his back pocket and gives it to Ava.

Ava   Thanks. I . . . hey. If you don't work in this club, why are you here?

Calvin   I'm English, too. Like the owner of this club. I don't know exactly where he's from, but it's someplace southern. And wealthy. I've been here a long time. Too long. Anyway, that's why I don't have an accent. I'm Calvin. Calvin Higgins.

Calvin and Ava shake hands.

Ava   Ava Coo. Answer my question. What are you doing here?

Calvin   What an unusual name. Ava. Coo. Lovely. Soft.

Ava   Yeah. I'm named after a French murderess.

Calvin   You're joking.

Ava   I'm not. Answer my question, Calvin.

Calvin   I'm looking for you.

Ava   That's a really tired line. And I remember asking if you could lend me a twenty for gas. I got places to get to.

Calvin   Well. That's just it, Ava Coo. I'm here to repossess your car.

*Shift to **Lester** and **Loretta** in their Earls Court hotel room. **Lester** obsessively polishes and repolishes his cowboy boots throughout the scene. **Loretta** holds **Baby Ray**. She reads very slowly and deliberately to **Ray** from a book. Both **Lester** and **Loretta** speak in quite broad Virginia (southern) accents.*

Loretta   'What did they look like? Early Romans came from a tribe called the Latins. Latins had olive skin and dark hair. When their empire spread across Europe, other people began to settle in Rome. As time went on, the Romans included people with lots of different looks.' (*Beat.*) I'm not sure I like this book, Lester.

Lester   Baby Ray's a leader. Leaders learn about everything, beginning with the Romans.

Loretta   The Romans weren't olive skinned. They were white.

Lester   I know that, Loretta. You don't got to tell me. And I don't think the book is suggesting that the Romans weren't white. The book is saying that the Romans were Italians.

Loretta   If you say so. (*She continues to read.*) 'Romans had many more baths and were a lot cleaner than people in other ancient civilizations. Both men and women loved wearing expensive perfume.' There is something wrong with this book, Lester. I will not have Baby Ray believing that it's right for men to wear expensive perfumes.

Lester   That ain't the point of the story, Loretta. You got no appreciation for the great cultures. But that doesn't mean Baby Ray ain't gonna have any.

Loretta   Well, what is the point of the story then, Lester? That the Romans were cleaner than everybody else?

Lester   Yeah. That's it.

Loretta   Where did you get this book?

Lester   Cleanliness is next to Godliness.

Loretta   We take showers, Lester. I change Baby Ray's diaper seventeen times a day. Believe me. I know all about cleanliness.

Lester   All I'm saying is, if you find out who the cleanest people are, they are always the smartest people.

Loretta   Such as?

Lester   Shit, Loretta. Why do you got to bother me when

I'm cleaning my boots? Why do you do this to me, woman?

Loretta   Such as? I am waiting for an example, Lester. Mr Mink says we learn by example.

Lester   For example. The Swiss. They are very clean. They are first-class inventors. The Germans. They're so clean, they all have blond eyelashes. Smartest people in the world. Have I proved my point?

Loretta   Only northern Germans are clean.

Lester   Who told you that?

Loretta   I read. I put two and two together.

Lester   Why don't you just . . . read some more to Baby Ray. He's got to know about the Romans.

Loretta   Fact: northerners everywhere are always cleaner. Look at America. Need I go on?

Lester   I swear you don't know your ass from a hole in the ground. Remember where we live?

Loretta   Virginia is not the south. Virginia is a rich state. Always has been. And we don't live in Roanoke any more, Lester. We live in a bed and breakfast in goddamned Earls Court in the goddamned United Kingdom. Get used to it.

Lester   We ain't gonna be clean for long. There's no shower.

Loretta   Adapt to circumstance. Assimilate. Conquer. Mr Mink's triple crown for success.

Lester   Fuck you, Loretta. I'm not sitting in my own dirt.

Loretta   The Roman generals took baths.

Lester   They had no choice. There was no electricity or water pressure.

Loretta   You talk shit, Lester. And I am not sitting in this hotel room like I'm some kind of prisoner. I am going out to see what I can see.

Lester   You can't do that, Loretta. You will not do that. We are waiting on Mr Mink's call.

Loretta   Three days and three nights. It's time to go, Lester.

Lester   Jesus waited forty days and forty nights.

Loretta   Jesus was in the desert, Lester, not London. There wasn't restaurants or entertainment available.

Lester   We wait for his call. Anyway. What do you think you're gonna see out there?

Loretta   Sights.

Lester   There's a couple of homos living across the airshaft. One of them dances around with weights, the other one eats. Go out. See the sights, Loretta.

Loretta   You don't got to look at it. See no evil.

Lester   You really ain't the smartest person in the world.

Loretta   No, Lester, I'm not the smartest. But I am the best person for you. And do you know why I am the best person for you? Because I believe that *you* are the smartest person in the world. Because I believe that *you* will be famous and in the process, you will make me a very rich woman. And when I am a very rich woman, I will send Baby Ray off to Oxford and I will eat Belgian chocolates until I am the fattest, most docile wife a man could hope for. I will be so fat, you will have to build extension after extension to our Georgian mansion. And then, Lester, I will be truly happy and I won't ask you another question about the Romans or about why I am cooped up in some dump of a hotel without a shower or why it is we no longer have a home.

Lester   I'm already famous.

Loretta   You're a fugitive. I don't think that qualifies.

Lester   You're a fugitive with me.

Loretta   No way. I didn't do nothing but slip a ring on my finger and give birth to your child.

The telephone rings. It rings again. And again. **Lester** *answers. He listens. He hangs up.*

Lester   Looks like we'll be testing out one of your finer sociological theories. We're going north.

Shift to **Tina** *on her hands and knees at the Tumbleweed Junction, Las Vegas. She uses a scrub-brush to clean the floor with one hand, and holds a small Dictaphone in the other hand. Distant sounds of slot machines, roulette wheels.* **Tina** *speaks into the Dictaphone.*

Tina   Dear Ava. I probably didn't get your last letter because when I married Mr Marshall, I moved house. Not that my split level wasn't nice enough for us but . . . well now I live on a one-hundred and fifty acre ranch with Mr Marshall. And before that, I was so busy at the casino I was hardly ever home to get my mail. But I know you wrote to me, Ava. And I know what you wrote about because let's face it honey, all our letters say the same thing. The weather is good, the weather is bad, and so on. I put pen to paper and I find myself writing the same old things, who knows why. So I am sending you a tape in the hope that it will change our routine. Mr Marshall gave me this Dictaphone as a wedding gift and you know I've always been a freer talker than a writer. You would like Mr Marshall. He's tall and rarely speaks. But he opens doors for me and buys me bunches of daisies from the Seven-Eleven and really, Ava, that's more than good enough. I miss your voice, honey. It's hard being a casino supervisor in Vegas, but it's rewarding. As you can imagine, I don't make many friends on the gaming floor, but I am a fair boss and last week I got Dolly Parton's autograph. Mr Marshall breeds horses. I keep an eye out for promising colts. So far there's no hint of a Secretariat, but his horses are strong and good-looking. Like him. I am babbling and so I better get to the point of this letter which is: I think I saw your daddy's picture in a newspaper last week. I say I think it was him because I haven't seen him in twenty years but it looked just like him. Except in the newspapers his name was Marquette and he looked much thinner than when I knew him. I think he killed twenty-seven people at a truck stop in Lynchburg. Well. That's all for now. I hope you are still enjoying success as a cabaret singer. I am so proud of you, Ava. With love, your mother, Mrs Tina Coo Marshall.

The casino sounds suddenly grow much louder, as **Otto** *enters. And then, just as suddenly, the sounds drop down to ther previous level.*

Otto   Mrs Marshall. A pleasure, as always.

Tina   You're not supposed to be in here, Mr Greene. This is the ladies' room.

Otto   I do own this establishment.

Tina   Yeah but . . . it's weird, you being in here.

Otto   This is my ladies' room, Mrs Marshall. And you are my primary lady.

Tina   Oh Mr Greene. You shouldn't flirt.

Otto   I'm not.

Tina   We're, uhm, running out of extra strength Lysol.

Otto   Are we?

Tina   I had to bring some from home today. Will we be getting it on delivery any time soon?

Otto   I'm afraid not.

Tina   Oh. Well. But how can I clean the toilets without it?

Otto   Be inventive, Mrs Marshall. Employee initiative brings its own reward.

Tina   We ran out of rubber gloves last week.

Otto   I'm aware of that.

Tina   I could use a raise. The plumbing in my trailer's been busted for months and you don't know how tired I am of taking sponge baths here. I can't get my clothes clean. They don't fit too good in these tiny sinks and my sweaters got soapy residue all over them. I itch all the time, Mr Greene.

Otto   Have you heard from Mr Marshall lately?

Tina   Not exactly.

Otto   These are hard times. We must make do with what we have.

Tina   What if we got nothing?

Otto   Why is your glass always half empty, Mrs Marshall, and never half full?

Tina   Because I drink a lot.

Otto   Have you finished with my Dictaphone?

Tina   Oh sure, I was just . . . you ever notice how when you play back a tape your voice doesn't sound like your voice?

Otto   I've had complaints from several guests. The loos aren't clean enough. The lavatory floor is grimy. There are standards to be upheld at Tumbleweed Junction, Mrs Marshall. Who hasn't been working hard enough?

Tina   I need this job. Please let me keep my job.

Otto   Who hasn't been working hard enough?

Tina   There's not another hotel in town that'll hire me. I'm trying to get a place at croupier school but they won't take me until I got some hotel experience. And no hotel will take me on unless I got experience at one of the big places. God. I wanna work at the Luxor, Mr Greene. I wanna know what it's like inside that pyramid.

Otto   Just tell me. Who hasn't been working hard enough?

Tina   I . . . me. Me. I haven't been working hard enough.

Otto   What happens when we don't work hard enough?

Tina We get docked. I get docked.

Otto *takes the Dictaphone away from* **Tina**.

Otto Thank you, Mrs Marshall. I believe a day's wages will be sufficient.

Otto *holds out his hand to* **Tina**.

Tina You want me to give you one day's pay. Now?

Otto Why not? What you no longer have can't hurt you.

Tina *digs some cash out of her shoe and gives it to* **Otto**.

Tina I don't understand you a lot of the time, Mr Greene. But I thank Christ you don't fire me.

Otto I'm inscrutable. Like the Sphinx.

Tina *resumes scrubbing the floor.*

Tina Whatever. (*Beat.*) My husband's a trucker. It's not unusual that I don't hear from him say, for a few weeks. Or months.

Otto *removes the tape from the Dictaphone. He bends down to give* **Tina** *the tape.*

Otto You shouldn't spend so much time on your knees, Mrs Marshall. It's bad for the circulation.

Shift to **Martin** *and* **Tom** *in their Earls Court flat.* **Martin** *sits on a straight-back chair. He wears only jockey briefs.* **Tom** *bathes* **Martin***'s feet. He uses an old-fashioned foot basin and a pitcher of water.* **Suzy** *does sit-ups. She's not expert.*

Suzy So I run this bloke's details through the software programme. He's a Gemini with Gemini rising and a moon in Capricorn. A complete mess. He's a bankrupt, his boyfriend's fucked off with a Chippendale and to make things worse, the bloody computer tells me he's got eight months to live. I don't know what to do. I mean, do I write to him and say, awfully sorry, but you have no future?

Martin Pouf.

Suzy   That's not very nice. He isn't dying because he's a pouf.

Martin   No, Suzy. You're a pouf. You do sit-ups like a pouf.

Tom   You're a pouf, Martin. You do sit-ups.

Martin   Shut up. (*Beat.*) Computer astrology software does not predict the future.

Suzy   Mine does. Don't ask me how. But it does.

Martin   That's impossible.

Tom   I've seen it work. Once I watched while Suzy ran an entire sixth form –

Martin   This water's tepid.

Tom   I'll fetch some hot. I'm sorry.

Martin   Never mind.

Suzy *stops doing sit-ups.* **Tom** *continues to bathe* **Martin***'s feet.*

Suzy   Anyway, I've been taking on too many mail-order jobs. Last month I got a letter from a very strange woman in America. Real nutter. A journalist . . . or something. She keeps writing. I think she has me confused with a lonely hearts' club.

Tom   How do you know she's a nutter if you've never met her?

Suzy   You can tell from a letter.

Tom   I couldn't.

Martin   You couldn't tell much now, could you, Tommy? (*Beat.*) You ought to do three sets of fifteen, Suzy. And what about those press-ups?

Suzy   I'm knackered, Martin. Really.

Martin   Pouf.

Tom   Stop saying that.

Martin Why? Why should I stop?

Tom Because it bothers me.

A beat, and then **Martin** *exits, dripping water everywhere.*

Tom He has a good heart.

Suzy You should get out more often.

Tom He misses his brother.

Suzy Don't be daft. Martin hasn't heard from his brother in years.

Tom He phoned up. Yesterday.

Suzy Calvin? You heard from Calvin?

Tom Said he was in love with a girl called Ava. She's a drag queen. Apparently.

Suzy And? What else did he have to say for himself?

Tom Nothing. That was all.

Suzy You fancy a curry? I do. I'm starved. I gave up waiting for Calvin's letters three years ago. December. The twelfth. Eight a.m. Central heating out. Enough jam for one croissant. Red notice from BT. And I stopped missing Calvin Higgins.

Tom What will you tell him?

Suzy Who? What?

Tom The bloke who's dying.

Suzy Him. Well. I don't know, do I?

Tom Tell him the stars suggest a configuration of rare fortune. Tell him he's the most stunning creature alive. Tell him he'll meet a man who will adore him. Who will mend his trousers and his broken heart. Tell it to him over and over.

Suzy *touches her hand to* **Tom**'s *forehead.*

Suzy You're sweating. Poor Tom.

Tom   Why does he hate me? Why?

Suzy   Why does my astrology software provide me with information nobody else has?

Tom   The stars are strange this month.

Suzy   Come on, then. Teach me a proper press-up.

Tom *demonstrates press-ups for* **Suzy**. *He does the press-ups very slowly, so she is able to follow his lead.*

Tom   It's really very simple. See.

Suzy   I wish I believed fitness could be fun.

Tom *suddenly accelerates. He's going very fast and breathing very hard.* **Suzy** *can't keep up.*

Suzy   Tom. TOM. YOU'RE WHEEZING. THAT'S ENOUGH.

But **Tom** *doesn't stop. He keeps going.* **Suzy** *pours the pitcher of water over* **Tom***'s head. He stops abruptly, and lets himself fall face down onto the floor.*

Tom   FuckhimfuckhimfuckhimfuckhimFUCKFUCKFUCK HIMHIMHIM.

Suzy*, at a complete loss, pats* **Tom***'s back tentatively.*

Suzy   Okay. Okay. Poor Tom. Okay. Sssh. Sssh. Poor Tom. Okay.

Shift to **Otto** *and* **Kate** *at* **Kate***'s office in Arlington, Virginia.* **Kate** *wears Walkman headphones. She carries a rather large purse.*

Kate   The leads you gave me don't check out.

Otto   I felt certain they would.

Kate   Well they don't. What do you make of that?

Otto   I haven't any notion. You are the reporter, Miss Buck. Report.

Kate   I wasn't an intestigative reporter, Murphy. I was a columnist. There's a difference.

Otto   Nonetheless. I hired you as a reporter.

Kate   I can't find Marquette. He's not in Roanoke. He's not anywhere in Virginia. Or in the Carolinas for that matter. Lynchburg cops got a positive ID on the prints found at the truck stop. And they are not Lester Marquette's prints.

Otto   I believe they are.

Kate   I will not report false information. I have a duty to our readership.

Otto   The Arlington Pennysaver is not The New York Times, Miss Buck.

Kate   It's still a newspaper. Even if it is a weekly. A free weekly. A free weekly shopper. Oh fuck. Why did I let you hire me?

Otto   I seem to recall a rather nasty incident involving your ethics at the Philadelphia Inquirer.

Kate   I was duped.

Otto   Pre-teen calculus genius with a crack habit plus disabled mum equals a prize-winning story. Heart-rending. Metaphorical. And a fabrication.

Kate   I WAS DUPED.

Otto *approaches* **Kate**. *He lifts up one of* **Kate**'s *headphone speakers and leans in close to listen to what she's listening to. A beat, before he replaces the headphone in* **Kate**'s *ear and steps back.*

Otto   If the fingerprints aren't Lester Marquette's, then to whom do they belong? You said there was a positive identification.

Kate   That's right. It's positively not Lester Marquette.

Otto   You favour sentimental popular music, Miss Buck.

Kate   I do not. I like . . . a little Motown, a little disco, this and that.

Otto   The sentimental are always duped. In journalism as

in life. I prefer jazz to pop. It resists false notions of a
single shared experience and is therefore unsentimental.
Your reportage has been flabby of late.

Kate   So I'm supposed to buy a Thelonius Monk tape
and that'll fix it? I don't think so. You want to know what
my problem is?

Otto   Not especially.

Kate   I track down leads about some twelve-year-old's
stolen Raleigh. I cover the grand openings of, let's see,
bingo halls, electrolysis clinics, Weight Watchers. You name
it, Murphy. I'm there. I'm hot. Mrs fucking Esposito's
blender disappears: Kate's got a few inches in Community
Corner for it. No problem not a problem hey I'm smiling
see me smile see me take a photo of this new-born or that
blue ribbon Alsatian no problem I'm happy I'm there and
I WAS A COLUMNIST GODDAMNIT.

Otto   Displays of excessive emotion bore me, Miss Buck.

Kate   I'm being watched by a person who lives in another
country.

Otto   Which country?

Kate   I don't know. Another one. Does it matter?

Otto   I should think it matters a great deal. Canada is
relatively nearby. England, on the other hand, is not.

Kate   England. Why do you say England?

Lights up on **Suzy**. *She works out on an exercise bike while writing
a letter.*

Otto   An obsession with unanswerable questions is the first
sign of insanity. Concern yourself with easy answers. Find
Lester Marquette and you will have the story of your life.

Otto *exits. Music in: 'Native New Yorker' (Odyssey).* **Kate***'s been
listening to this tune on her Walkman. She listens to the song
seriously for a moment, then removes a letter from her bag and reads
it as she bops along to the music.*

Suzy (*plugging away on the bicycle*)   Dear Kate Buck. My advert, which ought to have run in Astrology Monthly, mistakenly ran in Looking for Love, a publication I am not familiar with. My life is a bit of a mess just at the moment so I'm not surprised by odd occurrences. I think it has something to do with the upcoming solar eclipse and also my Mars is in Scorpio, which explains a great deal. But enough about me. Yes, I am interested in holistic healing, crystals, natural childbirth, macrobiotics and the lot, but I am fairly certain that I'm not a lesbian. I mean, I'm always receptive to new experiences. An astrologer has to be. But I have to admit I enjoy a good rogering every once in a while and therefore I feel your letters, however sensitive and entertaining, are quite missing their mark. I'm sorry, but since I've rarely been outside of London, I don't see how I could have been born in New York City. And as your dream date is a native New Yorker, I'm afraid that leaves me out. One of my ex-boyfriends lives somewhere near New York City, and he once sent me a miniature Statue of Liberty. But that's as close as I got, since he stopped writing to me shortly afterwards. Though I do thank you for the cassette. I have fond memories of dancing with my gay friend, Martin, to that song in the late seventies. Good luck in your search and I'd appreciate your not writing to me again. Unless, of course, you'd like me to prepare your chart. I'm sure we could agree on a rate. Sincerely, Suzy Bradfield.

Lights down on **Suzy**. **Kate** *folds up the letter carefully, kisses it, puts it back in her bag. She removes her 9mm. automatic pistol from the bag and once again begins the ritual of cleaning it. Music out.*

Shift focus to **Ava** *and* **Calvin** *on a street in Arlington, Virginia.* **Ava** *consults a map.*

Calvin   We should have headed west, Ava Coo.

Ava   Look. I got sick of you back in Pennsylvania in that that – what the hell was that loony tunes town you dragged me through –

Calvin   It was an Amish village.

Ava   Yeah, well, they were fucking out to lunch.

Calvin   I'm interested in the way they live.

Ava   What's to be interested in? They don't have zippers. What kind of people don't have zippers? I'll tell you, Calvin. Wackos. That's who.

Calvin   They do just as well with buttons, Ava Coo.

Ava   I'm gonna shove a button up your ass if you don't stop calling me Ava Coo like I'm some kind of . . . bug. Ava. A-V-A. Get it?

Calvin   Yours is a name that begs to be heard in its entirety. Like a Beethoven piano sonata.

Ava   Oh boy. Listen to me Liberace: THIS IS MY TRIP. Okay? It's my trip, it's my car, it's my map and we go where I say we go. And we are going south. As soon as I figure out why my friggin' car won't start.

Calvin   It's not your car any more.

Ava   Just . . . why do you do that? Huh? Never got anything good to say. Always bringing me down. DownDOWNDOWN.

Calvin   And actually, it's my map.

Ava   I'm gonna put my fist through your ugly fat face if you don't SHUT UP about it already. I swear to God those fruitcake Amish put some kind of fucking hex on me and my car.

Calvin   You shouldn't blame others for your own misfortune.

Ava   You know, you really ought to do some evangelising 'cause you'd make a fortune with this thine neighbour thy self thou holy shit. (*A beat.*) I shouldn't have laughed at that Amish kid's pants. I knew they were into that voodoo hoodoo crap. Shitshit. Where the hell are we?

Calvin   Arlington, Virginia. President Kennedy's buried here. Would you like to see his grave?

Ava Fuck off.

Calvin Respect history and it will respect you.

Ava You're unbelievable. It's like you drop a coin in your mouth and some stupid saying comes out your ass.

Calvin His grave has an eternal flame. I'd like to see it.

Ava Listen. I wasn't even born when Kennedy, you know, rest in peace and all that shit, and my mother didn't vote for him. So go yourself. Bye-bye.

Calvin The very thought of an eternal flame fills my heart with an inexplicable longing. Why don't you feel it?

Ava You're really freaking me out, Calvin. Why don't you take the car, okay, take the car and do . . . whatever you gotta do with it. I'll hitch.

Calvin I can't leave you.

Ava Sure you can. I'm like a doormat. People coming and going, breaking and entering, the whole time.

Calvin I'm sorry, but I'm meant to be with you.

Ava I'm pretty sure I was meant to be with Paul Newman, but I'm not so.

Calvin My face isn't fat. And I'm not ugly. At least I don't think I am. Am I?

Ava What – okay, no. You're not ugly. I'm sorry.

Calvin What about my face? Is it fat? Do you really think it's fat?

Ava I don't – it's just an expression. Like when you're mad at somebody you say, you know, you say, fuck you, you fat face bastard. Like that.

Calvin A figure of speech.

Ava Yeah. Whatever. (*Beat.*) How many phone books can we go through in how many hick towns looking for some dive that probably doesn't exist?

Calvin   It exists.

Ava   How do you know? How do you know that Mink guy wasn't pulling my pud? People always pull my pud. I have that kind of face.

Calvin   You're beautiful.

Ava   All right all right. Don't start up again. I'm warning you.

Kate *enters. She listens to her Walkman intently and dangles the pistol nonchalantly. She's in a world only she understands and therefore doesn't notice* **Ava** *and* **Calvin**.

Ava   Ohmygod I've read about this kind of right-wing southern lunatic with a gun. Ohmygod we're gonna die.

Calvin   She's just . . . walking. Thinking. Relax.

Ava   She's probably on her way to a . . . a post office or or . . . a McDonald's – yeah – some fast-food joint where she's gonna, I don't know, burn her bra and shoot till she ain't got any fingers left. Get me out of here, Calvin. Weirdos stick to me like I'm flypaper. I'm serious.

Calvin *approaches* **Kate**. **Ava** *drops to her knees. Crosses herself every which way.*

Ava   Now I lay me down to sleep . . . oh fuck that's not right. What is it? WHAT IS THE FUCKING PRAYER.

Calvin *puts his hand on* **Kate**'s *shoulder. She turns to him. A beat. She removes her headphones, puts them in her purse.*

Kate   You're from England, aren't you?

Calvin   I am.

Kate   I knew that.

Calvin   I'm impressed.

Kate   I was a Pulitzer prize-winning columnist for the Philadelphia Inquirer.

Calvin   I'm a repossessions man. Depressing, but it's a living.

Kate (*refers to* **Ava**)   Is your friend hurt?

Calvin   She's praying.

Kate   I like spiritual women.

Calvin   Do you have a Yellow Pages?

Kate   Yes. I do.

Calvin   Do you know anything about cars?

Kate   What make?

Calvin   Chevy Nova. 1974.

Kate   That's the same as mine. What colour?

A beat, before they answer simultaneously.

Kate *and* **Calvin**   Yellow.

Calvin   It's my friend's car. Well, I'm in the process of repossessing it, but . . . she's got a night-club engagement she's got to get to in the meantime. (*Refers to the gun.*) Are you afraid of something?

Kate   Everything. (*Refers to his hand on her shoulder.*) You have a very comforting touch.

Calvin   Thank you. I took a massage class on Long Island.

Kate   New York. You're here from New York?

Calvin   That's right.

Kate   Is your friend from New York?

Calvin   Born and bred.

Kate   Really.

Calvin   I feel I'm meant to marry her. But something tells me she doesn't want it to work out.

Kate   Really.

Kate *gently removes* **Calvin**'s *hand from her shoulder. She approaches* **Ava**, *who's been silently praying to herself, eyes shut tight against the threat of potential violence.* **Kate** *taps* **Ava** *with the pistol.*

Ava (*with great speed, as if she's been holding this in all the while*) I'm just as uncomfortable with blacks Jews democrats shriners Irish and you know whatever as you are please don't kill me I'm on the verge of a spectacular singing career if only I could find the Tumbleweed Junction.

Kate I'm a journalist. I don't take sides.

Ava (*she opens her eyes*) Oh. Thankyougod. (*Refers to the gun.*) Is it dangerous around here?

Kate No. Somebody's watching me, though. What's your name?

Ava Ava. Ava Coo.

Kate Ava Coo. Ava Coo. Hmmm.

Ava Fuck me, not another one who has a thing about my name.

Kate Are you going out with anybody?

Ava Oh sure. Maybe. Yeah . . . well. Not really. No. Definitely not.

Kate (*refers to the pistol*) I'll put this away now.

She does. She holds out her hand to **Ava**. *A beat, before* **Ava** *takes* **Kate**'s *hand.* **Kate** *lifts* **Ava** *to her feet.*

Kate I understand you have car trouble.

Ava You ever hear of a club called Tumbleweed Junction?

Kate Come home with me and we'll discuss it.

Music in: 'Follow Me' (Amanda Lear). Shift to **Martin** *and* **Lester** *in an Earls Court gay bar.* **Martin** *wears his best leathers.* **Lester** *wears his magnificently polished cowboy boots,* *ten-gallon hat, bolo tie: the works.* **Lester**'s *not aware he's in a gay bar. He drinks beer and drums his fingers along to the tune.* **Martin** *watches* **Lester** *take in his surroundings. Several moments pass.* **Martin** *approaches* **Lester**. *Silence.*

Lester Man, this place. Wow. Makes me homesick.

Martin Does it?

Lester Sure thing. I mean, back home, I got this local place right off the US 220 – called Tinker's. And it's just like this.

Martin Really? How so?

Lester Well, it's just about the only place in the entire Shenandoah Valley where a fella can hook up with his buddies, take a break from the missus and the kids. Relax. Shoot some pool. Well. Actually, it's where we have our Klan meetings so, you know, ladies just ain't allowed. (*Beat.*) Still. I didn't think I'd find a place like Tinker's in this neck of the woods. I mean, England's so, I don't know, refined.

Martin We here at the Coleherne take pride in the fact that ladies just aren't allowed. So. Welcome.

Lester Why, thank you kindly.

A pause, as they listen to the tune.

Great tune, huh? Whatsit. German or something?

Martin Well. It's certainly continental.

Lester Yeah. That's what I figured. Sounds like that, that actress.

Martin Dietrich.

Lester That's the one. Yeah. (*Beat.*) You look familiar to me. You look like someone I've seen.

Martin I doubt it. (*Beat.*) More lager?

Lester That's great, man. I've read that the English peoples have a reputation for hospitality.

Martin I think I've read that, too. (*Produces another lager as if from nowhere.*) Cheers.

Lester Yeah. Cheers (*Beat.*) Calfskin?

Martin Pardon?

Lester The chaps. Calfskin, right? The best.

Martin The best.

Lester Must have set you back a bundle.

Martin But don't you think it's worth it?

Lester You bet. Sure as hell a man's got to be in A-1 shape to wear leather well.

Martin I couldn't agree more.

Lester You sure we never met before? In an airport maybe? Strip joint?

Martin I don't travel.

Lester Right. Well. (*Beat.*) Is this some kind of biker bar? I mean, everybody's wearing the gear.

Martin We have what you might call theme nights. Sometimes one theme, sometimes another.

Lester You a biker?

Martin No. You a cowboy?

Lester Coulda been. But, uh, no. I'm in business.

Martin I manage a health club.

Lester I'm a politician. Well. I will be. Soon.

Martin Brilliant. You must have great strength. Of character. Do you . . . work out?

Lester Who, me? Nah. You got to be kidding.

Martin You look like you work out.

Lester Well, you know, in the old days. Boot camp. Infantry. The usual.

Martin I bet you really kicked some ass.

Lester Sure. Back then, hell, all the boys kicked a little ass. Now. Well, now I got responsibilities. Got no time for it, buddy.

Martin You ought to make time for it. A fit body is the first step on the road to strength of character.

Lester You know, I got to tell you that I truly admire that clean living thing. I do. But . . . there just ain't the hours in a day between the wife, the kid, the, what have you.

Martin The politics.

Lester The politics. Damn right. Listen, do you think you could fill me in on the local, you know, the local political scene? The, uh, affiliations and whatnot?

Martin I don't see why not. Another lager?

Lester Gee, thanks an awful lot mister. Don't mind if I do. (**Martin** *produces another lager out of thin air.*) I've been reading about the . . . Tories. That's the ruling party, ain't it?

Martin In a manner of speaking. Yes. The other major parties are Labour and the Liberal Democrats.

Lester Well now, we don't like the sound of them Liberal Democrats. Double welfare whammy smells like to me. Which one you belong to?

Martin None of them.

Lester So . . . what are you?

Martin You might say I'm a member of a clan.

Lester No shit. Who'd a thought . . . well. Ain't that something.

Martin Oh, yes. The American influence is rather strong in my clan.

Lester (*a brilliant idea occurs to* **Lester**) Listen. I'm in the process of teaching my son Ray about, well, just about all sorts of things. History, mainly. Wars. Russia. The important stuff. He's only tiny, you know, three, four months old, but it's crucial to get a head start.

Martin   Quite.

Lester   I was thinking you could tutor him in politics. Me and my wife, we're going to Liverpool for a couple of days. But then we'll be back. And we live, well, just around the corner. So. I mean, if you want to. I'll pay.

Martin   I've never been a tutor. But I must say, your proposition is intriguing. (*Beat.*) Do you arm wrestle?

Lester   Oh, now, no shit Sherlock. You're talking to a former Virginia state champeen arm wrestler.

Martin   Show me.

Lester   What? You mean, now? Here?

Martin   Show me your arm strength and I'll show you mine.

Lester (*considers it*)   Okay. Sure, you're on. Why not. Flex the old elbow grease.

Martin   I like spontaneity in a man. Another sign of character.

They prepare to arm wrestle.

Martin   On the count of three.

Lester   I'm cooking. I'm ready for you, man.

Martin (*drawing out the count*)   One ... two ... three.

He beats **Lester** *almost immediately.*

Now. Let's talk politics.

Shift to **Tom** *and* **Loretta** *in Greene & Greene pawn shop, Earls Court.* **Tom** *works there.* **Loretta**'s *browsing.* **Loretta** *carries* **Baby Ray.** *The kid's dressed up in* **Loretta**'s *ludicrous version of English infant aristocratic chic. So is* **Loretta**.

Loretta   Cheerio.

Tom   May I . . . assist you with . . . something?

Loretta   Tally ho.

Tom   We don't have much jewellery in at the moment, I'm afraid.

Loretta   Did you know that King Edward the Martyr was killed by his own stepmother in the year of our Lord 978? I think that is absolutely disgusting.

Tom   I don't know. It did happen a long time ago.

Loretta   Do you suppose he's called a martyr because his stepmother killed him? I mean, would he have been called a martyr had anybody killed him or was it just her? Or is it for some entirely different reason?

Tom   I'm sure I don't know. Can I help you with something in particular?

Loretta   I am immersing myself in the history and culture of your people. Were you aware that the Romans were olive complected?

Tom   Well. I think, yes, I may have studied that. Once.

Loretta   Huh. So you knew that? I didn't. Go figure. Are you Mr Greene?

Tom   No. I'm not. I'm Tom.

Loretta   Where is Mr Greene? Or the other Mr Greene?

Tom   Pardon?

Loretta   Greene and Greene. Two Greenes. If I'm gonna pawn my double solitaire diamond engagement ring, I'd best be speaking to one of the owners.

Tom   Ah. I'm sorry to disappoint you, but there is just one Mr Greene. And he doesn't visit the shop very often. He lives in America, you see.

Loretta   I knew I was attracted to this establishment for a damned good reason. I'm a great patriot. So's my husband. I guess you're in charge, then?

Tom   Yes. I'm the manager. Tom. As I said. Tom Warner.

Loretta   Oooo. I like that name. Like a movie studio. You're a good-looking guy, Tom Warner.

Tom   Why . . . thanks awfully. Really.

Loretta   I am Loretta, Lady Marquette. And this is my infant son, Baby Ray. Say hello to the nice man, Baby Ray.

Loretta *waves* **Ray***'s arm towards* **Tom***.*

Loretta   Ray's gonna be an Earl or something when he grows up.

Tom   Are you . . . on holiday?

Loretta   Hell, I ain't worked a day in my life, Mister Tom Warner. I am a lady.

Tom   Of course. You did say that. Of course.

Loretta   Every day's a holiday *chez* Marquette. I am currently learning several new languages. Shit, every language's a new language these days. So it's best to keep on top of the situation.

Tom   I'm not sure I understand.

Loretta   Every place you look there's a new country sprouting out the map like some kind of crabgrass. And they all got their own languages. My husband, Lester, he says there ain't no language worth talking but English. But I got this idea, see, that you got to know what your enemies are talking about.

Tom   I hadn't considered that. But you're absolutely, I mean, that's really perceptive.

Loretta   Damn right. Fact: you go to the UN, there's lots of meetings with these new countries, they're clucking away in their own languages and how do you know they ain't laughing at the USA behind your back?

Tom Well. I assume there's simultaneous translation.

Loretta You mean those headphone things?

Tom Mind you, I've not been to the United Nations but I have seen television clips. And . . . as I say, there are translators.

Loretta You tell me this, Tom Warner: how do you know those translators ain't laughing at you, too? Huh? Explain that to me.

Tom I suppose it's a matter of trust. Honour.

Loretta Uh-huh. Well. You go on and trust those headphones. You're a very nice young man, I can tell, you've got one eye bigger than the other and that's the surest sign of sincerity in my book. But you are naive, and I do hate to point that out to you.

Tom I speak a bit of Italian. That's all, I'm afraid. So I probably am naive. I'm sorry.

Loretta Now don't go apologising for the state of your human condition, honey. I just been around the block a few more times than you and it's my duty to pass on information. I like you very much, Tom.

Tom Thank you. Lady Marquette.

Loretta You got eyes like my Lester had before he turned mean.

Tom How many languages do you speak?

Loretta Fact: the meaner a man gets, the more his eyeballs shrink. (*Beat.*) I speak a little of this and a little of that. But I'm gonna buy myself some tapes. That's why I'm pawning my engagement ring. Me and Baby Ray, we're gonna listen to a shitload of tapes. How much you reckon you'll give me for the ring, Tom? Tom Warner with the beautiful eyes.

Tom   I'd have to examine it.

Loretta   Examine away, baby. Last time a man asked to examine something of mine, he found Baby Ray nestled up inside me.

She gives **Tom** *the ring with a flourish. He peers at it through a jeweller's glass.*

I am a student of history. I got to be because my Lester is a very important man and doesn't have the time to study it himself. Like Tammy Wynette says, stand by your man. Course, she also says D-I-V-O-R-C-E spells divorce. But never mind. Listen sugar, what's holding you up? You looking for gold in my double solitaire diamond?

Tom   I'm afraid there's a problem.

Loretta   Don't frown, Tom. It's not masculine. Open your eyes real big when you talk to me.

Tom   This isn't actually a double solitaire diamond.

Loretta   You're kidding.

Tom   I'm not an expert, but I do know that this is not what you say it is.

Loretta   Are you accusing me of lying?

Tom   I didn't say that. I must, however, point out that –

Loretta   You must nothing. You must hear me when I tell you that I was right there at the Sears Roebuck counter when Lester purchased that ring. I saw the label. It said: DOUBLE SOLITAIRE.

Tom   It's zircon, I'm afraid. Cubic zirconia. Double solitaire.

Loretta   What are you talking about?

Tom   It's a diamond substitute. It's very convincing, but ... it's not a diamond.

Loretta   Are you telling me that my engagement ring is made out of the stuff they sell to housewives who diddle themselves while watching Home Shopping Network?

Tom   I'm not familiar with Home Shopping Network. But I suppose, yes, that is probably what I'm telling you.

Loretta   Sears Roebuck is a reputable department store.

Tom   Yes, yes. Undoubtedly.

Loretta   You make much money, Tom?

Tom   I . . . pardon?

Loretta   Does Mr Greene or the other Mr Greene pay you enough money?

Tom   I'm on a fair wage.

Loretta   Uh-huh. But you ain't rolling in it, right?

Tom   I really can't discuss this with you.

Loretta   You don't make money. Okay. I won't judge. And I am sure nobody ever sent you to, you know, jewellery expert school, right?

Tom   I have been trained. I have had basic training and Mr Greene –

Loretta   You ain't no expert, Tom. Pretty as you are. So I don't think you oughtta be passing judgement on Lady Marquette's double solitaire engagement ring. That ring is a token of my husband's undying love and devotion to me. It is not a cheap piece of shit.

Tom   I didn't suggest it was. Look. Perhaps another shop will be happy to accommodate you.

Tom *holds out the ring to* **Loretta**. *She doesn't take it.*

Loretta   But I like *you*, Tom. Baby Ray likes you. He's a genius and communicates with me telepathically. What is your sun sign?

Tom   I don't see what it's got to do with anything. (*Beat.*) Taurus. I'm a Taurus.

Loretta   Baby Ray told me that, you know. A bull,

Mommy, that boy with the cock-eyes is a bull, he said.
And bulls are strong. But they are often stubborn. You owe
me and Baby Ray lunch, Tom.

Loretta *holds out her hand to* **Tom**. *She wiggles her fingers impatiently.*

Tom (*rather at a loss, refers to her hand*) Please, Mrs – Lady
– Marquette. I can't have fits in the shop. Please.

Loretta No, silly. It ain't a fit. Gimme my ring. (*Beat.*)
P-U-T the ring on my finger, darlin'.

Tom *slips the ring on* **Loretta**'s *finger. It's an awkward movement.*

Loretta Ooooo you have made my day, Tom. More
years ago than I care to recall, a gorgeous young man like
yourself slipped that ring on my finger. He took my breath
away. I got asthma now. Well. That was many many
stretch marks ago.

Tom You're not very old now.

Loretta Palm reader told me I am the reincarnation of
Cleopatra. I got her eyes. Snake eyes. And I got her heavy
heavy heart. Take me to lunch.

Tom Why does your son never make a sound? I mean,
babies usually cry or spit or . . . I'm sorry. It's none of my
concern.

Loretta Baby Ray talks to me the whole time, Tom.
You can't hear him is all. See? Just now, he said to me,
Mommy, that Taurus man doesn't want to take us to
lunch. He doesn't like us, Mommy. Don't you like us,
Tom? We're good solid people. You oughtta like us.

Tom It's not that. Really. But I . . . look, I barely know
you and I've got a shop to look after and you have no
idea, no idea at all what's been – I mean, it's true that I'm
wary of – some of my customers are most unsavoury types
you understand – and I don't know what to make of your
your – tales of Cleopatra and telepathy and the person I

live with despises me 'cos I can't do press-ups but I do try, I really do try to be interested, involved, you know, with his activities and and . . . bloody hell will you please just leave me alone I I I . . . fuck. Shit. I tell him, I do, I say please. Please just leave me. Alone.

A short, sharp cry is heard, presumably from **Baby Ray**.

Tom   What . . . what was that?

Loretta   Don't you get a lunch hour, Tom?

Tom   Yes I do. Of course I do. But that's not the – what was that sound? Did your son make that sound?

Loretta   I'm hungry. So hungry. Feed me.

She holds out **Baby Ray** *to* **Tom**. *A pause.*

Well. Come on, boy. Take him. I have an itch I got to scratch.

Tom   I'll drop him.

Loretta   Ain't you never held a baby, Tom?

Tom   No. Never.

Loretta   You do it just like you hold a woman. All soft and sure of yourself. I itch real bad, Tom. Take him.

Tom *takes* **Baby Ray** *from* **Loretta**. **Tom** *holds him as if he's a Martian.* **Loretta** *hikes up her skirt and has a long, slow satisfying scratch at her inner thigh.*

Loretta   Baby Ray doesn't vocalise, Tom. He never speaks out loud. You're just beginning to learn his language.

Shift to **Ava** *and* **Tina**. *Music in: 'I Will Always Love You' (Dolly Parton).* **Ava**'s *at* **Kate**'s *house.* **Tina**'s *in her crummy little trailer chopping vegetables, some of them quite inappropriate, for a salad. Far too many vegetables for one salad. During the course of the scene,* **Tina**'s *chopping becomes increasingly frenzied.* **Ava** *swigs from a bottle of whiskey. Her drinking intensifies as the scene progresses.*

Tina Mr Marshall's got this colt called Season's
Greetings, you know, on account it was foaled on
Christmas Eve? I was right there, knee-deep in hay, when
it happened. Colt plopped outta its mama and I swear,
Ava, I cried. I mean, I do have hay fever so I guess it's no
surprise I cried. But I think I was crying about the miracle
of birth or the mystery of life or something mystical like I
never think about but I should. You know, honey, I was
marvelling at this little new-born horse on Christmas Eve
and the words just rolled off my tongue: Season's
Greetings, I said to Mr Marshall. He laughed and wiped
some hay off my face and he didn't say nothing, as usual,
but later that day I noticed he signed the colt's papers with
that lovely name.

Ava We got a bad connection, Ma. I'm gonna hang up.

Tina No no honey – don't – don't do that. It's nice
hearing your voice.

Ava It ain't my phone, Ma. And I ain't paying the bill,
either. I can't hear a fucking thing you're saying, anyway.
Every time I call you I can't hear nothing. Bunch of
inbreds built the phone lines in Nevada. I swear.

Tina What? What's that you said, honey?

Ava I'm an alcoholic transvestite, Ma.

Tina That's real nice where you are, Ava. Mr Marshall's
been to Virginia many times because, as you may know,
it's an important thoroughbred racing state. Myself, I've
never been, but I'd like to. A working woman rarely
travels. Tell me all about it. Is the grass really blue?

Ava How did you – look, I didn't say a thing about
Virginia. Not one fucking word. And what are you talking
about? Huh? Kentucky in the bluegrass state, Ma. Not
Virginia. I'm dying here. I'm broke and some religious
fanatic's come to repossess my car but he won't take the
car and he won't leave my side and ... what in the fuck
are you doing over there? Sounds like you got a couple of
machetes dancing round your head.

Tina   Your daddy comes from Virginia. 'Course, I don't expect he's there any more. Not after the murders. Did you get my letter, Ava? Well, it isn't exactly a letter. It's a recording of my voice. It'd be wonderful if you could be here with me. The ranch is so peaceful this time of year. We could eat a salad. I'm eating real healthy. Nothing but vegetables, Ava. Grow 'em myself. Are you drinking much these days, honey?

Ava   *You're* a fucking vegetable, Ma. LISTEN TO ME.

Tina   Aren't you interested in your daddy? It isn't natural for a girl to lose interest in her father. I lost interest in mine and look where it's got me. Oh, sure, I got myself a fine life with Mr Marshall but he never talks to me. Sometimes I think if I had kept a healthy interest in my own daddy, I might have noticed I was marrying a man who never speaks. Isn't life funny? Isn't this song pretty? It's my favourite. I listen to it all the time when Mr Marshall's away. He gave it to me for an anniversary gift.

Ava   God forgive me and I don't know why but I love you Ma. I love you and I don't know where I'm going next and I don't give a shit about some drunk daddy I never met and I sure as fuck don't know how you know where I am but I wish you would just send me some cash and call it a day.

Tina   You still there, Ava? You say something about dinner? Oh honey, I'd love to have you over but Mr Marshall's bringing a couple of jockeys to the ranch and there just ain't the room for another mouth. Jockeys are funny men. So tiny and polite. You look real pretty today, Ava, that blouse becomes you. But you shouldn't drink whiskey out of a bottle. It isn't ladylike.

Ava   I'm going crazy. I'm going crazy and you're scaring me, Ma. I can't take this no more. I only called to fucking say HELLO.

Tina   Hello, honey. Hello. I love saying that word. Hello.

Ava   There's all sorts of things I got to understand. Like

... do you really think I can sing? And why do you call
the man you live with Mr Marshall? Don't he got a name,
Ma? I mean, a name you call him when you're, you know,
doing stuff with him? Private stuff? And why am I on the
road to some nowhere club I can't even locate?

Tina   Hello. Hello. Ava, that word, it thrills me so.

Ava   You ever hear of some place called Tumbleweed
Junction? Huh? Answer *one* of my friggin' questions, Ma,
okay?

Tina   Oh honey, what's the point. Tell me. What is the
point in answering questions when there are so many of
them? That whiskey will rot your gut. My tummy's
practically gone, I've drunk so much whisky.

Ava   I'm not like you. Don't ever say I'm like you.

Tina   And I wish you wouldn't wear so much black. It's
morbid. Your hair doesn't look healthy. Your skin's so pale.
Let me cook you some soup, honey. Or a stew. Please.

Ava   Look, I gotta go. I gotta ... this sucks, Ma.

Tina   Hello. Say hello, baby.

Ava   Goodbye, Ma.

Lights down on **Tina**. *Music out.* **Ava** *chugs the rest of the
whiskey.* **Kate** *enters. She holds a casserole dish.*

Kate   I made a stew.

Ava   I used your phone. Long-distance. But I don't have
any money, so I can't pay. Tough luck, huh?

Kate   I'm looking for a man.

Ava   Yeah? Well, you can bet he ain't looking for you.

Kate   My phone was disconnected three months ago.

Ava   Uh-uh. No way.

Kate   I don't like talking to people I can't see.

Ava   Well you may not like it, but I just called fucking

Las Vegas.

Kate Tell me about New York.

Ava It's big, it's filthy, it's got the World Trade Centre.
That about covers it.

Kate You'll help me find this man I'm looking for.

Ava Oh no. Nonono. See, me and Calvin are going
somewhere.

Kate You're lost. I found you. Eat some stew.

Ava I got a job in a club. I'm a night-club entertainer in
demand.

Kate I'm not much of a cook. But I know a few things.

Ava Hey, lady, you're making my skin crawl.

Kate I know where your club is. I'm not so bad.

Ava You what? You know this this . . . Tumbleweed
whatchamacalit place? So. Tell me already.

Kate Scratch my back and I'll scratch yours.

Ava Oh. Okay. I get it. All right. I'll chow down some of
your stew, make a little chit chat, be polite, I tell you
you're a great cook, you tell me where the club is. Blah
blah blah. I know how to scratch a little back same as the
next dope.

Kate Fine. Then do it.

Kate *sets down the casserole, lifts her shirt, turns her bare back to*
Ava.

Ava Whoa, hold on just a fucking minute. You mean . . .
like, you literally want me to scratch your back?

Kate It's extraordinarily relaxing. I need to be relaxed.

A pause before **Ava** *begins to tentatively scratch* **Kate**'s *back.*

Ava Where's Calvin?

Kate (*really enjoying this*) Ohgodohgodohgod a little higher yes yes no not there a little to the left ohyesyesyes –

Ava Hey. HEY. I said: where's Calvin?

Kate Arlington National cemetery.
Don'tstopdon'tstopdon't – theretherethere –
ahahahahyessss . . .

Ava Aw look, I don't like this shit one bit. Okay?

Kate *pulls away abruptly and pulls down her shirt. After wallowing in the luxury of the back scratch, she's suddenly all business.*

Kate Your turn.

Ava Thanks, really, but, um, no.

Kate We have a deal. You scratch my back, I scratch yours.

Ava Oh man, I'm surrounded by creeps and weirdos.

Bored, she turns her back to **Kate**. *She half-heartedly lifts up her shirt.*

I'm all yours. Hurry up.

Kate (*coming up very close to* **Ava**) I'll take you to Tumbleweed Junction. I'll drive. You'll sit next to me in the front seat. You'll wear your seat belt. Calvin will sit in the back. He doesn't have to wear his seat belt. I'll tell you stories about this man I'm looking for, you'll tell me about the Empire State building.

Ava Sure. Whatever.

Kate Not whatever. This. This, and only this.

Kate *begins to scratch* **Ava**'s *back slowly, carefully. Silence.*

Ava You know, this ain't half bad.

Kate I told you. It's relaxing.

Ava My mother's lost her mind. And the really weird thing is, I don't know if I should give a shit. Oh man, I'm such a loser. Christ. Look at me. I'm gonna cry. Gotta be PMS.

Ava *angrily wipes at her face.* **Kate** *gently places her arms around* **Ava**'s *waist. She rests her head carefully against* **Ava**'s *bare back. They stand together peacefully, in silence.*

Music in: 'Love Is in the Air' (John Paul Young). Lights up on **Otto** *in* **Loretta** *and* **Lester**'s *hotel room.* **Otto** *carries a gorgeous bunch of flowers.* **Baby Ray**'s *miniature hooded Klan robe is on the floor.* **Otto** *picks it up, examines it carefully, finds a ridiculously small portable telephone in one of its pockets. He drops the robe to the floor as if it's contaminated.*

Lights up on **Calvin** *at Arlington National Cemetery. John F. Kennedy's grave, with eternal flame. He's on all fours, crawling around the roped-off grave, trying to figure out how the flame works.*

Lights up on **Martin** *and* **Lester** *regarding a very scary looking multi-gym.* **Lester**'s *never seen one of these before, and is very much a kid in a candy shop.*

Lights up on **Tina** *in her trailer, surrounded by mountains of chopped vegetables. She sits engulfed by them. She eats salad out of a salad bowl. She watches a tiny portable television.*

Lights up on **Tom**, **Loretta** *and* **Suzy** *in* **Tom**'s *flat. They are using an Ouija board, its planchette moving furiously to and fro beneath their fingertips.* **Baby Ray** *is sat on* **Loretta**'s *lap. She's guided his baby-sized fingertips onto the planchette, as well.*

Ava My mother listens to songs that nobody else can hear. I think I'm hearing one of them right now.

Kate Sssh. I hear it too.

Ava Oh yeah? How do you know which one I'm listening to?

Otto *dials a number on the portable phone.*

Otto Reception? Mink here. Yes. Yes. That's right. Three days, you say? I see. But they haven't checked out. Yes yes I realise – the clothes on their backs are all they have. Nor have I seen or heard – that's why I'm here, you fool. How in the world can you lose track of them for three days?

Calvin *removes a small pamphlet from his back pocket. He reads from it.*

Calvin   The miracle of the eternal flame is, in fact, not so much a mystery as it is a remarkable feat of engineering and testament to man's enduring ingenuity. (*A beat as he considers this.*) Well. Go figure.

Lester   How long you reckon I got to fiddle with this stuff before there's, you know, an improvement?

Martin   You've wasted considerable time, Lester. All of it gone to indolence. Best to begin straight away. On your back.

Martin *pushes* **Lester** *firmly, but without real force, onto his back on the multi-gym.*

Lester   You know, I'm the kinda guy who just has to think about exercise and a couple of muscles pop out. Look. Here's one in my arm now.

Martin *looms over* **Lester**, *stands straddling him and the multi-gym.*

Martin   Been years since you've had a proper workout, though, hasn't it?

Tina (*chomping down salad and watching the telly avidly*)   You give it to the fat bastard crook, Oprah honey. You tell him. We ain't gonna take it any more from scumbags who cut out on their wives. Oh you look just great, Oprah. Trim and tight and lean. I hope you didn't suffer too much for it, honey. I hope you ate lots of salads. I hope that man you're marrying doesn't turn out to be a no account prick. Be careful.

And at **Tom**'s *place, the Ouija planchette's jerking about the board at an alarming rate.*

Suzy   K-A-T-E-B-U-C-K. Bugger. The bloody thing's spelling out the name of that nutter who's been writing to me.

Loretta   Hush, woman. Can't you see Baby Ray's concentrating? He's telling us things.

Tom L-I-V-E . . .

Suzy Fuck. I can't take my hand away from the damned thing. Fuck.

Loretta Come on, baby. That's a good baby. Tell us things, Ray.

Tom . . . R-P-O-O-L.

Martin (*to* **Lester**, *refers to the multi-gym*) Lift you arms, grab hold of the handles and pull down. Push up, pull down. Very simple.

Lester *does so with considerable difficulty.* **Martin** *lowers himself into a sitting position onto* **Lester***'s lap.*

Otto (*into the phone*) We had a date at the registry office for fuck's sake. Nono – you misunder – Marquette was unaware. Yes yes the divorce papers – look. The woman was to marry me today. Of course she didn't know. Why should she know? It was a bloody SURPRISE, man.

Otto *hurls the telephone down in disgust.*

Ava When's Calvin coming back?

Kate When the flame dies down.

The Ouija board's planchette movement is at a frenzied peak.

Tom Liverpool.

Loretta G-R-E-E-N-E-M-I-N-K.

Kate Greenemink?

Loretta Yup. Greenemink.

Tom Liverpool Greenemink. Huh?

Ava Hey. What's your name? I don't know your name.

Kate *turns* **Ava** *around to face her.*

Kate Kate. I'm Kate Buck.

Ava I'm sorry I used your phone.

Kate   Don't worry. There won't be a bill.

Lester (*pumping away*)   Man, this takes me back to the old days at Fort Bening. And Loretta's really gonna love the new me.

Martin *quite suddenly grabs* **Lester**'s *balls.* **Lester** *starts to let out a scream,* **Martin** *clamps his hand over* **Lester**'s *mouth.*

Martin   Is she? Well. I don't know when you're going to have the time to show Loretta the new you. You're such a busy boy, aren't you, between your male bonding at Klan meetings and your historical reading. And now, your new fitness regimen. No – don't make a sound. Don't you dare. This is character building, lesson one: take the pain. Oh my: I feel your muscle growing larger as I speak. Transform the pain, Lester. Just close your eyes and think of England. I do.

Martin *squeezes* **Lester**'s *balls tighter and tighter.*

Kate *leans in towards* **Ava**, *as if to kiss her.*

The Ouija's planchette begins to spin in uncontrollable circles.

Otto   LORETTA LORETTA I NEED LORETTA LORETTA I WANT LORETTA WHY LORETTA WHY HAVE YOU BETRAYED ME?

Otto *drops to his knees and lets out a quite unearthly and long cry of sorrow and deep deep pain. He flings the gorgeous bunch of flowers away. At the moment* **Otto** *lets out his cry, these things happen simultaneously:*

Kate, *about to plant a kiss on* **Ava**'s *lips, covers her ears as if reacting to the most piercing, painful sound she's ever heard.* **Ava** *faints, dead away.*

Martin, *squeezing* **Lester**'s *balls ever tighter, hurls himself off* **Lester** *and the multi-gym as if he's been hit in the stomach by some mammoth force.* **Lester** *hyperventilates.*

Tina's *tiny portable television set explodes.*

The Ouija board's planchette flies off violently and with great speed, up up and away.

Otto*'s bunch of flowers lands on JFK's grave at Arlington National Cemetery. The eternal flame is suddenly extinguished.*

And without warning or prelude, the sound of a tremendous approaching storm, like a hurricane or a tornado — wind, like a portent, overwhelms the space. **Ava** *sits up suddenly, wide awake.*

The space darkens ominously, as if it's closing in on its inhabitants. Everybody looks to the sky as if it holds some kind of common answer.

Blackout.

Act Two

Lester *and* **Martin** *in* **Lester***'s hotel room.* **Lester** *fidgets with* **Baby Ray***'s Klan robe.*

Lester I know where I seen you before. You're a homo.

Martin Do you think you're telling me something I haven't heard before?

Lester My wife's up and disappeared on me and I'm stuck with a homo fitness freak. (*Refers to the robe.*) This damned thing's soaked. Smells salty. Like somebody's been crying in it.

Lester *drops the robe to the floor.*

Martin You've a free will. Go.

Lester You're sitting in *my* hotel room, mister.

Martin I was invited.

Lester 'Cause I couldn't *move*. I couldn't move an inch after what you done to me. You had to help me get back to my hotel. You owed me that. Now, I got places to get to and I'm running way behind.

Martin Still. I was invited.

Lester You live across that air shaft. I seen homos across that air shaft. Therefore, you are a homo.

Martin Your analytical skills astound me.

Lester Don't look like anybody's home. I seen you there. You and your boyfriend.

Martin I knew you had voyeuristic tendencies. Good. We can work with that.

Lester Dancing around doing, I don't know, weird homo

shit with weights. I seen it.

Martin Your vocabulary is extremely limited, Lester. There are many more interesting words you could use. For instance: queer, pouf, faggot, nancy boy, ponce. To name but a few.

Lester I thought you was on the level with me, man. How could you . . . shit. You people disgust me.

Martin You entered my pub. So to speak. You honed right in. Like radar. It's uncanny, wouldn't you say?

Lester Hey, man, you caught me off guard.

Martin The refrain of weak men the world over. I could teach you something about overcoming weakness, Lester. If you'd let me.

Lester I got no time for you. I gotta find my wife and my son.

Martin She's gone. Done a runner on you, Lester. She smelled the weakness. Same as I do.

Lester I shoulda let her go out and catch a flick or something. I shoulda . . . you know, women are way unpredictable.

Martin Moody. Subject to erratic behaviour.

Lester Yeah, yeah . . . whoa. I ain't gonna start taking advice from you. You don't know shit about women.

Martin And why not? I probably know more about women than you. Considering how much time you spend at – what was it called? Tinker's?

Lester You're a mean motherfucker.

Martin But you like my meanness. Cowards always admire meanness. Though you wouldn't begin to question its source.

Lester Hell, I don't got to ask no more questions about you. I already got the answers.

Martin   Omnipotence is such an attractive quality.

Lester   You're talking mumbo jumbo, man, and my watch is ticking.

Martin *grabs* **Lester** *by his shirt front and pulls* **Lester** *very close to him.*

Martin   Listen to me you animal. I come from a place that's full of light. A light that you have tried to obliterate through the ravages of scorn and ignorance. Look at me closely, Lester. LOOK.

Lester   Don't hurt me, man, don't hurt me or I'll . . . I'll . . .

Martin   What? What will you do? Run back to your window and spy on another couple of queers? LOOK AT ME. What do you see, tell me. What do you see.

Lester   Hey, I don't know, you're . . . like, you're a good-looking guy, you're pretty tough and listen, I know you got lots of friends, okay, I know you got –

Martin   Do you see my defences, Lester? I have built an impenetrable core of darkness to replace all that lost bright light and believe me, it's wonderful to have you here like this, up-close and at my mercy.

Lester   HEY – I AIN'T NEVER DONE NOTHING TO YOU, MAN. I AIN'T DONE NOTHING.

Martin *very suddenly pulls* **Lester** *towards him and kisses him, a deep, long kiss. And just as suddenly,* **Martin** *releases him.* **Lester** *reels backwards.*

Lester (*frantically trying to wipe the kiss away*)   Oh shit I'm gonna die now. I'm gonna die I'm gonna die I'm gonna fucking die –

Martin   LOOK AT ME. I'M PERFECT. I'M A MAGNIFICENT MACHINE. DO I LOOK SICK? I'M FUCKING IMPERVIOUS.

Lester (*quite beside himself, tearing at the skin around his*

mouth)   You killed me killed me killed me and now I'm
gonna die I'm gonna die oh sweet Jesus where's my son oh
lord my son my wife my my my –

Martin *picks up* **Baby Ray**'s *robe from the floor.*

Martin   You know, Lester, I think the Roman generals
probably snogged each other as a form of greeting. (*Beat.*)
Your tongue is very rough. And salty. Excessive salt intake
is not consistent with the aims of any decent fitness
programme. (*Beat.*) Who would have thought we'd see the
day when a simple kiss, the purest act of tenderness, could
wreak such havoc among the ignorant, and at such cost?

Lester (*he's babbling*)   My son my wife my son my wife my
life for yours my life for nothing nothing everything
nothing ohohohoh –

Martin *helps* **Lester** *to his feet. He uses the Klan robe to wipe
away the spittle and general mess of* **Lester**'s *face.*

Martin   I feel the urge to fly. Don't you? I think . . .
America. Take me to your leader. Isn't that what you
people say when you're captured by the enemy? I do hope
you're a good travel companion, Lester.

He sneezes three times.

Must have picked up your bug, eh?

Shift focus to **Tom**, **Loretta** *and* **Suzy** *in Liverpool.* **Tom** *holds*
Baby Ray *like he's an old hand at infant care. The occasional
sound of a train rumbling beneath them.*

Loretta   This is it. Right here. This is where Baby Ray
wants us to be. Liverpool.

Suzy   How do you know?

Tom   She just knows, Suzy. Leave it at that, will you?

Loretta   Okay. We're here. We're ready. (*Beat.*) What are
we ready for?

Tom   Greenemink?

Suzy   There is no such thing as *green* mink. This is foolish. I'm shit scared.

Loretta   Whatcha scared of, sugar? We're alive and kicking and there ain't a thing can touch us now.

Suzy   How can you be so sure of that?

Loretta   I believe.

Suzy   In what for fucksake?

Loretta   In my belief.

Tom   She's got a point, Suzy. I haven't been afraid of anything since, well, since I've met Lady Marquette.

A particularly loud train passes beneath them.

Suzy   What are we waiting for?

Loretta   Instructions.

Suzy   From whom?

Loretta   Who really cares, sweetheart? It's a sunny day and we got ourselves stood in front of the prettiest building I've ever seen. Look. Look at the pretty columns, Baby Ray. They're Roman, I think. Baby Ray's learning lots about the Romans.

Suzy   This is too weird. It's the eclipse. Got to be the eclipse.

Tom   This is the old law courts, Lady Marquette.

Suzy   Would you *please* stop calling her that? It's driving me bonkers.

Loretta   This is the law courts. Fine. Let's go inside and get us a little justice.

Tom   Brilliant. I've wanted that for such a long time.

Suzy   They're shut down, Tom. *Abandoned.*

Loretta   Nonsense, woman. I hear them big ole wheels of justice spinning underneath our feet.

Suzy   Those are trains beneath us, daft bitch.

Loretta   Suzy the cynical. That figures. But you tell me this, missy: what's the point of having law courts if they're closed?

Suzy   How should I know? This is Liverpool. I never question anything that happens here.

Loretta   Fact: The wheels of justice never stop spinning, even if there's nobody home inside the law courts.

Tom   I'd like a hearing before a judge. There's lots I want to say.

Loretta   Take my hand, Tom. We're gonna walk together with our heads held high.

Tom   I'd like that.

Tom *and* **Loretta** *join hands.*

Suzy   This is absolutely absurd.

Loretta   Tell me what kinda justice you're gonna ask the judge for, Tom.

Tom   I . . . there's . . . so much. I mean, there's so much I can't begin to think of what to say.

Loretta   Okay. I'll start: I want the bastards who make fun of my accent shot through their hearts. Your turn.

Tom   I want . . . a position that matches my qualifications. Yes. That's it.

Loretta   And Lester will be forgiven for blowing up that truck stop with all them unfortunate people inside.

Tom   Your husband's a murderer?

Loretta   Well, it wasn't his fault. He didn't know what he was doing. See, we was sitting inside a Chevy Nova with this English fella, you know, he's kinda like Lester's patron or something, and this fella hands Lester something that looks like, whaddyacallit, one of them joysticks? And then he goes, here, Lester, push this button. So Lester pushes

the button and boom. Truck stop across the US Highway
blows like a geyser. Boom. Just like that, we're fugitives,
Lester and me. All 'cause of some crazy Brit who says
Lester's gonna be elected to the US House of
Representatives next year and we're all gonna get fat as
houses and rich as shit as a result.

Tom   Blimey.

Loretta   You bet your ass, honey. Okay. So what do we
want? One: A better job for my friend with the kind eyes.
Two: Me and Lester don't got to be fugitives. What else?

Tom   A satellite dish. A Moroccan holiday.

Loretta   A set of bone china. An Encyclopaedia
Britannica for Baby Ray. And I want . . . titties as sweet
and round as melons.

Tom   When I walk into a club, I want people to want
me.

Suzy (*reluctantly joining in*)   My own astrology column in the
Daily Mail. And two dates with Harrison Ford. Okay –
one. One f'n date with Harrison Ford.

Tom   To be the most brilliant medical researcher ever.
And to snog the bloke with the biggest cock in the world
whilst dining with a Royal.

Loretta   What did you just say, Tom Warner?

Tom   Well. It's justice, isn't it? I'm so happy, Lady
Marquette. I can't think why, though.

Loretta   Baby Ray ain't never been held by no gay.

Tom   Hasn't turned him into a pillar of salt yet, has it?

Suzy   Look. Over there. The doors are opening. The law
court is . . . open.

Loretta   There's the judge.

Suzy   Let's go, Tom. Now. Please.

Tom   She's right. It is a judge. He's bearing gifts.

Loretta (*calling out to the unseen presence*) COME ON OVER HERE, MISTER, AND SPREAD A LITTLE OF THAT JUSTICE AROUND.

Tom I don't believe it. It's Mr Greene.

Loretta No. No it ain't. It's Mr Mink.

Suzy Oh no. Greenemink. Minkgreene. It's like that film, you know, Redrum redrum. I'm out of here.

Otto *enters. He does bear gifts: a letter and some wilted flowers. He smiles an angelic smile. He holds out the letter to* **Suzy***.*

Otto Good afternoon, Miss Bradfield. I believe this letter is for you.

Suzy Who are you? Why have you come out from inside of an abandoned law court? How do you know –

Otto Never mind, my dear. You know, the chap who designed these courts committed suicide. A most unfortunate incident. Apparently, his plans called for a rather elaborate inner courtyard, very much like the courtyard which you now face. As luck would have it, our poor architect's fortunes blossomed and he could not supervise the building of these courts. When finally he arrived to witness the opening, he discovered that his inner courtyard had become an outer courtyard. Shortly afterwards, he topped himself. Take the letter, Miss Bradfield. Open it in private.

Suzy *takes the letter.*

Loretta That's a truly heartbreaking story, Mr Mink, but I sure as hell don't why you told it.

Otto It's a parable, Loretta.

Loretta I don't remember that being in the Bible.

Otto Hello, Tom. Have you decided on a bit of a holiday? Did you phone for permission to shut the shop?

Suzy *surreptitiously tries to open the letter.*

Otto (*without looking at her*)   Miss Bradfield. I said: you are to read the contents of that letter in private. (*Beat.*) Well, Tom. What have you to say for yourself?

Tom   I ... I don't ... I can't ... (*Suddenly gains in confidence.*) How is it you're both Mr Greene and Mr ... what was it?

Loretta   Mink. Otto Mink. He's a political media consultant.

Otto   Sometimes I'm one, sometimes the other. There's no harm in it. And it's really none of your concern.

Otto *holds out the flowers to* **Loretta**.

Loretta   Gee thanks a bundle. Just what I wanted. Dead daisies.

Otto   They are not daisies, Loretta. And you could not imagine what I've been through to get them to you. I moved heaven and earth.

Loretta   Why? What's the big occasion?

Tom   Did you bring something for me, Mr Greene?

A slight pause, as **Otto** *glares at* **Tom**.

Otto   Something quite astonishing's about to happen to you, Loretta. Come.

Otto *holds out his arm to* **Loretta**.

Loretta   Where we going?

Otto   To the courts, Loretta. The courts.

Loretta   In there? Is it safe?

Otto   It's what you want.

Loretta   Yeah, but, is it *safe*? We gonna get tons of plaster and shit falling on top of our heads? I seen a 911 Emergency episode like that.

Otto   What do you want? Safety? Or Justice?

Loretta You know, they ain't exactly mutually whaddyacallit whatever.

Otto Aren't they?

Loretta Okay. But I want Tom with me. And Baby Ray. They deserve whatever I end up getting

Otto As you wish. Come, then.

Loretta *slips her arm through his.*

Suzy You're not leaving me here, are you?

Loretta Find your own justice, sister.

Loretta, **Tom** *and* **Otto** *begin to exit. The light coming from the direction of the law courts darkens noticeably.*

Otto The doors are beginning to close. We must hurry.

Loretta, **Tom** *and* **Otto** *exit.* **Suzy** *looks after them as the light grows dimmer and dimmer.*

Suzy What am I to do? What can I – I've got no *money*. I can't get back. Ooooo FUCK.

Suzy *rips open the letter with some irritation. Several fifty-pound notes drop out.*

Lights up on **Kate**, *behind the wheel of a yellow Chevy Nova. Beside her,* **Ava** *sleeps, strapped in by her seat belt. In the back seat,* **Calvin** *peers alternatively at a map and at the road whizzing by them. They're driving due west.*

Calvin What's the town we just passed through?

Kate Tut's Hut, Idaho.

Calvin That's what I thought.

Kate Why do you ask?

Calvin Nothing important, really. It's just . . . it's not on the map.

Kate I know that.

Calvin Oh. All right. (*Beat.*) Why are we speeding? The road's empty.

Kate   You never know what's coming up behind you.

Suzy (*reading from the letter*)   Dear Suzy, who needs you.
Who. Not me. It's useless to pretend there was no
connection between us, nevertheless, who needs you. Not
me. Don't pretend you meant to run an ad in a magazine
that doesn't exist. I checked it out. Astrology Monthly
never existed. Your ad had my name written all over it.
But never mind. I have since found my very own personal
native New Yorker. We are touring the United States and
we are terribly happy together. She doesn't know this yet,
but she will in due time. So who needs you. Not me. I am
on a mission to find a dangerous terrorist and I feel certain
I am getting closer to him. I won't be in touch again
because, as you can tell, I am very very VERY busy
without you. I'm enclosing one hundred fifty pounds,
which, by the way, I had a great deal of difficulty getting
in Arlington. But I did get it because I am a decent
woman who wants to save you the hassle. The money is
not a gift, it's for my chart. If you're such a fucking good
astrologer, then you'll have no difficulty guessing my birth
details. Good luck. And Suzy, guess what: NOBODY
NEEDS YOU LEAST OF ALL ME. Kate Buck.

Kate *slams on the brakes. She blasts the car horn, holds it down.*

Calvin   What's wrong. WHAT'S WRONG.

Kate *continues to blast the horn;* **Suzy** *reacts as if she, too, hears the horn wailing away.*

Music in: 'I Don't Know How to Love Him' (Yvonne Elliman).
Shift focus to **Martin** *and* **Lester** *seated at a table in* **Martin**'s
flat. **Martin** *eats breakfast and reads a tabloid. He's enjoying the
music.* **Lester** *isn't eating. He just stares at* **Martin***. This goes on
for some time.* **Martin** *sneezes once.*

Martin   Eat something.

Lester   I'm on a hunger strike. All political martyrs do
hunger strikes.

Martin   Suit yourself.

More silence from **Lester***;* **Martin** *continues with breakfast, music and tabloid.*

Lester   You're holding me hostage.

Martin   Here's a sordid little story. Bloke in America plants a bomb in a truck stop. Kills twenty-seven Baptist ministers.

Martin *sneezes twice.*

Lester   Kidnapping is a federal offence, buddy.

Martin   So is murder. Why do you suppose twenty-seven Baptist ministers convened at a truck stop?

Lester   I could send you down on lots of charges. This ain't legal.

Martin   Are you able to walk, Lester?

Lester   Yeah, yeah. I can walk. What's it to you?

Martin   Then walk. Leave. I don't see that you're shackled or bound and gagged. Would you like to be bound and gagged?

A pause, as **Lester** *considers this.*

Lester   Maybe them Baptist preachers had it coming to them.

Martin   Why do you stay, Lester? Why did you follow me back to my flat? What's the fascination? (*Mocking* **Lester***, sings along to the song.*) I don't know how to love him . . . what to do . . . how to moooove him.

Martin *coughs a bit.*

Lester   Maybe them Baptist preachers was spies. Or traitors.

Martin   For whom were they spying?

Lester   You know, whoever . . . spies *spy* for. Other governments. Enemies.

Martin   Well. I'm sure they gathered loads of valuable information in Denny's Roadside Diner. (*Beat.*) The murderer will surely get the gas chamber, don't you think?

Lester   Yeah, well, he's a hero in my book. I mean, just twenty-seven less nigger preachers to deal with. Hardly a dent in the, you know, the iceberg.

Martin   The story does not refer to race one way or the other.

Lester   Sure, but, deep south, it stands to reason Baptists are . . . shit man, in Virginia every other Baptist's a nigger snake handler.

Martin   I didn't say where the truck stop was. In fact, it *was* in Virginia. Lynchburg, Virginia. How appropriate. And how perceptive of you.

Lester   I'm pretty fucking smart, mister. (*Beat.*) You been listening to this pussy song all morning. I'm gonna vomit all over your pristine faggot floors, you don't turn it off.

Martin *coughs a bit more.*

Martin   What's wrong, Lester, did you sleep through the seventies?

Lester   You think I'm stupid, right? I'm not stupid. I know this song. I know it comes from some fucked-up limey musical thee-a-ter thingamajig with a bunch of hippies humping Jesus and and . . . sacrilegious crap, that's what it is. People will buy any old shit but not me. No sir. I know what's what.

Martin   This from a man who applauds the murder of twenty-seven black Baptist ministers. Let me ponder that one. You're obviously way ahead of me.

Lester *overturns the table. Music out.* **Martin** *has a violent sneezing and coughing fit. A pause, as neither man moves.* **Suzy** *enters, carrying a tabloid. She looks very much worse for wear.*

Suzy   (*excitedly, referring to the tabloid*)   She really is looking for a man. A terrorist. Christ. She actually is a journalist.

Here. HERE. Kate Buck. Kate Buck. This story is
fantastic. Absolutely brilliant. A dangerous felon on the lam
and Kate Buck pursues his trail against the odds. Brilliant.
(*Notices, for the first time, the overturned table, etc.*) Have I
interrupted something important?

*A pause. The men ignore her. They are absolutely focused on one
another, neither moving the tiniest bit.* **Suzy** *isn't clocking anything,
though, and sets about cleaning up the mess, re-righting the table and
such.*

Suzy   Anyway, isn't it funny how things turn out? Here I
was thinking she was a first-rate nutter with an alias. I
mean, I hadn't any reason to think she was *actually* called
Kate Buck. It's got a sort of Mills and Boon ring to it, you
know? I'm impressed. Really. She's risking her all for . . .
for . . . well, I don't know exactly *why* she's doing it. God
knows I wouldn't, but I'm sure it's for the best.

Martin   (*without losing his focus on* **Lester**)   Where've you
been, Suzy?

Suzy   You look awful. Martin.

Martin   Bit of the flu.

Suzy   Ah. (*Beat.*) I think she's really admirable. In context.
She wants me to do her chart.

Martin   Where's you been, Suzy?

Suzy   Liverpool. (*Beat.*) Honestly, Martin, have I
interrupted . . . you know . . . (*Takes notice of* **Lester**.) Oh.
Hello. How rude of me not to have introduced myself.
Suzy Bradfield. Astrologer.

She offers her hand to **Lester**. *He doesn't take it.*

Lester   I got to go to Liverpool.

Suzy   Oh. Holiday?

Lester   Business. Big business.

Martin   Where's Tom?

Suzy   Tom. Well. Tom's been kidnapped.

Martin   He isn't worth the trouble.

Suzy   It's not really . . . look, I suppose he hasn't been kidnapped. But he has gone away. With a woman.

Lester   *I've* been kidnapped.

Suzy   How horrible for you. Was it terribly frightening?

Lester   I am Martin's hostage. Right now.

A pause, as **Suzy** *considers this. The men have kept their focus on each other.*

Suzy   Ah. Yes. Well, I'm sure you'll work it out between yourselves.

Martin   So. Tom's done a runner with a woman.

Suzy   And her child.

Martin   Oh. A tot, as well. Fucking brilliant. Who's going to do the washing-up now?

A pause, as **Martin** *smiles maliciously at* **Lester**.

Lester   I got to get to Liverpool. I got a job to do. I got to find my wife.

Suzy   Well, I suggest you catch a train from Euston. They run fairly regularly and it's not a bad journey, not really, considering . . . I'm sorry, I didn't catch your name . . .

Lester   Lester Marquette. Political candidate for election to the US House of Representatives, state of Virginia.

Suzy (*after a beat*)   Fucking hell. You're . . . no. It can't be. A coincidence, a really strange coincidence. Have you noticed the alarming rate of coincidences lately? Kate Buck says –

Lester   What coincidence? Why are you looking at me that way, lady? Huh? Whatcha looking at?

Suzy   The terrorist. In Kate Buck's story. He's called Lester Marquette, too. Isn't that weird? You know, I feel I know Kate Buck so well.

Martin *laughs.* **Lester** *snatches the tabloid from* **Suzy** *and scans it frantically.* **Martin** *continues to laugh.*

Lester   Oh shit. Oooooh shit. Man, I got to get in touch with Mink. Where the *fuck* is he? WHERE? No names. Supposed to be no names mentioned. NO NAMES. NO GODDAMNED NAMES.

Martin's *laughter is now mixed with coughs and sneezes.* **Lester** *slumps back, unable to cope with this new information.* **Suzy**, *at a complete loss, continues to clean.*

Suzy (*to* **Lester**)   Ehm. I hope you don't mind me asking, but, are you really a member of the Ku Klux Klan?

A pause, as **Lester** *regards* **Martin** *coolly.* **Martin**'s *coughing/ laughing seizure is now really alarming.*

Lester (*to* **Suzy**)   You got any cough syrup, lady?

Shift focus to **Tina**, *on the job in the ladies' room at Tumbleweed Junction. She scrubs at the floor with a pathetic, basically eaten-away foam sponge. She occasionally dips the sponge into a bucket of dirty water. Distant sounds from the casino: slot machines, bells, sirens.* **Tina** *speaks into the miniature Dictaphone.*

Tina   Dear Ava. As I can't seem to remember the details of our last telephone conversation, I thought I'd send along another tape. It's weird that I can't remember what we spoke about. There was an eighty-eight-year-old woman on Phil Donahue's show who woke up one morning unable to remember anything that happened to her after her tenth birthday party. A psychiatrist said she'd been traumatised. And I thought, well, why did the trauma wait eighty years to hit? Seems like everybody's traumatised these days and really, Ava, I am ashamed to say I do not buy it. But who am I? I'm not an expert, so maybe that's what happened to us. Trauma, which was carried by the telephone line. Like lightning, which I have heard does strike people through telephone lines more frequently than you might imagine. Ava, I will be honest. Things are not good and

I'm not sure I have the strength to continue at
Tumbleweed Junction. There hasn't been any toilet paper
here going on two weeks and Mr Greene hasn't turned up
in days. I don't got any cleaning materials, and the toilets
are in an awful mess. I mean, I tried to use some lye soap
I kept for emergencies in the trailer, but that ran out pretty
quick. I guess casino gambling gives people the runs. I
didn't get my last pay cheque and God knows when Mr
Marshall's gonna show up and really honey, I don't think
he's gonna turn up at all but I got to believe he will. So
most days I show up at the casino out of habit and I scrub
the floor with water, but it's no good. No good at all. It's
like my routine has become a memory of its former self but
since the memory ain't a fond one, what's the point? Oh
Ava, I fear I'm not making a damned bit of sense.

Lights up on **Calvin** *and* **Ava**. **Ava** *sorts through an open suitcase
full of outfits for her club routines. She hands one to* **Calvin**.

Ava   Whaddya think?

Calvin   It's very . . . Shirley Bassey.

Ava   You think?

Calvin   Yes, yes I do. It's not a bad way to go, Ava.
Goldfinger is a night-club classic.

Ava   Nah. It's too, you know, too queeny.

Calvin   But you're a female impersonator, Ava. There is
a certain logic to doing something queeny.

Ava   Yeah, but . . . I wanna do something, I don't know.
daring. Not expected.

Calvin   How about Joan Baez? I've always liked Joan
Baez. She's politically aware and I admire that in popular
singers.

Ava   Uh-huh. Well, I do Joan Baez and I'll bore the
audience to death. All that Gracias a la whatever shit.

Calvin (*clearly a bit hurt*)   I'm sorry. It was just a
suggestion.

Tina I been thinking about your daddy so much, Ava. I don't know why. And that was before I seen that newspaper story about his latest criminal activities. It's amazing how you can go for years without thinking of somebody and then ... well, there may be a reason for everything, but I can't figure out a reason for anything. I think that's why we have philosophers, to figure out those reasons. But I have noticed that most philosophers tend to be French or German, and not American, I guess 'cause in those countries way back when, there was nothing to do but think. Americans were busy building roads and putting the Injuns in their place and dealing with, you know, all the stuff we had to catch up with on account of us being a new country. So if we don't got philosophers here, I wonder if that means we are doomed never to think of the right answers for why stuff happens.

Ava Listen, Calvin. I like you. But you ain't the king of style, I gotta say. (*Beat.*) So what's she doing in there, palm readings or mind readings or whatever that scary stuff she does is? I swear, I wish the ground woulda swallowed me up back there in that, that ... what was that loony tunes place we was at yesterday?

Calvin Brighton Village. A reproduction early American settlement.

Ava Yeah, like Disneyland except instead of Mickey Mouse you got fucking Puritans or something and half naked yo-yos painted red to look like Indians except it's so hot the make up blisters all over their bodies and they end up looking like goddamned lepers and wacko Kate tells one of them he would end up in the fucking slammer before Christmas on grand theft auto charges and I coulda died, I coulda just died of embarrassment right there in front of the imitation ye oldee worldee Martha Washington.

Calvin (*after a beat*) Kate is not a wacko.

Ava No. Not exactly. She's more like a wackette.

Calvin She cares for you a great deal. Why do you

never notice when people care for you, Ava?

Ava (*after a beat*)   Okay. She's not so bad. Okay?

Calvin   And you should have paid more attention to Brighton Village. It's a remarkable piece of living history. Especially the silversmith's –

Ava (*extremely irritated with him*)   Why don't you just blow it out your ass already?

Tina   I know I said it before but I got to say it again and again so it makes sense to me: things are not good. They are not good at all, Ava. I'm too old to be on my knees all day and I don't like the way the hotel customers sneer at me on their way to the john, like they're saying, hell, that hag's too old to be scrubbing floors even though I ain't old at all, honey, hell, I'm barely past forty I think. It's just I look older than time itself and yes, maybe that's because I had one husband who fucked off when I gave birth to a girl and now I got another one who can't stand me so much he lives in his truck. But I can't help thinking it's also got something to do with the fact that I got a daughter who ain't interested in where she comes from any more. Those casino gamblers look at me while they're pissing out champagne and I hear them thinking. They think: why have the toilet scrubber's children let her get to that state? It's criminal. And I got to admit, Ava, I got to ask: don't you feel ashamed, honey?

Calvin   Kate's filing her new story. Information comes to her in dreams, in odd flashes of deduction while she's driving. She says it's like a thousand-piece jigsaw puzzle of a Jackson Pollock painting. Unfathomable but logical. And you've inspired that. I envy her.

Ava   I wouldn't spend too much time envying Kate I'm-Dreaming-As-Fast-As-I-Can Buck. Didn't she get fired from her last job for dreaming up information?

Calvin   That was a different situation, at a different time.

Ava   Facts are facts. Where I come from, newspaper types deal in facts, not in the twilight zone.

Calvin Fact is relative sometimes.

Ava Uh-huh. Well, my mother's a relative sometimes.

Tina I got fifteen dollars and thirty-nine cents in my checking account and Mr Marshall's absconded with the two hundred dollars in my Christmas Club account. So there's no gifts in your future this year, Ava. There's no gifts in mine, either. My TV blew up the other day and the trailer shook right off its foundation. And I don't know why I'm recording this stuff honey, because you and me both know I'm never gonna send you the tape. The truth ain't never been a help to neither one of us but oh God I sure wish I knew what could be a help to us 'cause we need it bad.

Tina *drops the Dictaphone into the bucket of dirty water.*

Ava (*clutches at her chest*) Christ. Feels like my lungs are filling up with water. Shit. I think I'm *drowning*.

Calvin *moves to help her.*

Tina Hell with it. I'm going for broke at the slots.

Tina *tosses the sponge into the bucket of dirty water. She begins to exit, turns back, retrieves the Dictaphone from the bucket and exits.*

Calvin Stress. Too much stress in one so young. You should read more often. Reading relaxes as well as informs.

Ava Get your hands off me. (*He does.*) You got cold hands, Calvin, and books give me a headache. (*A beat.*) Phew. I feel much better now.

She rummages through the suitcase, picks out an outfit.

Rosemary Clooney. That's original. Whaddya think?

Shift focus to **Tom**, **Loretta** *and* **Baby Ray** *in the Liverpool law courts.* **Loretta** *breast-feeds* **Baby Ray**. *They wander around in circles.*

Loretta Looky there. They got the stations of the cross up on the wall.

Tom   I don't think so. It's not a church.

Loretta   Honey, church, court – same thing back where I come from. Oh my, and they're three-dimensional stations, too. Look: you can see Jesus's blood trickling down from his crown of thorns.

Tom   I don't know how long we've been here. I've lost track of time.

Loretta   Coupla days, I reckon. Or maybe a week. Who knows? Mr Mink/Greene said we'd be provided for and I believe him. Ooooo look at Saint Veronica making a photocopy of Jesus's face with her handkerchief.

Tom   Do you miss your husband, Lady Marquette?

Loretta   You know, I don't. I expect he's doing okay for himself. Lester's kind of a weasel and I spend a lot of time convincing him he's smart when really he's got the IQ of a flea, but I like the way his hair stands on end in the morning like it's full of electricity.

Tom   But what's it like waking up next to a criminal?

Loretta   Lester's not a criminal, sweetheart, he just wants to be famous. Don't you want to be famous?

Tom   Not really.

Loretta   That's a true shame, Tom Warner.

Tom   Why?

Loretta   I don't know. It's just something solid to believe in, like when you call the talking clock and it tells you the exact time.

Tom   I've always wanted to own my own beauty salon, but it's a bit of a gay cliché, so . . . But I do like hair. Not to cut it, mind you, but to wash it, run my fingers through a really smashing head of hair, you know?

Loretta   Lester's going bald.

Tom I never feel close to a man until I run my fingers through his hair. I'd be able to do that all day long in my own beauty salon and never have to put up with the rest.

Loretta The rest of what?

Tom You know, the whole lot. Dating, clubbing, sex, possible commitment, more sex, more dating, too many clubs, bad performance art, disillusionment, less sex, no sex, the end.

Loretta Hell, that sounds just like real dating between men and women, except for the performance whatever. You got such pretty eyes, Tom. I bet you could have any sailor in port.

Tom My flatmate makes me feel inadequate. (*Beat.*) Sailors are a bit passé, Lady Marquette.

Loretta I am trying to make some social chit-chat around a difficult subject, okay? Don't make it harder on me.

Tom Don't you think it's strange that we've been here for rather a long time without getting hungry?

Loretta Nope. I figure it's a test.

Tom What sort of test?

Loretta A really hard one. (*Beat.*) Sailors in Roanoke are mighty handsome. Strong. Lean. Great heads of hair. God, I miss home. I mean, I like this submersion in alternative cultures just fine, but I hate being on the run and I'm a real mountain girl at heart.

Tom The Blue Ridge Mountains. (*Beat.*) I was always good at geography.

Loretta That means you got a wandering soul.

Tom Say – if Roanoke is basically a valley surrounded by mountains, why are sailors stationed there?

Loretta Beats me. Just another military mystery, I guess.

Tom   And most sailors I know are a bit short and pallid. Why are they so hunky in Roanoke?

Loretta   Well, probably 'cause they don't get to do naval duties much on account of the lack of water so they spend all their time in gyms or something.

Tom   Sound like paradise.

Loretta   Tom. Let's go. You and me and Baby Ray. Let's go home. To Roanoke.

Tom   It's ... very tempting. But I couldn't.

Loretta   Why the hell not? You tell me what's keeping you here.

Tom   Things. My job. Things.

Loretta   There's no gay running a beauty salon in Roanoke, Tom. Believe me. You'd be the first. Hell, it'd be kinda like a monopoly.

Tom   Well. I do love the idea of a monopoly.

The sound of a massive set of doors opening, straining, as if they've been shut for a thousand years. A brilliant shaft of golden light streams across **Tom**.

Loretta   Praise be something or other, Tom. Them doors are opening. And look at you, all bathed in sunlight.

Tom   The light. It's so warm. Gloriously warm. Why are the doors opening now?

Loretta   We found justice, that's why. Come on. We're going home.

Shift focus to **Suzy** *and* **Lester** *in* **Martin**'*s flat.* **Suzy** *is reading* **Lester**'*s palm.*

Lester   Can you see where my wife's at?

Suzy   It doesn't work that way.

Lester   Does it say something about my son?

Suzy   I'm afraid it doesn't *say* anything. Palms don't talk.

Lester Yeah, but them lines talk. That's what you said.

Suzy Well, yes, metaphorically speaking, the lines . . . speak.

Lester Well, then what's the problem, woman? Are my lines mutes?

Suzy No. It's . . . look. Lately, Mr Marquette, I seem to have been blessed with the power of second sight. I mean, I know that because I am an astrologer, people assume I have special gifts in all things paranormal. But let's be frank, we both know that all most astrologers do is buy a software programme, run a few dates through a PC, and end up with a twenty-page printout of platitudes for which some poor sod is out of pocket thirty quid. And that is exactly what I did until a fortnight ago. Now, I know when road accidents are about to happen, I know when certain people will develop pancreatic cancer, I know the eclipse has a huge role to play in my future, and I am now obsessed with a woman I had written off as a lesbian psychopath a mere fourteen days ago. So excuse me if I encounter a few problems in reading your palm.

Lester I can't leave Martin. I hate him, but every time I get up to walk out that door, I think, hey, man, you gotta do a few more dishes or there's dust under the couch I got to clean up.

Suzy He has that effect on people.

Lester I wanna strangle him and kind of like, you know, hang out with him. All at the same time. Used to be, a guy could rely on another guy. Hell, he could rely on *any* other guy, even a foreign guy, to share a similar viewpoint on most things. Like it was some big club where all the rituals was secret and yet every guy knew them. Now, well, who knows, you know?

Suzy Yeah. I know. (*A beat, as she scrutinises his palm.*) I'm seeing . . . jewellery.

Lester Jewellery?

Suzy   Yes. And . . . guitars. Electric guitars. Toasters. Bric-a-brac. How very odd.

Otto Mink *appears, as if from nowhere.*

Otto   Hello, Lester. You're looking remarkably shitty.

Lester   Fuck. I mean, Mr Mink – when – where – I mean –

Suzy (*to* **Lester**, *refers to* **Otto**)   You know this bloke?

Lester   Damn right. He's my my whaddycallit my . . .

Otto   Brains? (*Beat.*) Lovely to see you again, Miss Bradfield. Tell me, was that letter informative?

Suzy   I see bad things. Very bad things.

Otto   Pessimist. (*To* **Lester**.) I've got some good news and some bad news, old chap. The bad news is: there's been a change in plan. I will no longer be requiring your services in the US House of Representatives. The good news is: I've a new job for you and you won't have far to go to get it. Henceforth, you will refer to me as Mr Murphy Greene.

Lester   What the hell's going on here, Mink? You made promises. You made a lot of promises.

Otto   I promised you a job. That is all.

Lester   Yeah, but –

Otto   But nothing, Lester. (*He produces a sheet of paper out of thin air.*) I own a pawn shop. The shop is not far from here. The address of the shop is written down on this sheet of paper. You will take this sheet of paper and you will go to the shop.

Suzy   Toasters. Guitars. Jewellery.

Lester   Hey. I ain't no fucking cheap shop clerk.

Suzy   Bric-a-brac. Pancreatic cancer. Kate Buck.

Otto   No, Lester. But you will be a fucking cheap shop assistant. And soon.

Suzy   Fifteen-car pile-up on the M4. Jack-knifed semi. Bric-a-brac. Kate Buck. Kate Buck.

Otto   I believe Miss Bradfield's really rather lost it.

Otto *dangles the sheet of paper and the key for* **Lester**. *A beat.* **Lester**, *defeated, approaches* **Otto** *to accept them.*

Music in: 'Mesopotamia' (The B52s). Insistent sounds of casino gambling in full swing. Shift focus to **Kate**, **Ava** *and* **Calvin**. *They have arrived in Las Vegas and are admiring the formidable façade of the Luxor Hotel.* **Kate** *reclines against a telephone box which has been made up to resemble an Egyptian sarcophagus.* **Calvin** *furiously snaps photos of the pyramid and Sphinx.* **Ava** *wears a beaded gown – possibly her Shirley Bassey outfit. She chugs a Budweiser tallboy.*

Calvin (*to no one in particular, as he snaps away*)   The Sphinx. From Greek myth, an inscrutable beast with the body of a lion and the head of a woman, who killed travellers when they could not provide answers to the riddles she asked them.

Ava   Oh yeah? In that case, I got lots of riddles I'd like to ask lots of people. (*To* **Kate**, *referring to the phone box.*) What's up with you and that coffin, huh? It ain't exactly gonna fly away without you.

Kate   Aren't you a little overdressed?

Ava   This is Vegas. There's no clocks and no dress code.

Kate   I'm expecting a call.

Ava   Look. We been standing here three hours. I'm getting varicose veins.

Kate   If there's no clocks, how do you know we've been here three hours? (*Beat.*) I'm very close to him, Ava. I'm on my way.

Ava   Oh, you know, I've had it up to here with being on *your* way. I wanna *arrive*, all right?

Kate   By the way, Calvin, the Sphinx killed herself when

Oedipus answered one of her supposedly unsolvable riddles. So much for inscrutability.

Calvin (*pretty miffed*)   I knew that. I did. I just chose not to include it in my retelling. You can be such a bad sport, Kate.

Ava   Knock-Knock: who's there? Ava. Ava who? Ava I WANNA FUCKING ARRIVE ALREADY.

Kate   What's got two heads, a beer belly, a nasty disposition and yet is somehow entirely lovable?

Ava   I don't know. What?

Lights up on **Otto**. *Music out. The telephone rings. A pause, as* **Kate**, **Ava** *and* **Calvin** *regard the ringing sarcophagus.* **Kate** *jumps to answer it.* **Calvin** *and* **Ava** *are all ears.*

Otto   It's been too long since last we spoke, Miss Buck.

Kate   I'm close. Tell me I'm close.

Otto   Still listening to sentimental popular music, eh? Well, I must admit the events of the last two weeks have brought me somewhat closer to your point of view. (*Beat.*) Yes. You are close, Miss Buck.

Kate   I knew it I knew it I smelled his blood I KNEW it. Where do I go now?

Otto   Tell me, why are you so anxious to pursue this individual now that you've found love? You have found love, haven't you, Miss Buck?

Kate   Yes. I have. Or . . . as close as I can get. But that doesn't mean I can't have both.

Otto   You will catch the next flight to London. You will proceed to a certain pawn shop, Greene and Greene, in Earls Court.

Kate   Yes, but what about . . . (*Keenly aware that* **Ava** *and* **Calvin** *are listening.*) well, the matter we just discussed?

Otto   I have no answer, Miss Buck, except to suggest that the choice is more clear-cut than you imagine. I speak sentimentally. From experience.

Kate   She ... the matter we discussed is my sole inspiration. I can't leave her behind.

Otto   I am a businessman, Miss Buck. Inspiration is cheap. American Airlines, flight 666, three o'clock. Be on it.

Kate   Nono – wait – there's no clocks in Las Vegas. I can't tell time. I CAN'T TELL TIME.

Lights down on **Otto**. **Kate** *hangs up, remains inside the telephone box.*

Ava   You gonna tell me where this club is now? Come ON. Chop chop.

Kate   Do you believe in fate, Ava?

Ava   Fuck that. I got a gig.

Kate   Tumbleweed Junction's right behind you.

Ava   What? You mean, naaah. It's too big. It's too ... something.

Calvin   No, Kate. This isn't Tumbleweed Junction. It's the Luxor Hotel, the ninth wonder of the world.

Kate *exits the phone box, approaches* **Ava**.

Kate   You look magnificent in that gown, Ava Coo.

Ava   Jeez, hey, I don't need ... thanks. Really. I appreciate, you know, whatever.

Kate *takes* **Ava** *into her arms and kisses her, a long, gentle, sensual kiss.* **Calvin**, *at a bit of a loss, snaps photos of their kiss.* **Kate** *releases* **Ava**, *takes* **Ava**'s *Budweiser tallboy, and exits. A considerable pause, as they consider her leave-taking.*

Ava   Hey. She never did say what had two heads and a beer belly.

Sudden intensification of the casino gambling sounds. **Ava** *and*

Calvin *turn to face the Luxor Hotel. They walk towards its entrance.*

Shift focus to **Otto** *and* **Tina** *in* **Tina***'s trailer.* **Tina** *eats a bowl of salad and stares at her burnt-out portable television set.* **Otto** *regards his waterlogged Dictaphone.*

Otto   Tell me about love, Mrs Marshall.

Tina   Are you a philosopher?

Otto   I chose against it many years ago.

Tina   I'm sorry about the Dictaphone. I got a little, well, over excited.

Otto   Have you heard from Mr Marshall?

Tina   Yeah, sure. Maybe. Well, no. But I heard from my daughter. That's something.

Otto   Do you believe there is such a thing as a broken heart?

Tina   I think . . . I've got to be able to see something in order to know that it's broken. My TV's busted. I know that.

Otto   Therefore, if one has left behind the object of one's desire, if the love one harbours is no longer in sight, one doesn't really know if the love is destroyed.

Tina   Yeah, I guess that's right. And since I haven't *seen* Mr Marshall in a dog's age, I got nothing to worry about. (*Beat.*) Are you French or German by any chance, Mr Greene?

Otto *removes his wallet from his jacket pocket and sets it down beside* **Tina**.

Otto   For your television set. Thank you, Mrs Marshall. (*Beat.*) Is the salad tasty?

Tina   Mmmm. Fresh veggies. Grow 'em myself. You want some?

Otto   There's a perpetual order on loo paper and

cleaning supplies at Tumbleweed Junction. I shan't be returning.

Tina (*peeks inside the wallet*)   Mr Greene, this is way too much money for a TV repairman and really you don't got to –

Otto (*patting his hand over hers, an affectionate touch*)   Sssh. Are those cherry tomatoes?

Tina   Oh, sure. They're real easy to grow.

Otto   I'm suddenly quite famished.

Tina *feeds* **Otto** *salad out of her bowl. She uses her fork. He eats greedily, gratefully.*

Shift focus to **Martin**, *who stands before a full-length mirror. He wears only briefs and a peaked leather cap. He coughs. He's shivering, sweaty, sniffly, sneezy. He's very sick. He strikes various poses, à la Mr Universe.*

Martin   Steel steel steel steel steel steel steel steel steel rock rock rock rock rock rock hard hard hard hard hard hard march march march march forward forward forward back back back forward back forward back west west west west Calvin Calvin Calvin Calvin . . .

Otto *enters.*

Otto   Are you ready, Martin?

Martin   Ready ready west ready west ready fly fly fly fly fly up up down up down up up down down fly fly fly fly west west west west . . .

Shift focus to **Ava**. *She stands at a microphone, ready for her big act. She wears a rather strange outfit and a ridiculous blonde wig. She looks like nobody in particular. She holds an electric guitar. She taps the microphone a couple of times and gets feedback.*

Ava   Shit. Whoops. I mean, hey, it's really great, really outstanding to be with y'all here tonight. It's taken me a while to get here and lemme tell you, I learned more than I ever wanted to know about the Revolutionary War, the

Amish, and other assorted religious types who don't have sex. But I'm with you now, and that's the important thing.

Lights up on **Tina** *and* **Calvin** *playing the slots side by side at the Luxor.* **Tina** *hits a small jackpot.*

Calvin   You're very lucky.

Tina   Somebody gave me a bunch of money today. I have this theory about money coming to money. So I'm investing all the cash I got in the slots.

Calvin   Gambling isn't an investment.

Tina   Says who?

Ava   I'm gonna sing a special tune for you tonight. It's for this friend of mine, see, who kinda took off sudden, you know, without advance warning. I hate when that happens, don't you?

Calvin   I've lost ten dollars.

Tina   That's nothing, son. A drop in the bucket. I know all about buckets. Use 'em a lot in my line of work.

Calvin   You remind me of somebody.

Tina   Well I sure hope it's Zsa Zsa Gabor.

Ava   I thought I hated her a lot but then she scratched my back and I felt, I don't know, a connection, a safety, and it was confusing to me because I thought I hated her and . . . well, I mean, it wasn't sexual or nothing 'cause, shit, what do I know about sex anyway? I'm just some chick who pretends to be a chick so people will look at me in a different light so, Christ, you know, what's *that* about?

Calvin   I was interested in the socio-political implications of gambling in the late twentieth century.

Tina   And now you're not interested?

Calvin   I put a quarter in the slot and suddenly I no longer cared about the implications.

Ava   Anyways, this is for my friend who I didn't think I liked at all but then she scratched my back and later on she kissed me and though it was nothing sexual it was something sexual and fuck knows I don't understand it at all and all I really know is I miss her now she's gone and I ask you, ain't that always the way?

Calvin   My friend's performing in the Euphrates Lounge. She's a female impersonator. She's quite good.

Tina   Does she do Dolly Parton?

Calvin   Uhm, no. I don't think she does. But she does others. Many others.

Tina   No, honey, I'm not interested. I have no time for unknown quantities.

Ava   Okay. So. Here it is. My song for you.

Music in: 'Bette Davis Eyes' (Kim Carnes). **Ava** *begins her lip-synch routine. For some reason, she's amazingly convincing.* **Calvin** *and* **Tina** *continue on at the slots.* **Ava** *grows in confidence as the song progresses. She's really having a good time. And then, the music suddenly cuts out and* **Ava**'s *left singing the song on her own. For a moment, she doesn't realise the music's abandoned her. When she does, she croaks on in a panic.*

Ava   (*singing, not terribly well*)   She'll tease you . . . she'll appease you . . . she'll expose you . . . she's got . . . Bette Davis eyes.

And on and on she sings, in a haphazard, tuneless manner. **Tina** *cocks her head, as if she hears* **Ava** *singing.*

Tina   I recognise that voice.

Calvin   What voice?

Ava   (*completely breaking down*)   Oh fuck damn damn DAMN. Why does NOTHING ever turn out right for me?

She smashes the guitar to the floor repeatedly.

Okay okay – you want a show? I'll give you a show. This is my Pete Townsend imitation. See. It's good, right? SEE. SEE.

Calvin   My brother's in trouble. (*Beat.*) Why do I say that?

Tina   I *know* that voice.

Ava   All right, you happy you motherfuckers? This is my generation. MY GENERATION. MY GENERATION.

Lights upon **Suzy** *and* **Lester** *at Greene and Greene pawn shop, Earls Court.* **Lester** *wears an ill-fitting suit. His hair is slicked back and generally, he's made an attempt to look business-like and oddly stylish.* **Suzy** *wears a sandwich board sign with the words 'Kate Buck' written all over it. She speaks through a megaphone.*

Suzy   Something's coming don't know when don't know why something's coming don't know how don't know where watch your back watch your toasters your guitars your electric blankets something's coming.

Lester   Would you shut that door and come back on in here, woman? Hell. Pawn shop's an awful sad place to conduct business without some screaming harpy discouraging customers.

Suzy (*speaks to* **Lester** *through the megaphone*)   Why is it sad?

Lester   We got other people's sad old stuff all over the place. It's like limbo.

Tina   That voice is a voice that's close to me.

Lights up on the interior of a jumbo jet. **Tom**, **Loretta** *and* **Baby Ray** *are passengers. So are* **Martin** *and* **Otto**. **Martin** *is even sicker. He still wears only his briefs and peaked cap.*

Loretta   I can't believe the only flight we could get was a flight to Vegas.

Tom   I don't mind. I like deserts.

Loretta   Maybe I can get one of them quickie divorces in Vegas.

Martin   Senator Higgins Congressman Higgins Governor Higgins President Martin . . . Martin . . . Martin . . . HIGGINS.

Otto Aren't you putting the cart before the horse?

Calvin *hits a jackpot. It's a big one. Lights, bells, sirens.*

Calvin Ohmygod I've won. To hell with history. I'VE WON.

Tina I can't place the voice, though. Why can't I place something so near to me?

Ava (*ripping the strings from the guitar*) My generation my generation my generation MY GENERATION.

Kate *enters the pawn shop. She clocks* **Suzy**'s *sandwich board sign.* **Suzy** *clocks* **Kate**. **Suzy** *drops her megaphone.*

Lester You maybe wanna buy a ring, Miss? We got 'em real cheap.

Suzy (*to* **Kate**) It's you. It's really you. It's you. It's always been you.

Suzy *moves towards* **Kate**. **Calvin**'s *jackpot grows and grows. He's delighted.* **Tina** *strains to identify a voice she can't place.* **Ava**'s *sunk to the ground, the broken pieces of her guitar gathered in her arms. She rocks back and forth, back and forth – a steady rhythm. The lights begin a slow and persistent dimming.*

Suzy The eclipse. It's here.

Kate Not yet. Please. Not yet.

Loretta Oooo Tom, look at the sun. Look at it growing bigger in the sky.

Tom Are we in Egypt? I see a pyramid.

Loretta Baby Ray, looky: the sun's getting bigger and darker and ain't it just *something* to witness?

Martin Almost home Senator Higgins almost home Congressman Higgins almost home home there there home there home there.

Otto Spectacular. Sunset over the land that time forgot.

The lights dim ever more quickly, the casino sounds intensify, the very

*sky seems to close in on itself. Quick blackout. Music in: 'Go West'
(Pet Shop Boys version). Lights up suddenly on* **Tina** *and* **Baby
Ray**, *alone in the landscape.* **Baby Ray** *is on the ground.* **Tina**
picks him up.

Tina   Sweet baby. Awww. Sweetie-pie. Where'd you come
from, honey? You drop out of the sky or something? I had
a baby once. Yes indeedy, sugar lips, I had one and I lost
one and now I found one again. You like salad, pretty
baby?

And two by two, the others, except for **Otto**, *wander in from every
conceivable entrance, shaken and dazed and unsure of where they are.
The pairs should be:* **Ava** *and* **Suzy**; **Tom** *and* **Lester**;
Loretta *and* **Calvin**; **Kate** *and* **Martin**. **Suzy** *holds a
toaster.*

Ava (*clocks* **Tina**)   Ma? Ma?

Tina (*to* **Baby Ray**)   I got a trailer and a portable TV
and my oh my I know that voice, pretty baby. I know it.
Coo coo coo coo, little sunshine.

Loretta   Lester. Is that you, Lester?

Lester   Loretta. It's me. It's . . . impossible. Where are
we, Loretta?

Tom   Is this Roanoke?

Kate   Ava. Where've we got to?

Ava   Ma. Ma. MA?

Tom   Suzy. We went someplace, didn't we?

Suzy   We went back. Or forwards. I'm not sure. (*Beat; she
holds out the toaster to* **Tom**.) In any event, I brought a gift.

Tom *takes the toaster.*

Calvin   Martin. Martin, I'm here.

Martin (*he's the sickest he's ever been*)   You're there. I feel
good, Calvin. Strong. Some bastard made me sick, so sick.
But now I'm fine and full of purpose.

Calvin   Whenever I see you I have the urge to cry. But I don't.

Martin   What time is it, Calvin? Every time I see you, you look the same.

Calvin   And you look different. That's probably why I feel I should cry.

Martin   Where's my time? Where is it?

Martin and **Calvin** *move towards each other tentatively. A beat, before they embrace as if they're holding on for dear life. And then, a sudden unearthly rumbling sound from the deepest bowels of the earth. The sphinx/pyramid splits open to reveal* **Otto**, *like Samson, pushing its walls apart.*

Otto   What's your desire what's the situation I'll tell you the situation: I've got booze I've got car stereos I've got fax modems I've got what you want I've got what you want I've got what you WANT.

Otto *laughs, a deep, malevolent, continuous laugh. The very walls seem to shake. And then: Music out, as* **Baby Ray** *begins to cry, a wail, a pent-up burst of furstrated emotion. Everybody turns to look at* **Baby Ray**.

Tina (*to* **Baby Ray**)   Oh little boy, you can't cry. Dontcha know you're in *Vegas*? You're gonna love it here. There's lots of action. And chance. So much chance it gives you goose bumps. How about I call you Marshall? Would you like that, baby? You know what we got, Marshall? We got possibilities, little fella, endless possibilities.

And then there is stillness, as they all listen to **Baby Ray**'*s oddly unsettling cry.*

Blackout.

Printed in the United Kingdom
by Lightning Source UK Ltd.
100316UKS00001B/32